AJAX and PHP

Building Responsive Web Applications

Enhance the user experience of your PHP website
using AJAX with this practical tutorial featuring detailed
case studies

Cristian Darie
Bogdan Brinzarea
Filip Chereches-Toşa
Mihai Bucica

BIRMINGHAM - MUMBAI

AJAX and PHP
Building Responsive Web Applications

First published: March 2006

Production Reference: 1210206

Published by Packt Publishing Ltd.
32 Lincoln Road
Olton
Birmingham, B27 6PA, UK.

ISBN 1-904811-82-5

www.packtpub.com

Cover Design by www.visionwt.com

Credits

Authors
Cristian Darie
Brinzarea Bogdan
Filip Chereches-Toşa
Mihai Bucica

Reviewers
Emilian Balanescu
Paula Badascu

Technical Editor
Jimmy Karumalil

Editorial Manager
Dipali Chittar

Development Editor
Cristian Darie

Indexer
Ashutosh Pande

Proofreader
Chris Smith

Production Coordinator
Manjiri Nadkarni

Cover Designer
Helen Wood

About the Authors

Cristian Darie is a software engineer with experience in a wide range of modern technologies, and the author of numerous technical books, including the popular "Beginning E-Commerce" series. Having worked with computers since he was old enough to press the keyboard, he initially tasted programming success with a first prize in his first programming contest at the age of 12. From there, Cristian moved on to many other similar achievements, and now he is studying distributed application architectures for his PhD degree. He always loves hearing feedback about his books, so don't hesitate dropping a "hello" message when you have a spare moment. Cristian can be contacted through his personal website at www.cristiandarie.ro.

Cristian would like to express a big "thank you!" to his co-authors, Bogdan, Filip, and Mihai and to the Technical Editor of the book, Jimmy, for the hard work they've put into building this wonderful book.

Bogdan Brinzarea has a strong background in Computer Science holding a Master and Bachelor Degree at the Automatic Control and Computers Faculty of the Politehnica University of Bucharest, Romania and also an Auditor diploma at the Computer Science department at Ecole Polytechnique, Paris, France.

His main interests cover a wide area from embedded programming, distributed and mobile computing, and new web technologies. Currently, he is employed as an Alternative Channels Specialist at Banca Romaneasca, Member of National Bank of Greece, where he is responsible for the Internet Banking project and coordinates other projects related to security applications and new technologies to be implemented in the banking area.

Filip Cherecheş-Toşa is a web developer with a firm belief in the future of web-based software. He started his career at the age of 9, when he first got a Commodore 64 with tape-drive.

Back home in Romania, Filip runs a web development company named eXigo www.exigo.ro, which is actively involved in web-based application development and web design. He is currently a student at the University of Oradea, studying Computer Science, and also an active member of the Romanian PHP Community www.phpromania.net.

Mihai Bucica started programming and competing in programming contests (winning many of them), all at age twelve. With a bachelor's degree in computer science from the Automatic Control and Computers Faculty of the Politehnica University of Bucharest, Romania, Bucica works on building communication software with various electronic markets.

Even after working with a multitude of languages and technologies, Bucica's programming language of choice remains C++, and he loves the LGPL word. Mihai also co-authored *Beginning PHP 5 and MySQL E-Commerce* and he can be contacted through his personal website, www.valentinbucica.ro.

About the Reviewers

Emilian Balanescu is a programmer experienced in many technologies, including PHP, Java, .NET, PostgreSQL, MS SQL Server, MySQL, and others. He currently works as a Wireless Network Administrator at accessNET International S.A. Romania, a company that provides fixed wireless access services operating a point-to-multipoint digital radio communication network with national coverage. His latest project in this position was developing an AJAX-enabled real-time Network Management System (using SNMP, Perl, PHP, and PostgreSQL) used for remote debugging, monitoring system performance, and isolating and troubleshooting system problems. You can reach Emilian at http://www.emilianbalanescu.ro.

Paula Badascu is in the third year of studies at Politehnica University of Bucharest, one of the most famous technical universities in Romania, studying Electronics, Telecommunications, and Information Technology. Paula is currently working as an analyst/programmer for NCH Advisors Romania, building web applications using UML, OOP, PHP, SQL, JavaScript, and CSS. She contributed decisively to the analysis and development of a framework used for tracking and monitoring the Romanian capital market.

Table of Contents

Preface

AJAX is a complex phenomenon that means different things to different people. Computer users appreciate that their favorite websites are now friendlier and feel more responsive. Web developers learn new skills that empower them to create sleek web applications with little effort. Indeed, everything sounds good about AJAX!

At its roots, AJAX is a mix of technologies that lets you get rid of the evil page reload, which represents the dead time when navigating from one page to another. Eliminating page reloads is just one step away from enabling more complex features into websites, such as real-time data validation, drag and drop, and other tasks that weren't traditionally associated with web applications. Although the AJAX ingredients are mature (the XMLHttpRequest object, which is the heart of AJAX, was created by Microsoft in 1999), their new role in the new wave of web trends is very young, and we'll witness a number of changes before these technologies will be properly used to the best benefit of the end users. At the time of writing this book, the "AJAX" name is about just one year old.

AJAX isn't, of course, the answer to all the Web's problems, as the current hype around it may suggest. As with any other technology, AJAX can be overused, or used the wrong way. AJAX also comes with problems of its own: you need to fight with browser inconsistencies, AJAX-specific pages don't work on browsers without JavaScript, they can't be easily bookmarked by users, and search engines don't always know how to parse them. Also, not everyone likes AJAX. While some are developing enterprise architectures using JavaScript, others prefer not to use it at all. When the hype is over, most will probably agree that the middle way is the wisest way to go for most scenarios.

In *AJAX and PHP: Building Responsive Web Applications*, we took a pragmatic and safe approach by teaching relevant patterns and best practices that we think any web developer will need sooner or later. We teach you how to avoid the common pitfalls, how to write efficient AJAX code, and how to achieve functionality that is easy to integrate into current and future web applications, without requiring you to rebuild the whole solution around AJAX. You'll be able to use the knowledge you learn from this book right away, into your PHP web applications.

We hope you'll find this book useful and relevant to your projects. For the latest details and updates regarding this book, please visit its mini-site at http://ajaxphp.packtpub.com.

The book's mini-site also contains additional free chapters and resources, which we recommend you check out when you have the time.

What This Book Covers

Chapter 1: *AJAX and the Future of Web Applications* is an initial incursion into the world of AJAX and the vast possibilities it opens up for web developers and companies, to offer a better experience to their users. In this chapter you'll also build your first AJAX-enabled web page, which will give you a first look of the component technologies.

Chapter 2: *Client-Side Techniques with Smarter JavaScript* will guide you through the technologies you'll use to build AJAX web clients, using JavaScript, the DOM, the XMLHttpRequest object, and XML. While not being a complete tutorial for these technologies, you'll be put on the right track for using them together to build a solid foundation for your future applications.

Chapter 3: *Server-Side Techniques with PHP and MySQL* completes the theoretical foundation by presenting how to create smart servers to interact with your AJAX client. You'll learn various techniques for implementing common tasks, including handling basic JavaScript security and error-handling problems.

Chapter 4: *AJAX Form Validation* guides you through creating a modern, responsive, and secure form validation system that implements both real-time AJAX validation and server-side validation on form submission.

Chapter 5: *AJAX Chat* presents a simple online chat that works exclusively using AJAX code, without using Java applets, Flash code, or other specialized libraries as most chat applications do these days.

Chapter 6: *AJAX Suggest and Autocomplete* builds a Google Suggest-like feature, that helps you quickly find PHP functions, and forwards you to the official help page for the chosen function.

Chapter 7: *AJAX Real-Time Charting with SVG* teaches you how to implement a real-time charting solution with AJAX and SVG. SVG (Scalable Vector Graphics) is a text-based graphics language that can be used to draw shapes and text.

Chapter 8: *AJAX Grid* teaches you how to build powerful AJAX-enabled data grids. You'll learn how to parse XML documents using XSLT to generate the output of your grid.

Chapter 9: *AJAX RSS Reader* uses the SimpleXML PHP library, XML, and XSLT to build a simple RSS aggregator.

Chapter 10: *AJAX Drag and Drop* is a demonstration of using the script.aculo.us framework to build a simple list of elements with drag-and-drop functionality.

Appendix A: *Preparing Your Working Environment* teaches you how to install and configure the required software: Apache, PHP, MySQL, phpMyAdmin. The examples in this book assume that you have set up your environment and sample database as shown here.

At the book's mini-site at http://ajaxphp.packtpub.com, you can find the online demos for all the book's AJAX case studies.

What You Need for This Book

To go through the examples of this book you need PHP 5, a web server, and a database server. We have tested the code under several environments, but mostly with the Apache 2 web server, and MySQL 4.1 and MySQL 5 databases.

You can choose, however, to use another web server, or another database product, in which case the procedures presented in the chapters might not be 100% accurate. It is important to have PHP 5 or newer, because we use some features, such as Object Oriented Programming support, which aren't available in older versions.

Please read Appendix A for more details about setting up your machine. If your machine already has the required software, you still need to read the final part of Appendix A, where you are instructed about creating a database that is used for the examples in this book.

Conventions

In this book, you will find a number of styles of text that distinguish between different kinds of information. Here are some examples of these styles, and an explanation of their meaning.

There are three styles for code. Code words in text are shown as follows: "We can include other contexts through the use of the include directive."

A block of code will be set as follows:

```
// function calls the server using the XMLHttpRequest object
function process()
{
  // retrieve the name typed by the user on the form
  name = document.getElementById("myName").value;
  // execute the quickstart.php page from the server
  xmlHttp.open("GET", "quickstart.php?name=" + name, false);
  // make synchronous server request
  xmlHttp.send(null);
  // read the response
  handleServerResponse();
}
```

When we wish to draw your attention to a particular part of a code block, the relevant lines or items will be made bold:

```
// function calls the server using the XMLHttpRequest object
function process()
{
  // retrieve the name typed by the user on the form
  name = document.getElementById("myName").value;
  // execute the quickstart.php page from the server
  xmlHttp.open("GET", "quickstart.php?name=" + name, false);
  // make synchronous server request
  xmlHttp.send(null);
  // read the response
  handleServerResponse();
}
```

Any command-line input and output is written as follows:

```
./configure --prefix=/usr/local/apache2 --enable-so --enable-ssl --with-ssl --enable-auth-digest
```

New terms and **important words** are introduced in a bold-type font. Words that you see on the screen, in menus or dialog boxes for example, appear in our text like this: "clicking the Next button moves you to the next screen".

Warnings or important notes appear in a box like this.

Tips and tricks appear like this.

Reader Feedback

Feedback from our readers is always welcome. Let us know what you think about this book, what you liked or may have disliked. Reader feedback is important for us to develop titles that you really get the most out of.

To send us general feedback, simply drop an email to feedback@packtpub.com, making sure to mention the book title in the subject of your message.

If there is a book that you need and would like to see us publish, please send us a note in the SUGGEST A TITLE form on www.packtpub.com or email suggest@packtpub.com.

If there is a topic that you have expertise in and you are interested in either writing or contributing to a book, see our author guide on www.packtpub.com/authors.

Customer Support

Now that you are the proud owner of a Packt book, we have a number of things to help you to get the most from your purchase.

Downloading the Example Code for the Book

Visit http://www.packtpub.com/support, and select this book from the list of titles to download any example code or extra resources for this book. The files available for download will then be displayed.

The downloadable files contain instructions on how to use them.

Errata

Although we have taken every care to ensure the accuracy of our contents, mistakes do happen. If you find a mistake in one of our books—maybe a mistake in text or code—we would be grateful if you would report this to us. By doing this you can save other readers from frustration, and help to improve subsequent versions of this book. If you find any errata, report them by visiting http://www.packtpub.com/support, selecting your book, clicking on the Submit Errata link, and entering the details of your errata. Once your errata have been verified, your submission will be accepted and the errata added to the list of existing errata. The existing errata can be viewed by selecting your title from http://www.packtpub.com/support.

Questions

You can contact us at questions@packtpub.com if you are having a problem with some aspect of the book, and we will do our best to address it.

1

AJAX and the Future of Web Applications

"Computer, draw a robot!" said my young cousin to the first computer he had ever seen. (Since I had instructed it not to listen to strangers, the computer wasn't receptive to this command.) If you're like me, your first thought would be "how silly" or "how funny"—but this is a mistake. Our educated and modeled brains have learned how to work with computers to a certain degree. People are being educated to accommodate computers, to compensate for the lack of ability of computers to understand humans. (On the other hand, humans can't accommodate very well themselves, but that's another story.)

This little story is relevant to the way people instinctively work with computers. In an ideal world, that spoken command should have been enough to have the computer please my cousin. The ability of technology to be user-friendly has evolved very much in the past years, but there's still a long way till we have real intelligent computers. Until then, people need to learn how to work with computers—some to the extent that they end up loving a black screen with a tiny command prompt on it.

Not incidentally, the computer-working habits of many are driven by software with user interfaces that allow for intuitive (and enjoyable) human interaction. This probably explains the popularity of the right mouse button, the wonder of fancy features such as drag and drop, or that simple text box that searches content all over the Internet for you in just 0.1 seconds (or so it says). The software industry (or the profitable part of it, anyway) has seen, analyzed, and learned. Now the market is full of programs with shiny buttons, icons, windows, and wizards, and people are *paying a lot of money for them*.

What the software industry has learned is that the equivalent of a powerful engine in a red sports car is *usability and accessibility* for software. And it's wonderful when what is good from the business point of view is also good from a human point of view, because the business profits are more or less proportional to customers' satisfaction.

We plan to be very practical and concise in this book, but before getting back to your favorite mission (writing code) it's worth taking a little step back, just to remember what we are doing and why we are doing it. We love technology to the sound made by each key stroke, so it's very easy to forget that the very reason technology exists is to serve people and make their lives at home more entertaining, and at work more efficient.

Understanding the way people's brains work would be the key to building the ultimate software applications. While we're far from that point, what we do understand is that end users need intuitive user interfaces; they don't really care what operating system they're running as long as the functionality they get is what they *expect*. This is a very important detail to keep in mind, as many programmers tend to think and speak in technical terms even when working with end users (although in a typical development team the programmer doesn't interact directly with the end user). If you disagree, try to remember how many times you've said the word *database* when talking to a non-technical person.

By observing people's needs and habits while working with computer systems, the term **software usability** was born—referring to the *art* of meeting users' interface expectations, understanding the nature of their work, and building software applications accordingly.

Historically, usability techniques were applied mainly to **desktop applications**, simply because the required tools weren't available for **web applications**. However, as the Internet gets more mature, the technologies it enables are increasingly potent.

Modern Internet technologies not only enable you to build a better online presence, but also allow building better intranet/dedicated applications. Having friendly websites is crucial for online business, because *the Internet never sleeps*, and customers frequently migrate to the next "big thing" that looks better or *feels* to move faster. At the same time, being able to build friendly web interfaces gives alternative options for intranet software solutions, which were previously built mainly as desktop applications.

Building user-friendly software has always been easier with desktop applications than with web applications, simply because the Web was designed as a means for delivering text and images, and not complex functionality. This problem has gotten significantly more painful in the last few years, when more and more software services and functionality are delivered via the Web.

Consequently, many technologies have been developed (and are still being developed) to add flashy lights, accessibility, and power to web applications. Notable examples include **Java applets** and **Macromedia Flash**, which require the users to install separate libraries into their web browsers.

Delivering Functionality via the Web

Web applications are applications whose functionality is processed on a web server, and is delivered to the end users over a network such as the Internet or an intranet. The end users use a **thin client** (web browser) to run web applications, which knows how to display and execute the data received from the server. In contrast, desktop applications are based on a **thick client** (also called a rich client or a fat client), which does most of the processing.

Web applications evolve dreaming that one day they'll look and behave like their mature (and powerful) relatives, the desktop applications. The behavior of any computer software that interacts with humans is now even more important than it used to be, because nowadays the computer user base varies much more than in the past, when the users were technically sound as well. Now you need to display good looking reports to Cindy, the sales department manager, and you need to provide easy-to-use data entry forms to Dave, the sales person.

Because end-user satisfaction is all that matters, the software application you build must be satisfactory to all the users that interact with it. As far as web applications are concerned, their evolution-to-maturity process will be complete when the application's interface and behavior will not reveal whether the functionality is delivered by the local desktop or comes through fiber or air. Delivering usable interfaces via the Web used to be problematic simply because features that people use with their desktop application, such as drag and drop, and performing multiple tasks on the same window at the same time, were not possible.

Another problem with building web applications is **standardization**. Today, everything web-accessible must be verified with at least two or three browsers to ensure that all your visitors will get the full benefit of your site.

Advantages of Web Applications

Yes, there are lots of headaches when trying to deliver functionality via the Web. But why bother trying to do that in the first place, instead of building plain desktop applications? Well, even with the current problems that web applications have with being user-friendly, they have acquired extraordinary popularity because they offer a number of major technological advantages over desktop applications.

- **Web applications are easy and inexpensive to deliver**. With web applications, a company can reduce the costs of the IT department that is in charge of installing the software on the users' machines. With web applications, all that users need is a computer with a working web browser and an Internet or intranet connection.

- **Web applications are easy and inexpensive to upgrade**. Maintenance costs for software have always been significant. Because upgrading an existing piece of software is similar to installing a new one, the web applications' advantages mentioned above apply here as well. As soon as the application on the server machine is upgraded, everyone gets the new version.

- **Web applications have flexible requirements for the end users**. Just have your web application installed on a server—any modern operating system will do—and you'll be able to use it over the Internet/Intranet on any Mac, Windows, or Linux machine and so on. If the application is properly built, it will run equally well on any modern web browser, such as Internet Explorer, Mozilla Firefox, Opera, or Safari.

- **Web applications make it easier to have a central data store**. When you have several locations that need access to the same data, having all that data stored in one place is much easier than having separate databases in each location. This way you avoid potential data synchronization operations and lower security risks.

In this book we'll further investigate how to use modern web technologies to build better web applications, to make the most out of the possibilities offered by the Web. But before getting into the details, let's take a *short* history lesson.

Building Websites Since 1990

Although the history of the Internet is a bit longer, 1991 is the year when **HyperText Transfer Protocol (HTTP)**, which is still used to transfer data over the Internet, was invented. In its first few initial versions, it didn't do much more than opening and closing connections. The later versions of HTTP (version 1.0 appeared in 1996 and version 1.1 in 1999) became the protocol that now we all know and use.

HTTP and HTML

HTTP is supported by all web browsers, and it does very well the job it was conceived for—retrieving simple web content. Whenever you request a web page using your favorite web browser, the HTTP protocol is assumed. So, for example, when you type www.mozilla.org in the location bar of Firefox, it will assume by default that you meant http://www.mozilla.org.

The standard document type of the Internet is **HyperText Markup Language (HTML)**, and it is built of markup that web browsers *understand*, *parse*, and *display*. HTML is a language that describes documents' formatting and content, which is basically composed of static text and images. HTML wasn't designed for building complex web applications with interactive content or user-friendly interfaces. When you need to get to another HTML page via HTTP, you need to initiate a full page reload, and the HTML page you requested must exist at the mentioned location, as a static document, prior to the request. It's obvious that these restrictions don't really encourage building anything interesting.

Nevertheless, HTTP and HTML are still a very successful pair that both web servers and web clients (browsers) understand. They are the foundation of the Internet as we know it today. Figure 1.1 shows a simple transaction when a user requests a web page from the Internet using the HTTP protocol:

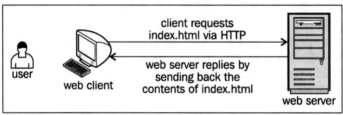

Figure 1.1: A Simple HTTP Request

Three points for you to keep in mind:

1. HTTP transactions always happen between a *web client* (the software making the request, such as a web browser) and a *web server* (the software responding to the request, such as **Apache** or **IIS**). *From now on in this book, when saying 'client' we refer to the web client, and when saying 'server' we refer to the web server.*

2. The user is the person using the client.

3. Even if HTTP (and its secure version, **HTTPS**) is arguably the most important protocol used on the Internet, it is not the only one. Various kinds of web servers use different protocols to accomplish various tasks, usually unrelated to simple web browsing. The protocol we'll use most frequently in this book is HTTP, and when we say 'web request' we'll assume a request using HTTP protocol, unless other protocol will be mentioned explicitly.

Sure thing, the HTTP-HTML combination is very limited in what it can do—it only enables users to retrieve static content (HTML pages) from the Internet. To complement the lack of features, several technologies have been developed.

While all web requests we'll talk about from now on still use the HTTP protocol for transferring the data, the data itself can be built dynamically on the web server (say, using information from a database), and this data can contain more than plain HTML allowing the client to perform some functionality rather than simply display static pages.

The technologies that enable the Web to act smarter are grouped in the following two main categories:

- **Client-side technologies** enable the web client to do more interesting things than displaying static documents. Usually these technologies are extensions of HTML, and don't replace it entirely.
- **Server-side technologies** are those that enable the server to store logic to build web pages on the fly.

PHP and Other Server-Side Technologies

Server-side web technologies enable the web server to do much more than simply returning the requested HTML files, such as performing complex calculations, doing object-oriented programming, working with databases, and much more.

Just imagine how much data processing Amazon must do to calculate personalized product recommendations for each visitor, or Google when it searches its enormous database to serve your request. Yes, server-side processing is the engine that caused the web revolution, and the reason for which Internet is so useful nowadays.

The important thing to remember is that no matter what happens on the server side, the response received by the client must be a language that the client understands (obviously)—such as HTML, which has many limits, as mentioned earlier.

PHP is one of the technologies used to implement server-side logic. Chapter 3 will serve an introduction to PHP, and we'll use PHP in this book when building the **AJAX** case studies. It's good to know, though, that PHP has many competitors, such as **ASP.NET** (Active Server Pages, the web development technology from Microsoft), **Java Server Pages (JSP)**, **Perl**, **ColdFusion**, **Ruby on Rails**, and others. Each of these has its own way of allowing programmers to build server-side functionality.

PHP is not only a server-side technology but a scripting language as well, which programmers can use to create PHP scripts. Figure 1.2 shows a request for a PHP page called index.php. This time, instead of sending back the contents of index.php, the server executes index.php and sends back the results. These results must be in HTML, or in other language that the client understands.

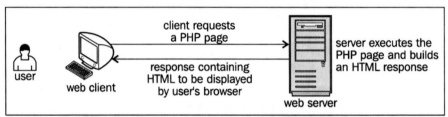

Figure 1.2: Client Requests a PHP Page

On the server side you'll usually need a **database server** as well to manage your data. In the case studies of this book we'll work with **MySQL**, but the concepts are the same as any other server. You'll learn the basics of working with databases and PHP in Chapter 3.

However, even with PHP that can build custom-made database-driven responses, the browser still displays a static, boring, and not very smart web document.

The need for smarter and more powerful functionality on the web client generated a separated set of technologies, called client-side technologies. Today's browsers know how to parse more than simple HTML. Let's see how.

JavaScript and Other Client-Side Technologies

The various client-side technologies differ in many ways, starting with the way they get loaded and executed by the web client. **JavaScript** is a scripting language, whose code is written in plain text and can be embedded into HTML pages to empower them. When a client requests an HTML page, that HTML page can contain JavaScript. JavaScript is supported by all modern web browsers without requiring users to install new components on the system.

JavaScript is a language in its own right (theoretically it isn't tied to web development), it's supported by most web clients under any platform, and it has some object-oriented capabilities. JavaScript is not a compiled language so it's not suited for intensive calculations or writing device drivers and it must arrive in one piece at the client browser to be interpreted so it is not secure either, but it does a good job when used in web pages.

With JavaScript, developers could finally build web pages with snow falling over them, with client-side form validation so that the user won't cause a whole page reload (incidentally losing all typed data) if he or she forgot to supply all the details (such as password, or credit card number), or if the email address had an incorrect format. However, despite its potential, JavaScript was never used consistently to make the web experience truly user friendly, similar to that of users of desktop applications.

Other popular technologies to perform functionality at the client side are Java applets and Macromedia Flash. Java applets are written in the popular and powerful Java language, and are executed through a **Java Virtual Machine** that needs to be installed separately on the system. Java applets are certainly the way to go for more complex projects, but they have lost the popularity they once had over web applications because they consume many system resources. Sometimes they even need long startup times, and are generally too heavy and powerful for the small requirements of simple web applications.

Macromedia Flash has very powerful tools for creating animations and graphical effects, and it's the de-facto standard for delivering such kind of programs via the Web. Flash also requires the client to install a browser *plug-in*. Flash-based technologies become increasingly powerful, and new ones keep appearing.

Combining HTML with a server-side technology and a client-side technology, one can end up building very powerful web solutions.

What's Been Missing?

So there are options, why would anyone want anything new? What's missing?

As pointed out in the beginning of the chapter, technology exists to serve existing market needs. And part of the market wants to deliver more powerful functionality to web clients without using Flash, Java applets, or other technologies that are considered either too flashy or heavy-weight for certain purposes. For these scenarios, developers have usually created websites and web applications using HTML, JavaScript, and PHP (or another server-side technology). The typical request with this scenario is shown in Figure 1.3, which shows an HTTP request, the response made up of HTML and JavaScript built programmatically with PHP.

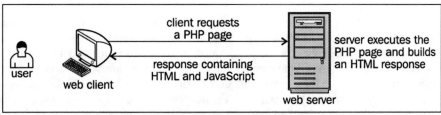

Figure 1.3: HTTP, HTML, PHP, and JavaScript in Action

The hidden problem with this scenario is that each time the client needs new data from the server, a new HTTP request must be made to reload the page, freezing the user's activity. The **page reload** is the new evil in the present day scenario, and AJAX comes in to our rescue.

Understanding AJAX

AJAX is an acronym for **Asynchronous JavaScript and XML**. If you think it doesn't say much, we agree. Simply put, AJAX can be read "empowered JavaScript", because it essentially offers a technique for client-side JavaScript to make background server calls and retrieve additional data as needed, updating certain portions of the page without causing full page reloads. Figure 1.4 offers a visual representation of what happens when a typical AJAX-enabled web page is requested by a visitor:

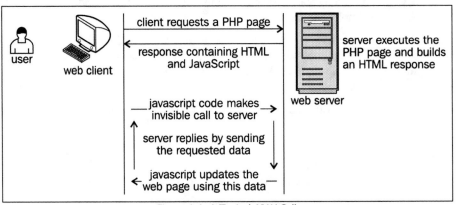

Figure 1.4: A Typical AJAX Call

When put in perspective, AJAX is about reaching a better balance between client functionality and server functionality when executing the action requested by the user. Up until now, client-side functionality and server-side functionality were regarded as separate bits of functionality that work one at a time to respond to user's actions. AJAX comes with the solution to balance the load between the client and the server by allowing them to communicate in the background *while the user is working* on the page.

To explain with a simple example, consider web forms where the user is asked to write some data (such as name, email address, password, credit card, etc) that has to be validated before reaching the business tier of your application. Without AJAX, there were two form validation techniques. The first was to let the user type all the required data, let him or her *submit* the page, and perform the validation on the server. In this scenario the user experiences a *dead time* while waiting for the new page to load. The alternative was to do this verification at the client, but this wasn't always possible (or feasible) because it implied loading too much data on the client (just think if you needed to validate that the entered city and the entered country match).

In the AJAX-enabled scenario, the web application can validate the entered data by making server calls in the background, while the user keeps typing. For example, after the user selects a country, the web browser calls the server to load on the fly the list of cities for that country, without interrupting the user from his or her current activity. You'll find an example of AJAX form validation in Chapter 4.

The examples where AJAX can make a difference are endless. To get a better feeling and understanding of what AJAX can do for you, have a look at these live and popular examples:

- **Google Suggest** helps you with your **Google** searches. The functionality is pretty spectacular; check it out at `http://www.google.com/webhp?complete=1`. Similar functionality is offered by **Yahoo! Instant Search**, accessible at `http://instant.search.yahoo.com/`. (You'll learn how to build similar functionality in Chapter 6.)

- **GMail** (`http://www.gmail.com`). GMail is very popular by now and doesn't need any introduction. Other web-based email services such as **Yahoo! Mail** and **Hotmail** have followed the trend and offer AJAX-based functionality.

- **Google Maps** (`http://maps.google.com`), **Yahoo Maps** (`http://maps.yahoo.com`), and **Windows Live Local** (`http://local.live.com`).

- Other services, such as `http://www.writely.com` and `http://www.basecamphq.com`.

You'll see even more examples over the course of this book.

> Just as with any other technology, AJAX can be *overused*, or used the wrong way. Just having AJAX on your website doesn't guarantee your website will be better. It depends on you to make good use of the technology.

So AJAX is about creating more versatile and interactive web applications by enabling web pages to make asynchronous calls to the server transparently while the user is working. AJAX is a tool that web developers can use to create smarter web applications that behave better than traditional web applications when interacting with humans.

The technologies AJAX is made of are already implemented in all modern web browsers, such as Mozilla Firefox, Internet Explorer, or Opera, so the client doesn't need to install any extra modules to run an AJAX website. AJAX is made of the following:

- JavaScript is the essential ingredient of AJAX, allowing you to build the client-side functionality. In your JavaScript functions you'll make heavy use of the **Document Object Model (DOM)** to manipulate parts of the HTML page.

- The **XMLHttpRequest** object enables JavaScript to access the server asynchronously, so that the user can continue working, while functionality is performed in the background. Accessing the server simply means making a simple HTTP request for a file or script located on the server. HTTP requests are easy to make and don't cause any firewall-related problems.

- A server-side technology is required to handle the requests that come from the JavaScript client. In this book we'll use PHP to perform the server-side part of the job.

For the client-server communication the parts need a way to *pass data* and *understand* that data. Passing the data is the simple part. The client script accessing the server (using the XMLHttpRequest object) can send name-value pairs using **GET** or **POST**. It's very simple to read these values with any server script.

The server script simply sends back the response via HTTP, but unlike a usual website, the response will be in a format that can be simply parsed by the JavaScript code on the client. The suggested format is XML, which has the advantage of being widely supported, and there are many libraries that make it easy to manipulate XML documents. But you can choose another format if you want (you can even send plain text), a popular alternative to XML being **JavaScript Object Notation** (**JSON**).

This book assumes you already know the taste of the AJAX ingredients, except maybe the XMLHttpRequest object, which is less popular. However, to make sure we're all on the same page, we'll have a look together at how these pieces work, and how they work together, in Chapter 2 and Chapter 3. Until then, for the remainder of this chapter we'll focus on the big picture, and we will also write an AJAX program for the joy of the most impatient readers.

> None of the AJAX components is new, or revolutionary (or at least evolutionary) as the current buzz around AJAX might suggest: all the components of AJAX have existed since sometime in 1998. The name AJAX was born in 2005, in Jesse James Garret's article at http://www.adaptivepath.com/publications/essays/archives/000385.php, and gained much popularity when used by Google in many of its applications.
>
> What's new with AJAX is that for the first time there is enough energy in the market to encourage standardization and focus these energies on a clear direction of evolution. As a consequence, many AJAX libraries are being developed, and many AJAX-enabled websites have appeared. Microsoft through its Atlas project is pushing AJAX development as well.

AJAX brings you the following potential benefits when building a new web application:

- It makes it possible to create better and more responsive websites and web applications.
- Because of its popularity, it encourages the development of patterns that help developers avoid reinventing the wheel when performing common tasks.
- It makes use of existing technologies.
- It makes use of existing developer skills.
- Features of AJAX integrate perfectly with existing functionality provided by web browsers (say, re-dimensioning the page, page navigation, etc).

Common scenarios where AJAX can be successfully used are:

- Enabling immediate server-side form validation, very useful in circumstances when it's unfeasible to transfer to the client all the data required to do the validation when the page initially loads. Chapter 4 contains a form validation case study.

- Creating simple online chat solutions that don't require external libraries such as the Java Runtime Machine or Flash. You'll build such a program in Chapter 5.

- Building Google Suggest-like functionality, like an example you'll build in Chapter 6.

- More effectively using the power of other existing technologies. In Chapter 7, you'll implement a real-time charting solution using **Scalable Vector Graphics (SVG)**, and in Chapter 10, you'll use an external AJAX library to create a simple drag-and-drop list.

- Coding responsive **data grids** that update the server-side database on the fly. You'll create such an application in Chapter 8.

- Building applications that need real-time updates from various external sources. In Chapter 9, you'll create a simple **RSS** aggregator.

Potential problems with AJAX are:

- Because the page address doesn't change while working, you can't easily bookmark AJAX-enabled pages. In the case of AJAX applications, bookmarking has different meanings depending on your specific application, usually meaning that you need to save state somehow (think about how this happens with desktop applications—there's no bookmarking there).

- Search engines may not be able to index all portions of your AJAX application site.

- The Back button in browsers, doesn't produce the same result as with classic web applications, because all actions happen inside the same page.

- JavaScript can be disabled at the client side, which makes the AJAX application non-functional, so it's good to have another plan in your site, whenever possible, to avoid losing visitors.

Finally, before moving on to write your first AJAX program, here are a number of links that may help you in your journey into the exciting world of AJAX:

- `http://ajaxblog.com` is an AJAX dedicated blog.

- `http://www.fiftyfoureleven.com/resources/programming/xmlhttprequest` is a comprehensive article collection about AJAX.

- `http://www.ajaxian.com` is the AJAX website of Ben Galbraith and Dion Almaer, the authors of Pragmatic AJAX.

- `http://www.ajaxmatters.com` is an informational site about AJAX, containing loads of very useful links.

- `http://ajaxpatterns.org` is about reusable AJAX design patterns.

- `http://www.ajaxinfo.com` is a resource of AJAX articles and links.

- `http://dev.fiaminga.com` contains many links to various AJAX resources and tutorials.

- `http://ajaxguru.blogspot.com` is a popular AJAX-related web blog.
- `http://www.sitepoint.com/article/remote-scripting-ajax` is Cameron Adams' excellent article *AJAX: Usable Interactivity with Remote Scripting*.
- `http://developer.mozilla.org/en/docs/AJAX` is Mozilla's page on AJAX.
- `http://en.wikipedia.org/wiki/AJAX` is the Wikipedia page on AJAX.

The list is by no means complete. If you need more online resources, Google will surely be available to help. In the following chapters, you'll be presented with even more links, but more specific to the particular technologies you'll be learning about.

Building a Simple Application with AJAX and PHP

Let's write some code then! In the following pages you'll build a simple AJAX application.

> This exercise is for the most impatient readers willing to start coding ASAP, but it assumes you're already familiar with JavaScript, PHP, and XML. If this is not the case, or if at any time you feel this exercise is too challenging, feel free to skip to Chapter 2. In Chapter 2 and Chapter 3 we'll have a much closer look at the AJAX technologies and techniques and everything will become clear.

You'll create here a simple AJAX web application called **quickstart** where the user is requested to write his or her name, and the server keeps sending back responses while the user is writing. Figure 1.5 shows the initial page, `index.html`, loaded by the user. (Note that `index.html` gets loaded by default when requesting the `quickstart` web folder, even if the file name is not explicitly mentioned.)

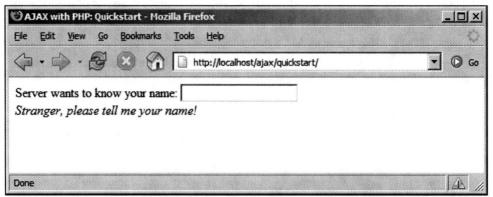

Figure 1.5: The Front Page of Your Quickstart Application

While the user is typing, the server is being called asynchronously, at regular intervals, to see if it recognizes the current name. The server is called automatically, approximately one time per second, which explains why we don't need a button (such as a 'Send' button) to notify when we're done typing. (This method may not be appropriate for real log-in mechanisms but it's very good to demonstrate some AJAX functionality.)

Depending on the entered name, the message from the server may differ; see an example in Figure 1.6.

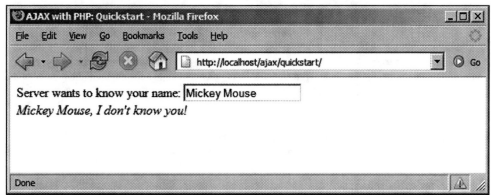

Figure 1.6: User Receives a Prompt Reply From the Web Application

Check out this example online at http://ajaxphp.packtpub.com/ajax/quickstart

Maybe at first sight there's nothing extraordinary going on there. We've kept this first example simple on purpose, to make things easier to understand. What's special about this application is that the displayed message comes automatically from the server, without interrupting the user's actions. (The messages are displayed as the user types a name). **The page doesn't get reloaded to display the new data, even though a server call needs to be made to get that data.** This wasn't a simple task to accomplish using non-AJAX web development techniques.

The application consists of the following three files:

1. index.html is the initial HTML file the user requests.
2. quickstart.js is a file containing JavaScript code that is loaded on the client along with index.html. This file will handle making the asynchronous requests to the server, when server-side functionality is needed.
3. quickstart.php is a PHP script residing on the server that gets called by the JavaScript code in quickstart.js file from the client.

Figure 1.7 shows the actions that happen when running this application:

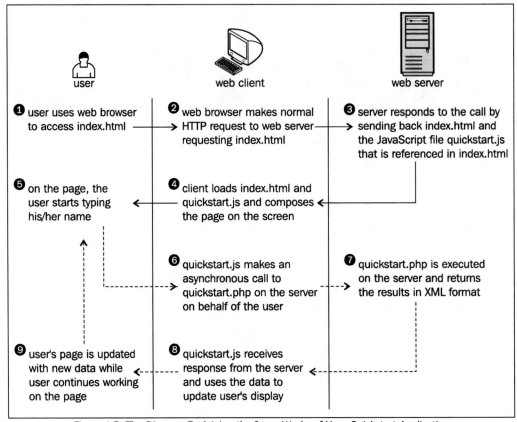

Figure 1.7: The Diagram Explaining the Inner Works of Your Quickstart Application

Steps 1 through 5 are a typical HTTP request. After making the request, the user needs to wait until the page gets loaded. With typical (non-AJAX) web applications, such a page reload happens every time the client needs to get new data from the server.

Steps 5 through 9 demonstrate an AJAX-type call—more specifically, a sequence of asynchronous HTTP requests. The server is accessed in the background using the XMLHttpRequest object. During this period the user can continue to use the page normally, as if it was a normal desktop application. No page refresh or reload is experienced in order to retrieve data from the server and update the web page with that data.

Now it's about time to implement this code on your machine. Before moving on, ensure you've prepared your working environment as shown in Appendix A, where you're guided through how to install and set up PHP and Apache, and set up the database used for the examples in this book. (You won't need a database for this quickstart example.)

All exercises from this book assume that you've installed your machine as shown in Appendix A. If you set up your environment differently you may need to implement various changes, such as using different folder names, and so on.

Time for Action—Quickstart AJAX

1. In Appendix A, you're instructed to set up a web server, and create a web-accessible folder called ajax to host all your code for this book. Under the ajax folder, create a new folder called quickstart.

2. In the quickstart folder, create a file called index.html, and add the following code to it:

```
<!DOCTYPE html PUBLIC "-//W3C//DTD XHTML 1.0 Transitional//EN"
"http://www.w3.org/TR/xhtml1/DTD/xhtml1-transitional.dtd">
<html xmlns="http://www.w3.org/1999/xhtml">
  <head>
    <title>AJAX with PHP: Quickstart</title>
    <script type="text/javascript" src="quickstart.js"></script>
  </head>
  <body onload='process()'>
    Server wants to know your name:
    <input type="text" id="myName" />
    <div id="divMessage" />
  </body>
</html>
```

3. Create a new file called quickstart.js, and add the following code:

```
// stores the reference to the XMLHttpRequest object
var xmlHttp = createXmlHttpRequestObject();

// retrieves the XMLHttpRequest object
function createXmlHttpRequestObject()
{
  // will store the reference to the XMLHttpRequest object
  var xmlHttp;
  // if running Internet Explorer
  if(window.ActiveXObject)
  {
    try
    {
      xmlHttp = new ActiveXObject("Microsoft.XMLHTTP");
    }
    catch (e)
    {
      xmlHttp = false;
    }
  }
  // if running Mozilla or other browsers
  else
  {
    try
    {
      xmlHttp = new XMLHttpRequest();
    }
    catch (e)
    {
      xmlHttp = false;
    }
  }
  // return the created object or display an error message
  if (!xmlHttp)
```

21

```
        alert("Error creating the XMLHttpRequest object.");
    else
        return xmlHttp;
}

// make asynchronous HTTP request using the XMLHttpRequest object
function process()
{
    // proceed only if the xmlHttp object isn't busy
    if (xmlHttp.readyState == 4 || xmlHttp.readyState == 0)
    {
        // retrieve the name typed by the user on the form
        name = encodeURIComponent(document.getElementById("myName").value);
        // execute the quickstart.php page from the server
        xmlHttp.open("GET", "quickstart.php?name=" + name, true);
        // define the method to handle server responses
        xmlHttp.onreadystatechange = handleServerResponse;
        // make the server request
        xmlHttp.send(null);
    }
    else
        // if the connection is busy, try again after one second
        setTimeout('process()', 1000);
}

// executed automatically when a message is received from the server
function handleServerResponse()
{
    // move forward only if the transaction has completed
    if (xmlHttp.readyState == 4)
    {
        // status of 200 indicates the transaction completed successfully
        if (xmlHttp.status == 200)
        {
            // extract the XML retrieved from the server
            xmlResponse = xmlHttp.responseXML;
            // obtain the document element (the root element) of the XML structure
            xmlDocumentElement = xmlResponse.documentElement;
            // get the text message, which is in the first child of
            // the the document element
            helloMessage = xmlDocumentElement.firstChild.data;
            // update the client display using the data received from the server
            document.getElementById("divMessage").innerHTML =
                                    '<i>' + helloMessage + '</i>';
            // restart sequence
            setTimeout('process()', 1000);
        }
        // a HTTP status different than 200 signals an error
        else
        {
            alert("There was a problem accessing the server: " +
xmlHttp.statusText);
        }
    }
}
```

4. Create a file called `quickstart.php` and add the following code to it:

```php
<?php
// we'll generate XML output
header('Content-Type: text/xml');
// generate XML header
echo '<?xml version="1.0" encoding="UTF-8" standalone="yes"?>';
// create the <response> element
echo '<response>';
```

```
    // retrieve the user name
    $name = $_GET['name'];
    // generate output depending on the user name received from client
    $userNames = array('CRISTIAN', 'BOGDAN', 'FILIP', 'MIHAI', 'YODA');
    if (in_array(strtoupper($name), $userNames))
      echo 'Hello, master ' . htmlentities($name) . '!';
    else if (trim($name) == '')
      echo 'Stranger, please tell me your name!';
    else
      echo htmlentities($name) . ', I don\'t know you!';
    // close the <response> element
    echo '</response>';
    ?>
```

5. Now you should be able to access your new program by loading http://localhost/ajax/quickstart using your favorite web browser. Load the page, and you should get a page like those shown in Figures 1.5 and 1.6.

> Should you encounter any problems running the application, check that you correctly followed the installation and configuration procedures as described in Appendix A. Most errors happen because of small problems such as typos. In Chapter 2 and Chapter3 you'll learn how to implement error handling in your JavaScript and PHP code.

What Just Happened?

Here comes the fun part—understanding what happens in that code. (Remember that we'll discuss much more technical details over the following two chapters.)

Let's start with the file the user first interacts with, index.html. This file references the mysterious JavaScript file called quickstart.js, and builds a very simple web interface for the client. In the following code snippet from index.html, notice the elements highlighted in bold:

```
<body onload='process()'>
  Server wants to know your name:
  <input type="text" id="myName" />
  <div id="divMessage" />
</body>
```

When the page loads, a function from quickstart.js called process() gets executed. This somehow causes the <div> element to be populated with a message from the server.

Before seeing what happens inside the process() function, let's see what happens at the server side. On the web server you have a script called quickstart.php that builds the XML message to be sent to the client. This XML message consists of a <response> element that packages the message the server needs to send back to the client:

```
<?xml version="1.0" encoding="UTF-8" standalone="yes"?>
<response>
  ... message the server wants to transmit to the client ...
</response>
```

If the user name received from the client is empty, the message will be, "Stranger, please tell me your name!". If the name is Cristian, Bogdan, Filip, Mihai, or Yoda, the server responds with "Hello, master <user name>!". If the name is anything else, the message will be "<user name>, I don't know you!". So if Mickey Mouse types his name, the server will send back the following XML structure:

```
<?xml version="1.0" encoding="UTF-8" standalone="yes"?>
<response>
  Mickey Mouse, I don't know you!
</response>
```

The `quickstart.php` script starts by generating the XML document header and the opening `<response>` element:

```php
<?php
// we'll generate XML output
header('Content-Type: text/xml');
// generate XML header
echo '<?xml version="1.0" encoding="UTF-8" standalone="yes"?>';
// create the <response> element
echo '<response>';
```

The highlighted header line marks the output as an XML document, and this is important because the client expects to receive XML (the **API** used to parse the XML on the client will throw an error if the header doesn't set `Content-Type` to `text/xml`). After setting the header, the code builds the XML response by joining strings. The actual text to be returned to the client is encapsulated in the `<response>` element, which is the root element, and is generated based on the name received from the client via a GET parameter:

```php
// retrieve the user name
$name = $_GET['name'];
// generate output depending on the user name received from client
$userNames = array('CRISTIAN', 'BOGDAN', 'FILIP', 'MIHAI', 'YODA');
if (in_array(strtoupper($name), $userNames))
  echo 'Hello, master ' . htmlentities($name) . '!';
else if (trim($name) == '')
  echo 'Stranger, please tell me your name!';
else
  echo htmlentities($name) . ', I don\'t know you!';
// close the <response> element
echo '</response>';
?>
```

The text entered by the user (which is supposed to be the user's name) is sent by the client to the server using a GET parameter. When sending this text back to the client, we use the `htmlentities` PHP function to replace special characters with their HTML codes (such as &, or >), making sure the message will be safely displayed in the web browser eliminating potential problems and security risks.

> Formatting the text on the server for the client (instead of doing this directly at the client) is actually a bad practice when writing production code. Ideally, the server's responsibility is to send data in a generic format, and it is the recipient's responsibility to deal with security and formatting issues. This makes even more sense if you think that one day you may need to insert exactly the same text into a database, but the database will need different formatting sequences (in that case as well, a database handling script would do the formatting job, and not the server). For the quickstart scenario, formatting the HTML in PHP allowed us to keep the code shorter and simpler to understand and explain.

If you're curious to test `quickstart.php` and see what it generates, load `http://localhost/ajax/quickstart/quickstart.php?name=Yoda` in your web browser. The advantage of sending parameters from the client via GET is that it's very simple to emulate such a request using your web browser, since GET simply means that you append the parameters as name/value pairs in the URL query string. You should get something like this:

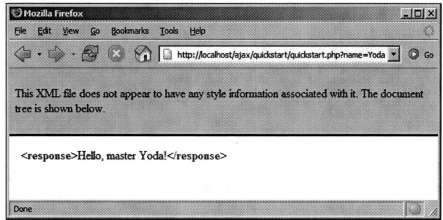

Figure 1.8: The XML Data Generated by quickstart.php

This XML message is read on the client by the `handleServerResponse()` function in `quickstart.js`. More specifically, the following lines of code extract the "Hello, master Yoda!" message:

```
// extract the XML retrieved from the server
xmlResponse = xmlHttp.responseXML;
// obtain the document element (the root element) of the XML structure
xmlDocumentElement = xmlResponse.documentElement;
// get the text message, which is in the first child of
// the document element
helloMessage = xmlDocumentElement.firstChild.data;
```

Here, `xmlHttp` is the XMLHttpRequest object used to call the server script `quickstart.php` from the client. Its `responseXML` property extracts the retrieved XML document. XML structures are hierarchical by nature, and the root element of an XML document is called the *document element*. In our case, the document element is the `<response>` element, which contains a single child, which is the text message we're interested in. Once the text message is retrieved, it's displayed on the client's page by using the DOM to access the `divMessage` element in `index.html`:

```
// update the client display using the data received from the server
document.getElementById('divMessage').innerHTML = helloMessage;
```

`document` is a default object in JavaScript that allows you to manipulate the elements in the HTML code of your page.

The rest of the code in `quickstart.js` deals with making the request to the server to obtain the XML message. The `createXmlHttpRequestObject()` function creates and returns an instance of the XMLHttpRequest object. This function is longer than it could be because we need to make it cross-browser compatible—we'll discuss the details in Chapter 2, for now it's important to know what it does. The XMLHttpRequest instance, called xmlHttp, is used in process() to make the asynchronous server request:

```
// make asynchronous HTTP request using the XMLHttpRequest object
function process()
{
    // proceed only if the xmlHttp object isn't busy
    if (xmlHttp.readyState == 4 || xmlHttp.readyState == 0)
    {
        // retrieve the name typed by the user on the form
        name = encodeURIComponent(document.getElementById("myName").value);
        // execute the quickstart.php page from the server
        xmlHttp.open("GET", "quickstart.php?name=" + name, true);
        // define the method to handle server responses
        xmlHttp.onreadystatechange = handleServerResponse;
        // make the server request
        xmlHttp.send(null);
    }
    else
        // if the connection is busy, try again after one second
        setTimeout('process()', 1000);
}
```

What you see here is, actually, the heart of AJAX—the code that makes the asynchronous call to the server.

Why is it so important to call the server asynchronously? Asynchronous requests, by their nature, don't freeze processing (and user experience) while the call is made, until the response is received. Asynchronous processing is implemented by *event-driven* architectures, a good example being the way graphical user interface code is built: without events, you'd probably need to check continuously if the user has clicked a button or resized a window. Using events, the button notifies the application automatically when it has been clicked, and you can take the necessary actions in the event handler function. With AJAX, this theory applies when making a server request—you are automatically notified when the response comes back.

If you're curious to see how the application would work using a synchronous request, you need to change the third parameter of xmlHttp.open to false, and then call handleServerResponse manually, as shown below. If you try this, the input box where you're supposed to write your name will freeze when the server is contacted (in this case the freeze length depends largely on the connection speed, so it may not be very noticeable if you're running the server on the local machine).

```
// function calls the server using the XMLHttpRequest object
function process()
{
    // retrieve the name typed by the user on the form
    name = encodeURIComponent(document.getElementById("myName").value);
    // execute the quickstart.php page from the server
    xmlHttp.open("GET", "quickstart.php?name=" + name, false);
    // make synchronous server request (freezes processing until completed)
    xmlHttp.send(null);
    // read the response
    handleServerResponse();
}
```

The process() function is supposed to initiate a new server request using the XMLHttpRequest object. However, this is only possible if the XMLHttpRequest object isn't busy making another request. In our case, this can happen if it takes more than one second for the server to reply, which could happen if the Internet connection is very slow. So, process() starts by verifying that it is clear to initiate a new request:

```
// make asynchronous HTTP request using the XMLHttpRequest object
function process()
{
    // proceed only if the xmlHttp object isn't busy
    if (xmlHttp.readyState == 4 || xmlHttp.readyState == 0)
    {
```

So, if the connection is busy, we use setTimeout to retry after one second (the function's second argument specifies the number of milliseconds to wait before executing the piece of code specified by the first argument:

```
// if the connection is busy, try again after one second
setTimeout('process()', 1000);
```

If the line is clear, you can safely make a new request. The line of code that prepares the server request but doesn't commit it is:

```
// execute the quickstart.php page from the server
xmlHttp.open("GET", 'quickstart.php?name=' + name, true);
```

The first parameter specifies the method used to send the user name to the server, and you can choose between GET and POST (learn more about them in Chapter 3). The second parameter is the server page you want to access; when the first parameter is GET, you send the parameters as name/value pairs in the query string. The third parameter is true if you want the call to be made asynchronously. When making asynchronous calls, you don't wait for a response. Instead, you define another function to be called *automatically* when the state of the request changes:

```
// define the method to handle server responses
xmlHttp.onreadystatechange = handleServerResponse;
```

Once you've set this option, you can rest calm—the handleServerResponse function will be executed by the system when anything happens to your request. After everything is set up, you initiate the request by calling XMLHttpRequest's send method:

```
// make the server request
xmlHttp.send(null);
}
```

Let's now look at the handleServerResponse function:

```
// executed automatically when a message is received from the server
function handleServerResponse()
{
    // move forward only if the transaction has completed
    if (xmlHttp.readyState == 4)
    {
        // status of 200 indicates the transaction completed successfully
        if (xmlHttp.status == 200)
        {
```

The handleServerResponse function is called multiple times, whenever the status of the request changes. Only when xmlHttp.readyState is 4 will the server request be completed so you can move forward to read the results. You can also check that the HTTP transaction reported a status of 200, signaling that no problems happened during the HTTP request. When these conditions are met, you're free to read the server response and display the message to the user.

After the response is received and used, the process is restarted using the `setTimeout` function, which will cause the `process()` function to be executed after one second (note though that it's not necessary, or even AJAX specific, to have repetitive tasks in your client-side code):

```
// restart sequence
setTimeout('process()', 1000);
```

Finally, let's reiterate what happens after the user loads the page (you can refer to Figure 1.7 for a visual representation):

1. The user loads `index.html` (this corresponds to steps 1-4 in Figure 1.7).

2. User starts (or continues) typing his or her name (this corresponds to step 5 in Figure 1.7).

3. When the `process()` method in `quickstart.js` is executed, it calls a server script named `quickstart.php` asynchronously. The text entered by the user is passed on the call as a query string parameter (it is passed via GET). The `handeServerResponse` function is designed to handle request state changes.

4. `quickstart.php` executes on the server. It composes an XML document that encapsulates the message the server wants to transmit to the client.

5. The `handleServerResponse` method on the client is executed multiple times as the state of the request changes. The last time it's called is when the response has been successfully received. The XML is read; the message is extracted and displayed on the page.

6. The user display is updated with the new message from the server, but the user can continue typing without any interruptions. After a delay of one second, the process is restarted from step 2.

Summary

This chapter was all about a quick introduction to the world of AJAX. In order to proceed with learning how to build AJAX applications, it's important to understand why and where they are useful. As with any other technology, AJAX isn't the answer to all problems, but it offers means to solve some of them.

AJAX combines client-side and server-side functionality to enhance the user experience of your site. The `XMLHttpRequest` object is the key element that enables the client-side JavaScript code to call a page on the server asynchronously. This chapter was intentionally short and probably has left you with many questions—that's good! Be prepared for a whole book dedicated to answering questions and demonstrating lots of interesting functionality!

2

Client-Side Techniques with Smarter JavaScript

It is said that one picture is worth a thousand words. And so is a well-written piece of code, we would say. You will get plenty of both, while building the foundations for your future AJAX-enabled applications, in this chapter and the next.

Hopefully, the first chapter has developed your interest in AJAX well enough that you will endure a second chapter with lots of theory to be learned. On the other hand, if you found the first exercise too challenging, be assured that this time we will advance a bit slower. We will learn the theory in parts by going through many short examples. In this chapter, we will meet client AJAX technologies, which include:

- JavaScript
- The JavaScript DOM
- Cascading Style Sheets (CSS)
- The XMLHttpRequest object
- Extensible Markup Language (XML)

You will learn how to make these components work together smoothly, and form a strong foundation for your future AJAX applications. You will see how to implement efficient error handling techniques, and how to write code efficiently. Chapter 3 will complete the foundations by presenting the techniques and technologies that you use on the server; in our case, PHP, MySQL, and others.

To be a good AJAX developer you need to know very well how its ingredients work separately, and then master how to make them work together. In this book, we assume you have some experience with at least a part of these technologies.

Depending on your experience level, take some time—before, while, or after reading Chapter 2 or Chapter 3, to have a look at Appendix B on http://ajaxphp.packtpub.com, which shows you a number of tools that make a programmer's life much easier. Don't skip it, because it's important, as having the right tools and using them efficiently can make a very big difference.

You can see all the example applications from this book online at http://ajaxphp.packtpub.com/.

JavaScript and the Document Object Model

As mentioned in Chapter 1, JavaScript is the heart of AJAX. JavaScript has a similar syntax to the good old C language. JavaScript is a *parsed language* (not compiled), and it has some **Object-Oriented Programming (OOP)** capabilities. JavaScript wasn't meant for building large powerful applications, but for writing simple scripts to implement (or complement) a web application's client-side functionality (however, new trends are tending to transform JavaScript into an enterprise-class language—it remains to be seen how far this will go).

JavaScript is fully supported by the vast majority of web browsers. Although it is possible to execute JavaScript scripts by themselves, they are usually loaded on the client browsers together with HTML code that needs their functionality. The fact that the entire JavaScript code must arrive unaltered at the client is a strength and weakness at the same time, and you need to consider these aspects before deciding upon a framework for your web solution. You can find very good introductions to JavaScript at the following web links:

- `http://www.echoecho.com/javascript.htm`
- `http://www.devlearn.com/javascript/jsvars.html`
- `http://www.w3schools.com/js/default.asp`

Part of JavaScript's power on the client resides in its ability to manipulate the parent HTML document, and it does that through the DOM interface. The DOM is available with a multitude of languages and technologies, including JavaScript, Java, PHP, C#, C++, and so on. In this chapter, you will see how to use the DOM with both JavaScript and PHP. The DOM has the ability to manipulate (create, modify, parse, search, etc.) XML-like documents, HTML included.

On the client side, you will use the DOM and JavaScript to:

- Manipulate the HTML page while you are working on it
- Read and parse XML documents received from the server
- Create new XML documents

On the server side, you can use the DOM and PHP to:

- Compose XML documents, usually for sending them to the client
- Read XML documents received from various sources

Two good introductions to DOM can be found at `http://www.quirksmode.org/dom/intro.html` and `http://www.javascriptkit.com/javatutors/dom.shtml`. Play a nice DOM game here: `http://www.topxml.com/learning/games/b/default.asp`. A comprehensive reference of the JavaScript DOM can be found at `http://krook.org/jsdom/`. The Mozilla reference for the JavaScript DOM is available at `http://www.mozilla.org/docs/dom/reference/javascript.html`.

In the first example of this chapter, you will use the DOM from JavaScript to manipulate the HTML document. When adding JavaScript code to an HTML file, one option is to write the JavaScript code in a `<script>` element within the `<body>` element. Take the following HTML file for example, which executes some simple JavaScript code when loaded. Notice the `document` object, which is a default object in JavaScript that interacts with the DOM of the HTML page. Here we use its `write` method to add content to the page:

```
<!DOCTYPE html PUBLIC "-//W3C//DTD XHTML 1.1//EN"
"http://www.w3.org/TR/xhtml11/DTD/xhtml11.dtd">
<html>
  <head>
    <title>AJAX Foundations: JavaScript and DOM</title>
    <script type="text/javascript">
      // declaring new variables
      var date = new Date();
      var hour = date.getHours();
      // demonstrating the if statement
      if (hour >= 22 || hour <= 5)
        document.write("You should go to sleep.");
      else
        document.write("Hello, world!");
    </script>
  </head>
  <body>
  </body>
</html>
```

The document.write commands generate output that is added to the <body> element of the page when the script executes. The content that you generate becomes part of the HTML code of the page, so you can add HTML tags in there if you want.

We advise you try to write well-formed and valid HTML code when possible. Writing code compliant to HTML format maximizes the chances that your pages will work fine with most existing and future web browsers. A useful article about following web standards can be found at http://www.w3.org/QA/2002/04/web-quality. You can find a useful explanation of the DOCTYPE element at http://www.alistapart.com/stories/doctype/. The debate on standards seems to be an endless one, with one group of people being very passionate about strictly following the standards, while others are just interested in their pages looking good on a certain set of browsers. The examples in this book contain valid HTML code, with the exception of a few cases where we broke the rules a little bit in order to make the code easier to understand. A real fact is that very few online websites follow the standards, for various reasons.

You will usually prefer to write the JavaScript code in a separate .js file that is referenced from the .html file. This allows you to keep the HTML code clean and have all the JavaScript code organized in a single place. You can reference a JavaScript file in HTML code by adding a child element called <script> to the <head> element, like this:

```
<html>
  <head>
    <script type="text/javascript" src="file.js"></script>
  </head>
</html>
```

Even if you don't have any code between <script> and </script> tags, don't be tempted to use the short form <script type="text/javascript" src="file.js" />

This causes problems with Internet Explorer 6, which doesn't load the JavaScript page.

Let's do a short exercise.

Time for Action—*Playing with JavaScript and the DOM*

1. Create a folder called `foundations` in your `ajax` folder. This folder will be used for all the examples in this chapter and the next chapter.

2. In the `foundations` folder, create a subfolder called `jsdom`.

3. In the `jsdom` folder, add a file called `jsdom.html`, with the following code in it:

```
<!DOCTYPE html PUBLIC "-//W3C//DTD XHTML 1.1//EN"
"http://www.w3.org/TR/xhtml11/DTD/xhtml11.dtd">
<html>
  <head>
    <title>AJAX Foundations: JavaScript and DOM</title>
    <script type="text/javascript" src="jsdom.js"></script>
  </head>
  <body>
    I love you!
  </body>
</html>
```

4. In the same folder create a file called `jsdom.js`, and write this code in the file:

```
// declaring new variables
var date = new Date();
var hour = date.getHours();
// demonstrating the if statement
if (hour >= 22 || hour <= 5)
  document.write("Goodnight, world!");
else
  document.write("Hello, world!");
```

5. Load `http://localhost/ajax/foundations/jsdom/jsdom.html` in your web browser, and assuming it's not late enough, expect to see the message as shown in Figure 2.1 (if it's past 10 PM, the message would be a bit different, but equally romantic).

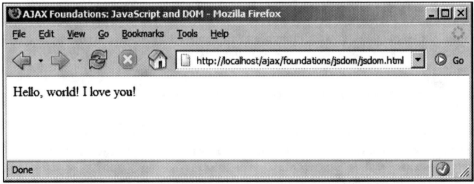

Figure 2.1: The Hello World Example with JavaScript and the DOM

What Just Happened?

The code is very simple indeed and hence it doesn't need too many explanations. Here are the main ideas you need to understand:

- Because there is no server-side script involved (such as PHP code), you can load the file in your web browser directly from the disk, locally, instead of accessing it through an HTTP web server. If you execute the file directly from disk, a web browser would likely open it automatically using a local address such as `file:///C:/Apache2/htdocs/ajax/foundations/jsdom/jsdom.html`.

- When loading an HTML page with JavaScript code from a local location (`file://`) rather than through a web server (`http://`), Internet Explorer may warn you that you're about to execute code with high privileges (more on security in Chapter 3).

- JavaScript doesn't require you to declare the variables, so in theory you can avoid the var keywords. This isn't a recommended practice though.

- The JavaScript script executes automatically when you load the HTML file. You can, however, group the code in JavaScript functions, which only execute when called explicitly.

- The JavaScript code is executed *before* parsing the other HTML code, so its output is displayed before the HTML output. Notice that "Hello World!"appears before "I love you!".

One of the problems of the presented code is that you have no control in the JavaScript code over where the output should be displayed. As it is, the JavaScript output appears first, and the contents of the <body> element come next. Needless to say, this scenario isn't relevant even to the simplest of applications.

Except for the most simple of cases, having just JavaScript code that executes unconditionally when the HTML page loads is not enough. You will usually want to have more control over when and how portions of JavaScript code execute, and the most typical scenario is when you use JavaScript *functions*, and execute these functions when certain *events* (such as clicking a button) on the HTML page are triggered.

JavaScript Events and the DOM

In the next exercise, we will create an HTML structure from JavaScript code. When preparing to build a web page that has dynamically generated parts, you first need to create its *template* (which contains the static parts), and use placeholders for the dynamic parts. The placeholders must be uniquely identifiable HTML elements (elements with the ID attribute set). So far we have used the <div> element as placeholder, but you will meet more examples over the course of this book.

Take a look at the following HTML document:

```
<!DOCTYPE html PUBLIC "-//W3C//DTD XHTML 1.1//EN"
"http://www.w3.org/TR/xhtml11/DTD/xhtml11.dtd">
<html>
  <head>
    <title>AJAX Foundations: More JavaScript and DOM</title>
  </head>
  <body>
    Hello Dude! Here's a cool list of colors for you:
    <br/>
    <ul>
      <li>Black</li>
```

```
        <li>Orange</li>
        <li>Pink</li>
      </ul>
   </body>
</html>
```

Suppose that you want to have everything in the `<ul>` element generated dynamically. The typical way to do this in an AJAX application is to place a named, empty `<div>` element in the place where you want something to be generated dynamically:

```
<!DOCTYPE html PUBLIC "-//W3C//DTD XHTML 1.1//EN"
"http://www.w3.org/TR/xhtml11/DTD/xhtml11.dtd">
<html>
   <head>
      <title>AJAX Foundations: More JavaScript and DOM</title>
   </head>
   <body>
      Hello Dude! Here's a cool list of colors for you:
      <br/>
      <div id="myDivElement"/>
   </body>
</html>
```

In this example we will use the `<div>` element to populate the HTML document from JavaScript code, but keep in mind that you're free to assign `id`s to all kinds of HTML elements. When adding the `<ul>` element to the `<div>` element, after the JavaScript code executes, you will end up with the following HTML structure:

```
<!DOCTYPE html PUBLIC "-//W3C//DTD XHTML 1.1//EN"
"http://www.w3.org/TR/xhtml11/DTD/xhtml11.dtd">
<html>
   <head>
      <title>Colors</title>
   </head>
   <body>
      Hello Dude! Here's a cool list of colors for you:
      <br/>
      <div id="myDivElement">
        <ul>
          <li>Black</li>
          <li>Orange</li>
          <li>Pink</li>
        </ul>
      </div>
   </body>
</html>
```

Your goals for the next exercise are:

- Access the named `<div>` element programmatically from the JavaScript function.

- Having the JavaScript code execute *after* the HTML template is loaded, so you can access the `<div>` element (no HTML elements are accessible from JavaScript code that executes referenced from the `<head>` element). You will do that by calling JavaScript code from the `<body>` element's `onload` event.

- Group the JavaScript code in a function for easier code handling.

Time for Action—Using JavaScript Events and the DOM

1. In the `foundations` folder that you created in the previous exercise, create a new folder called `morejsdom`.

2. In the `morejsdom` folder, create a file called `morejsdom.html`, and add the following code to it:

```
<!DOCTYPE html PUBLIC "-//W3C//DTD XHTML 1.1//EN"
"http://www.w3.org/TR/xhtml11/DTD/xhtml11.dtd">
<html>
  <head>
    <title>AJAX Foundations: More JavaScript and DOM</title>
    <script type="text/javascript" src="morejsdom.js"></script>
  </head>
  <body onload="process()">
    Hello Dude! Here's a cool list of colors for you:
    <br />
    <div id="myDivElement" />
  </body>
</html>
```

3. Add a new file called `morejsdom.js`, with the following contents:

```
function process()
{
  // Create the HTML code
  var string;
  string = "<ul>"
         + "<li>Black</li>"
         + "<li>Orange</li>"
         + "<li>Pink</li>"
         + "</ul>";
  // obtain a reference to the <div> element on the page
  myDiv = document.getElementById("myDivElement");
  // add content to the <div> element
  myDiv.innerHTML = string;
}
```

4. Load `morejsdom.html` in a web browser. You should see a window like the one in Figure 2.2:

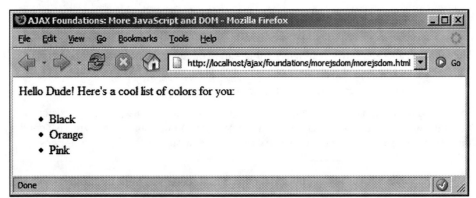

Figure 2.2: Your Little HTML Page in Action

What Just Happened?

The code is pretty simple. In the HTML code, the important details are highlighted in the following code snippet:

```
<!DOCTYPE html PUBLIC "-//W3C//DTD XHTML 1.1//EN"
"http://www.w3.org/TR/xhtml11/DTD/xhtml11.dtd">
<html>
  <head>
    <title>AJAX Foundations: More JavaScript and DOM</title>
    <script type="text/javascript" src="morejsdom.js"></script>
  </head>
  <body onload="process()">
    Hello Dude! Here's a cool list of colors for you:
    <br/>
    <div id="myDivElement" />
  </body>
</html>
```

Everything starts by referencing the JavaScript source file using the `<script>` element. The JavaScript file contains a function called `process()`, which is used as an event-handler function for the body's `onload` event. The `onload` event fires after the HTML file is fully loaded, so when the `process()` function executes, it has access to the whole HTML structure. Your `process()` function starts by creating the HTML code you want to add to the `div` element:

```
function process()
{
    // Create the HTML code
    var string;
    string = "<ul>"
           + "<li>Black</li>"
           + "<li>Orange</li>"
           + "<li>Pink</li>"
           + "</ul>";
```

Next, you obtain a reference to `myDivElement`, using the `getElementById` function of the document object. Remember that `document` is a default object in JavaScript, referencing the body of your HTML document.

```
    // obtain a reference to the <div> element on the page
    myDiv = document.getElementById("myDivElement");
```

> Note that JavaScript allows you to use either single quotes or double quotes for string variables. The previous line of code can be successfully written like this:
>
> ```
> myDiv = document.getElementById('myDivElement');
> ```
>
> In the case of JavaScript, both choices are equally good, as long as you are consistent about using only one of them. If you use both notations in the same script you risk ending up with parse errors. In this book, we will use double quotes in JavaScript programs.

Finally, you populate `myDivElement` by adding the HTML code you built in the `string` variable:

```
    // add content to the <div> element
    myDiv.innerHTML = string;
}
```

In this example, you have used the `innerHTML` property of the DOM to add the composed HTML to your document.

Even More DOM

In the previous exercise, you have created the list of elements by joining strings to compose a simple HTML structure. The same HTML structure can be built programmatically using the DOM. In the next exercise, you will generate this content programmatically:

```
<div id="myDivElement">
    Hello Dude! Here's a cool list of colors for you:
    <br/>
    <ul>
        <li>Black</li>
        <li>Orange</li>
        <li>Pink</li>
    </ul>
</div>
```

A DOM document is a hierarchical structure of elements, where each element can have one or more attributes. In this HTML fragment, the single element with an attribute is <div>, which has an attribute called id with the value myDivElement. The root node that you can access through the document object is <body>. When implementing the above HTML document, you will end up with a structure such as the one in the figure below:

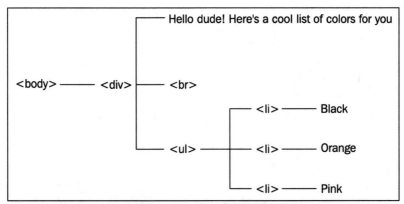

Figure 2.3: A Hierarchy of HTML Elements

In Figure 2.3, you see an HTML structure formed of <body>, <div>, <br>, <ul>, and <li> elements, and four text nodes ("Hello...", "Black", "Orange", "Pink"). In the next exercise, you will create this structure using the DOM functions createElement, createTextNode, and appendChild.

Time for Action—Even More DOM

1. In the foundations folder, create a subfolder called evenmorejsdom.

2. In the evenmorejsdom folder, create a file called evenmorejsdom.html, and add the following code to it:

```
<!DOCTYPE html PUBLIC "-//W3C//DTD XHTML 1.1//EN"
"http://www.w3.org/TR/xhtml11/DTD/xhtml11.dtd">
<html>
    <head>
        <title>AJAX Foundations: Even More JavaScript and DOM</title>
        <script type="text/javascript" src="evenmorejsdom.js"></script>
    </head>
```

```
    <body onload="process()">
      <div id="myDivElement" />
    </body>
</html>
```

3. Add a new file called evenmorejsdom.js, with the following contents:

```
function process()
{
    // create the first text node
    oHello = document.createTextNode
                        ("Hello Dude! Here's a cool list of colors for you:");

    // create the <ul> element
    oUl = document.createElement("ul")

    // create the first <ui> element and add a text node to it
    oLiBlack = document.createElement("li");
    oBlack = document.createTextNode("Black");
    oLiBlack.appendChild(oBlack);

    // create the second <ui> element and add a text node to it
    oLiOrange = document.createElement("li");
    oOrange = document.createTextNode("Orange");
    oLiOrange.appendChild(oOrange);

    // create the third <ui> element and add a text node to it
    oLiPink = document.createElement("li");
    oPink = document.createTextNode("Pink");
    oLiPink.appendChild(oPink);

    // add the <ui> elements as children to the <ul> element
    oUl.appendChild(oLiBlack);
    oUl.appendChild(oLiOrange);
    oUl.appendChild(oLiPink);

    // obtain a reference to the <div> element on the page
    myDiv = document.getElementById("myDivElement");

    // add content to the <div> element
    myDiv.appendChild(oHello);
    myDiv.appendChild(oUl);
}
```

4. Load evenmoredom.html in a web browser. The result should look like Figure 2.4:

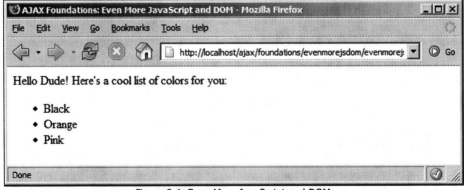

Figure 2.4: Even More JavaScript and DOM

What Just Happened?

Well, what just happened is exactly what happened after the previous exercise, but this time with much more code, as you can see by having a look at the process() function. Although there are many lines of code, the functionality is pretty simple. This suggests clearly enough that using the DOM to create HTML structures may not always be the best option. However, in certain circumstances it can actually make programming easier, for the following reasons:

- It's fairly easy to programmatically create dynamic HTML structures, such as building elements in for loops, because you're not concerned about text formatting but about building the structural elements.

- As a consequence, you don't need, for example, to manually add closing tags. When you add a 'ui' element, the DOM will take care to generate the <ui> tag and an associated closing </ui> tag for you.

- You can treat the nodes as if they were independent nodes, and decide later how to build the hierarchy. Again, the DOM takes care of the implementation details; you just need to tell it what you want.

JavaScript, DOM, and CSS

CSS (Cascading Style Sheets) is certainly a familiar term for you. CSS allows setting formatting options in a centralized document that is referenced from HTML files. If the job is done right, and CSS is used consistently in a website, CSS will allow you to make visual changes to the entire site (or parts of the site) with very little effort, just by editing the CSS file. There are many books and tutorials on CSS, including the free ones you can find at http://www.w3.org/Style/CSS/ and http://www.w3schools.com/css/default.asp. Although the article that invented the name AJAX (http://www.adaptivepath.com/publications/essays/archives/000385.php) mentions CSS as one of the AJAX ingredients, technically CSS is not required to build successful dynamic web applications. However, its usage is highly recommended because of the significant benefits it brings.

We will do a simple exercise to demonstrate using CSS, and manipulating HTML elements' styles using the DOM. These are usual tasks you will do when building AJAX applications. In the following exercise, you will draw a nice table, and you will have two buttons named Set Style 1 and Set Style 2. These buttons will change the table's colors and appearance by just switching the current styles. See Figure 2.5 to get a feeling about what you're about to create.

Time for Action—Working with CSS and JavaScript

1. In the foundations folder, create a new subfolder called csstest.

2. In your newly created csstest folder, create a new file called csstest.html, with the following contents:

```
<!DOCTYPE html PUBLIC "-//W3C//DTD XHTML 1.1//EN"
"http://www.w3.org/TR/xhtml11/DTD/xhtml11.dtd">
<html>
  <head>
    <title>AJAX Foundations: CSS</title>
    <script type="text/javascript" src="csstest.js"></script>
    <link href="styles.css" type="text/css" rel="stylesheet"/>
  </head>
```

```html
    <body>
      <table id="table">
        <tr>
          <th id="tableHead">
            Product Name
          </th>
        </tr>
        <tr>
          <td id="tableFirstLine">
            Airplane
          </td>
        </tr>
        <tr>
          <td id="tableSecondLine">
            Big car
          </td>
        </tr>
      </table>
      <br />
      <input type="button" value="Set Style 1" onclick="setStyle1();" />
      <input type="button" value="Set Style 2" onclick="setStyle2();" />
    </body>
</html>
```

3. Create a file called csstest.js and write the following code in it:

```javascript
// Change table style to style 1
function setStyle1()
{
  // obtain references to HTML elements
  oTable = document.getElementById("table");
  oTableHead = document.getElementById("tableHead");
  oTableFirstLine = document.getElementById("tableFirstLine");
  oTableSecondLine = document.getElementById("tableSecondLine");
  // set styles
  oTable.className = "Table1";
  oTableHead.className = "TableHead1";
  oTableFirstLine.className = "TableContent1";
  oTableSecondLine.className = "TableContent1";
}

// Change table style to style 2
function setStyle2()
{
  // obtain references to HTML elements
  oTable = document.getElementById("table");
  oTableHead = document.getElementById("tableHead");
  oTableFirstLine = document.getElementById("tableFirstLine");
  oTableSecondLine = document.getElementById("tableSecondLine");
  // set styles
  oTable.className = "Table2";
  oTableHead.className = "TableHead2";
  oTableFirstLine.className = "TableContent2";
  oTableSecondLine.className = "TableContent2";
}
```

4. Finally create the CSS file, styles.css:

```css
.Table1
{
  border: DarkGreen 1px solid;
  background-color: LightGreen;
}
.TableHead1
{
  font-family: Verdana, Arial;
  font-weight: bold;
```

```
      font-size: 10pt;
    }
    .TableContent1
    {
      font-family: Verdana, Arial;
      font-size: 10pt;
    }

    .Table2
    {
      border: DarkBlue 1px solid;
      background-color: LightBlue;
    }
    .TableHead2
    {
      font-family: Verdana, Arial;
      font-weight: bold;
      font-size: 10pt;
    }
    .TableContent2
    {
      font-family: Verdana, Arial;
      font-size: 10pt;
    }
```

5. Load `http://localhost/ajax/foundations/css/css.html` in your web browser, and test that your buttons work as they should.

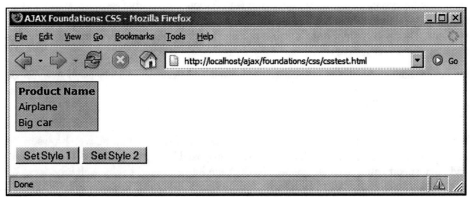

Figure 2.5: Table with CSS and JavaScript

What Just Happened?

Your `styles.css` file contains two sets of styles that can be applied to the table in `csstest.html`. When the user clicks one of the Set Style buttons, the JavaScript DOM is used to assign those styles to the elements of the table.

In the first part of the `setStyle` methods, we use the `getElementByID` function to obtain references to the HTML elements that we want to apply CSS styles to:

```
// obtain references to HTML elements
oTable = document.getElementById("table");
oTableHead = document.getElementById("tableHead");
oTableFirstLine = document.getElementById("tableFirstLine");
oTableSecondLine = document.getElementById("tableSecondLine");
```

As with many other web development tasks, manipulating CSS can be the subject of significant inconsistencies between different browsers. For example, in the previous code snippet, try to rename the object names to be the same as their associated HTML elements (such as renaming oTable to table) to see Internet Explorer stop working. Internet Explorer doesn't like it if there's already an object with that ID in the HTML file. This problem doesn't make much sense because the objects have different scopes, but better watch out if you want your code to work with Internet Explorer as well.

Once initializing these objects, the safe way that works with all browsers to set the elements' CSS style is to use their className property:

```
// set styles
oTable.className = "Table1";
oTableHead.className = "TableHead1";
oTableFirstLine.className = "TableContent1";
oTableSecondLine.className = "TableContent1";
```

Using the XMLHttpRequest Object

XMLHttpRequest is the object that enables the JavaScript code to make asynchronous HTTP server requests. This functionality allows you to make HTTP requests, receive responses, and update parts of the page completely in the background, without the user experiencing any visual interruptions. This is very important because one can keep the user interface responsive while interrogating the server for data.

The XMLHttpRequest object was initially implemented by Microsoft in 1999 as an ActiveX object in Internet Explorer, and eventually became *de facto* standard for all the browsers, being supported as a native object by all modern web browsers except Internet Explorer 6.

Note that even if XMLHttpRequest has become a *de facto* standard in the web browsers, it is not a W3C standard. Similar functionality is proposed by the W3C DOM Level 3 Load and Save specification standard, which hasn't been implemented yet by web browsers.

The typical sequence of operations when working with XMLHttpRequest is as follows:

1. Create an instance of the XMLHttpRequest object.
2. Use the XMLHttpRequest object to make an asynchronous call to a server page, defining a callback function that will be executed automatically when the server response is received.
3. Deal with server's response in the callback function.
4. Go to step 2.

Let's now see how to do these steps with real code.

Creating the XMLHttpRequest Object

The XMLHttpRequest is implemented in different ways by the browsers. In Internet Explorer 6 and older, XMLHttpRequest is implemented as an ActiveX control, and you instantiate it like this:

```
xmlhttp = new ActiveXObject("Microsoft.XMLHttp");
```

For the other web browsers, XMLHttpRequest is a native object, so you create instances of it like this:

```
xmlhttp = new XMLHttpRequest();
```

> The ActiveX XMLHttp library comes is many more flavors and versions that you could imagine. Each piece of Microsoft software, including Internet Explorer and MDAC, came with new versions of this ActiveX control. Microsoft.XMLHTTP is the oldest and can be safely used for basic operations, while the newer versions have performance and feature improvements. You will learn how to automatically use a more recent version.

A simplified version of the code we will use for cross-browser XMLHttpRequest instantiation throughout this book is:

```
// creates an XMLHttpRequest instance
function createXmlHttpRequestObject()
{
  // will store the reference to the XMLHttpRequest object
  var xmlHttp;
  // this should work for all browsers except IE6 and older
  try
  {
    // try to create XMLHttpRequest object
    xmlHttp = new XMLHttpRequest();
  }
  catch(e)
  {
    // assume IE6 or older
    try
    {
      xmlHttp = new ActiveXObject("Microsoft.XMLHttp");
    }
    catch(e) { }
  }
  // return the created object or display an error message
  if (!xmlHttp)
    alert("Error creating the XMLHttpRequest object.");
  else
    return xmlHttp;
}
```

This function is supposed to return an instance of the XMLHttpRequest object. The functionality relies on the JavaScript try/catch construct.

The try/catch construct, initially implemented with OOP languages, offers a powerful exception-handling technique in JavaScript. Basically, when an error happens in JavaScript code, an exception is thrown. The exception has the form of an object that contains the error's (exception's) details. Using the try/catch syntax, you can *catch* the exception and handle it locally, so that the error won't be propagated to the user's browser.

The try/catch syntax is as follows:

```
try
{
    // code that might generate an exception
}
catch (e)
{
    // code that is executed only if an exception was thrown by the try block
    // (exception details are available through the e parameter)
}
```

You place any code that might generate errors inside the try block. If an error happens, the execution is passed immediately to the catch block. If no error happens inside the try block, then the code in the catch block never executes.

Run-time exceptions propagate from the point they were raised, up through the call stack of your program. If you don't handle the exception locally, it will end up getting caught by the web browser, which may display a not very good looking error message to your visitor.

The way you respond to each exception depends very much on the situation at hand. Sometimes you will simply ignore the error, other times you will flag it somehow in the code, or you will display an error message to your visitor. Rest assured that in this book you will meet all kinds of scenarios.

In our particular case, when we want to create an XMLHttpRequest object, we will first try to create the object as if it was a native browser object, like this:

```
// this should work for all browsers except IE6 and older
try
{
    // try to create XMLHttpRequest object
    xmlHttp = new XMLHttpRequest();
}
```

Internet Explorer 7, Mozilla, Opera, and other browsers will execute this piece of code just fine, and no error will be generated, because XMLHttpRequest is a natively supported. However, Internet Explorer 6 and its older versions won't recognize the XMLHttpRequest object, an exception will be generated, and the execution will be passed to the catch block. For Internet Explorer 6 and older versions, the XMLHttpRequest object needs to be created as an ActiveX control:

```
catch(e)
{
    // assume IE6 or older
    try
    {
        xmlHttp = new ActiveXObject("Microsoft.XMLHttp");
    }
    catch(e) { }
}
```

The larger the number of JavaScript programmers, the more XMLHttpRequest object creation methods you will see, and surprisingly enough, they will all work fine. In this book, we prefer the method that uses try and catch to instantiate the object, because we think it has the best chance of working well with future browsers, while doing a proper error checking without consuming too many lines of code.

You could, for example, check whether your browser supports XMLHttpRequest before trying to instantiate it, using the typeof function:

```
if (typeof XMLHttpRequest != "undefined")
   xmlHttp = new XMLHttpRequest();
```

Using typeof can often prove to be very helpful. In our particular case, using typeof doesn't eliminate the need to guard against errors using try/catch, so you would just end up typing more lines of code.

An alternative way to achieve the same functionality is by using a JavaScript feature called **object detection**. This feature allows you to check whether a particular object is supported by the browser, and works like this:

```
if (window.XMLHttpRequest)
  xmlHttp = new XMLHttpRequest();
```

For example, by checking for window.activex you can find if the browser is Internet Explorer. Once again, we're not using this technique because it would simply add more lines of code without bringing any benefits; but the ideas are good to keep nevertheless.

If you decide to use object detection, please be sure to check for XMLHttpRequest first before checking for ActiveX support. The reason for this recommendation is Internet Explorer 7, which supports both ActiveX and XMLHttpRequest; the latter is better because it gives you the latest object version. With ActiveX, as you will see, you need to write quite a bit of code to ensure that you get a recent version, although you still are not guaranteed to get the latest one.

At the end of our createxmlHttpRequestobject function, we test that after all the efforts, we have ended up obtaining a valid XMLHttpRequest instance:

```
// return the created object or display an error message
if (!xmlHttp)
   alert("Error creating the XMLHttpRequest object.");
else
   return xmlHttp;
```

> The reverse effect of object detection is even nicer than the feature itself. Object detection says that JavaScript will evaluate a valid object instance, such as (xmlHttp), to true. The nice thing is that (!xmlHttp) expression returns true not only if xmlHttp is false, but also if it is null or undefined.

Creating Better Objects for Internet Explorer

The one thing that can be improved about the createxmlHttpRequestobject function is to have it recognize the latest version of the ActiveX control, in case the browser is Internet Explorer 6. In most cases, you can rely on the basic functionality provided by ActivexObject("Microsoft.XMLHttp"), but if you want to try using a more recent version, you can.

The typical solution is to try creating the latest known version, and if it fails, ignore the error and retry with an older version, and so on until you get an object instead of an exception. The latest *prog ID* of the XMLHTTP ActiveX Object is MSXML2.XMLHTTP.6.0. For more details about these prog IDs, or to simply get a better idea of the chaos that lies behind them, feel free to read a resource such as http://puna.net.nz/etc/xml/msxml.htm.

Here is the upgraded version of createXmlHttpRequestObject. The new bits are highlighted.

```
// creates an XMLHttpRequest instance
function createXmlHttpRequestObject()
{
  // will store the reference to the XMLHttpRequest object
  var xmlHttp;
  // this should work for all browsers except IE6 and older
  try
  {
    // try to create XMLHttpRequest object
    xmlHttp = new XMLHttpRequest();
  }
  catch(e)
  {
    // assume IE6 or older
    var XmlHttpVersions = new Array('MSXML2.XMLHTTP.6.0',
                                    'MSXML2.XMLHTTP.5.0',
                                    'MSXML2.XMLHTTP.4.0',
                                    'MSXML2.XMLHTTP.3.0',
                                    'MSXML2.XMLHTTP',
                                    'Microsoft.XMLHTTP');
    // try every prog id until one works
    for (var i=0; i<XmlHttpVersions.length && !xmlHttp; i++)
    {
      try
      {
        // try to create XMLHttpRequest object
        xmlHttp = new ActiveXObject(XmlHttpVersions[i]);
      }
      catch (e) {} // ignore potential error
    }
  }
  // return the created object or display an error message
  if (!xmlHttp)
    alert("Error creating the XMLHttpRequest object.");
  else
    return xmlHttp;
}
```

If this code looks a bit scary, rest assured that the functionality is quite simple. First, it tries to create the MSXML2.XMLHttp.6.0 ActiveX object. If this fails, the error is ignored (note the empty catch block there), and the code continues by trying to create an MSXML2.XMLHTTP.5.0 object, and so on. This continues until one of the object creation attempts succeeds.

Perhaps, the most interesting thing to note in the new code is the way we use object detection (!xmlHttp) to ensure that we stop looking for new prog IDs after the object has been created, effectively interrupting the execution of the for loop.

Initiating Server Requests Using XMLHttpRequest

After creating the XMLHttpRequest object you can do lots of interesting things with it. Although, it has different ways of being instantiated, depending on the version and browser, all the instances of XMLHttpRequest are supposed to share the same API (Application Programming Interface) and support the same functionality. (In practice, this can't be guaranteed, since every browser has its own separate implementation.)

You will learn the most interesting details about XMLHttpRequest by practice, but for a quick reference here are the object's methods and properties:

Method/Property	Description
abort()	Stops the current request.
getAllResponseHeaders()	Returns the response headers as a string.
getResponseHeader("headerLabel")	Returns a single response header as a string.
open("method", "URL"[, asyncFlag[, "userName"[, "password"]]])	Initializes the request parameters.
send(content)	Performs the HTTP request.
setRequestHeader("label", "value")	Sets a label/value pair to the request header.
onreadystatechange	Used to set the callback function that handles request state changes.
readyState	Returns the status of the request: 0 = uninitialized 1 = loading 2 = loaded 3 = interactive 4 = complete
responseText	Returns the server response as a string.
responseXML	Returns the server response as an XML document.
Status	Returns the status code of the request.
statusText	Returns the status message of the request.

The methods you will use with every server request are open and send. The open method configures a request by setting various parameters, and send makes the request (accesses the server). When the request is made asynchronously, before calling send you will also need to set the onreadystatechange property with the callback method to be executed when the status of the request changes, thus enabling the AJAX mechanism.

The open method is used for initializing a request. It has two required parameters and a few optional ones. The open method doesn't initiate a connection to the server; it is only used to set the connection options. The first parameter specifies the method used to send data to the server page, and it can have a value of GET, POST, or PUT. The second parameter is URL, which specifies where you want to send the request. The URL can be complete or relative. If the URL doesn't specify a resource accessible via HTTP, the first parameter is ignored.

The third parameter of open, called async, specifies whether the request should be handled asynchronously; true means that script processing carries on after the send() method returns without waiting for a response; false means that the script waits for a response before continuing processing, freezing the web page functionality. To enable asynchronous processing, you will seed to set async to true, and handle the onreadystatechange event to process the response from the server.

When using GET to pass parameters, you send the parameters using the URL's query string, as in http://localhost/ajax/test.php?param1=x&param2=y. This server request passes two parameters—a parameter called param1 with the value x, and a parameter called param2 with the value y.

```
// call the server page to execute the server side operation
xmlHttp.open("GET", "http://localhost/ajax/test.php?param1=x&param2=y", true);
xmlHttp.onreadystatechange = handleRequestStateChange;
xmlHttp.send(null);
```

When using POST, you send the query string as a parameter of the send method, instead of joining it on to the base URL, like this:

```
// call the server page to execute the server side operation
xmlHttp.open("POST", "http://localhost/ajax/test.php", true);
xmlHttp.onreadystatechange = handleRequestStateChange;
xmlHttp.send("param1=x&param2=y");
```

The two code samples should have the same effects. In practice, using GET can help with debugging because you can simulate GET requests with a web browser, so you can easily see with your own eyes what your server script generates. The POST method is required when sending data larger than 512 bytes, which cannot be handled by GET.

In our examples, we will place the code that makes the HTTP request inside a function called process() in the JavaScript file. The minimal implementation, which is quite fragile and doesn't implement any error-handling techniques, looks like this:

```
function process()
{
    // call the server page to execute the server side operation
    xmlHttp.open("GET", "server_script.php", true);
    xmlHttp.onreadystatechange = handleRequestStateChange;
    xmlHttp.send(null);
}
```

This method has the following potential problems:

- process() may be executed even if xmlHttp doesn't contain a valid XMLHttpRequest instance. This may happen if, for example, the user's browser doesn't support XMLHttpRequest. This would cause an unhandled exception to happen, so our other efforts to handle errors don't help very much if we aren't consistent and do something about the process function as well.

- process() isn't protected against other kinds of errors that could happen. For example, as you will see later in this chapter, some browsers will generate a security exception if they don't like the server you want to access with the XMLHttpRequest object (more on security in Chapter 3).

The safer version of process() looks like that:

```
// called to read a file from the server
function process()
{
    // only continue if xmlHttp isn't void
    if (xmlHttp)
    {
        // try to connect to the server
        try
        {
            // initiate reading the a file from the server
            xmlHttp.open("GET", "server_script.php", true);
            xmlHttp.onreadystatechange = handleRequestStateChange;
            xmlHttp.send(null);
        }
        // display the error in case of failure
        catch (e)
        {
            alert("Can't connect to server:\n" + e.toString());
        }
    }
}
```

If xmlHttp is null (or false) we don't display yet another message, as we assume a message was already displayed by the createxmlHttpRequestobject function. We make sure to display any other connection problems though.

Handling Server Response

When making an asynchronous request (such as in the code snippets presented earlier), the execution of xmlHttp.send() doesn't freeze until the server response is received; instead, the execution continues normally. The handleRequestStateChange method is the callback method that we set to handle request state changes. Usually this is called four times, for each time the request enters a new stage. Remember the readyState property can be any of the following:

```
0 = uninitialized
1 = loading
2 = loaded
3 = interactive
4 = complete
```

Except state 3, all the others are pretty self-explaining names. The *interactive* state is an intermediate state when the response has been partially received. In our AJAX applications we will only use the *complete* state, which marks that a response has been received from the server.

The typical implementation of handleRequestStateChange is shown in the following code snippet, which highlights the portion where you actually get to read the response from the server:

```
// function executed when the state of the request changes
function handleRequestStateChange()
{
    // continue if the process is completed
    if (xmlHttp.readyState == 4)
    {
        // continue only if HTTP status is "OK"
        if (xmlHttp.status == 200)
        {
            // retrieve the response
            response = xmlHttp.responseText;
```

```
      // (use xmlHttp.responseXML to read an XML response as a DOM object)
      // do something with the response
      // ...
      // ...
    }
  }
}
```

Once again we can successfully use try/catch to handle errors that could happen while initiating a connection to the server, or while reading the response from the server.

A safer version of the handleRequestStateChange method looks like this:

```
// function executed when the state of the request changes
function handleRequestStateChange()
{
  // continue if the process is completed
  if (xmlHttp.readyState == 4)
  {
    // continue only if HTTP status is "OK"
    if (xmlHttp.status == 200)
    {
      try
      {
        // retrieve the response
        response = xmlHttp.responseText;
        // do something with the response
        // ...
        // ...
      }
      catch(e)
      {
        // display error message
        alert("Error reading the response: " + e.toString());
      }
    }
    else
    {
      // display status message
      alert("There was a problem retrieving the data:\n" +
            xmlHttp.statusText);
    }
  }
}
```

OK, let's see how these functions work in action.

Time for Action—Making Asynchronous Calls with XMLHttpRequest

1. In the foundations folder, create a subfolder named async.

2. In the async folder, create a file called async.txt, and add the following text to it:
    Hello client!

3. In the same folder create a file called async.html, and add the following code to it:
    ```
    <!DOCTYPE html PUBLIC "-//W3C//DTD XHTML 1.1//EN"
    "http://www.w3.org/TR/xhtml11/DTD/xhtml11.dtd">
    <html>
      <head>
        <title>AJAX Foundations: Using XMLHttpRequest</title>
        <script type="text/javascript" src="async.js"></script>
      </head>
      <body onload="process()">
        Hello, server!
    ```

```
      <br/>
      <div id="myDivElement" />
   </body>
</html>
```

4. Create a file called async.js with the following contents:

```javascript
// holds an instance of XMLHttpRequest
var xmlHttp = createXmlHttpRequestObject();

// creates an XMLHttpRequest instance
function createXmlHttpRequestObject()
{
  // will store the reference to the XMLHttpRequest object
  var xmlHttp;
  // this should work for all browsers except IE6 and older
  try
  {
    // try to create XMLHttpRequest object
    xmlHttp = new XMLHttpRequest();
  }
  catch(e)
  {
    // assume IE6 or older
    var XmlHttpVersions = new Array("MSXML2.XMLHTTP.6.0",
                                    "MSXML2.XMLHTTP.5.0",
                                    "MSXML2.XMLHTTP.4.0",
                                    "MSXML2.XMLHTTP.3.0",
                                    "MSXML2.XMLHTTP",
                                    "Microsoft.XMLHTTP");
    // try every prog id until one works
    for (var i=0; i<XmlHttpVersions.length && !xmlHttp; i++)
    {
      try
      {
        // try to create XMLHttpRequest object
        xmlHttp = new ActiveXObject(XmlHttpVersions[i]);
      }
      catch (e) {}
    }
  }
  // return the created object or display an error message
  if (!xmlHttp)
    alert("Error creating the XMLHttpRequest object.");
  else
    return xmlHttp;
}


// called to read a file from the server
function process()
{
  // only continue if xmlHttp isn't void
  if (xmlHttp)
  {
    // try to connect to the server
    try
    {
      // initiate reading the async.txt file from the server
      xmlHttp.open("GET", "async.txt", true);
      xmlHttp.onreadystatechange = handleRequestStateChange;
      xmlHttp.send(null);
    }
    // display the error in case of failure
    catch (e)
```

```
        {
          alert("Can't connect to server:\n" + e.toString());
        }
      }
    }

    // function that handles the HTTP response
    function handleRequestStateChange()
    {
      // obtain a reference to the <div> element on the page
      myDiv = document.getElementById("myDivElement");
      // display the status of the request
      if (xmlHttp.readyState == 1)
      {
        myDiv.innerHTML += "Request status: 1 (loading) <br/>";
      }
      else if (xmlHttp.readyState == 2)
      {
        myDiv.innerHTML += "Request status: 2 (loaded) <br/>";
      }
      else if (xmlHttp.readyState == 3)
      {
        myDiv.innerHTML += "Request status: 3 (interactive) <br/>";
      }
      // when readyState is 4, we also read the server response
      else if (xmlHttp.readyState == 4)
      {
        // continue only if HTTP status is "OK"
        if (xmlHttp.status == 200)
        {
          try
          {
            // read the message from the server
            response = xmlHttp.responseText;
            // display the message
            myDiv.innerHTML +=
                        "Request status: 4 (complete). Server said: <br/>";
            myDiv.innerHTML += response;
          }
          catch(e)
          {
            // display error message
            alert("Error reading the response: " + e.toString());
          }
        }
        else
        {
          // display status message
          alert("There was a problem retrieving the data:\n" +
              xmlHttp.statusText);
        }
      }
    }
```

5. Load the async.html file through the HTTP server by loading http://localhost/ ajax/foundations/async/async.html in your browser (you *must* load it through HTTP; local access won't work this time). Expect to see the results similar to those shown in Figure 2.6:

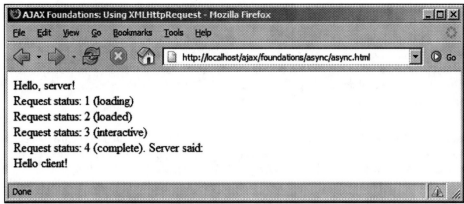

Figure 2.6: The Four HTTP Request Status Codes

> Don't worry if your browser doesn't display exactly the same message. Some XMLHttpRequest implementations simply ignore some status codes. Opera, for example, will only fire the event for status codes 3 and 4. Internet Explorer will report status codes 2, 3, and 4 when using a more recent XMLHttp version.

What Just Happened?

To understand the exact flow of execution, let's start from where the processing begins—the async.html file:

```html
<html>
  <head>
    <title>AJAX Foundations: Using XMLHttpRequest</title>
    <script type="text/javascript" src="async.js"></script>
  </head>
  <body onload="process()">
```

This bit of code hides some interesting functionality. First, it references the async.js file, the moment at which the code in that file is parsed. Note that the code residing in JavaScript functions does not execute automatically, but the rest of the code does. All the code in our JavaScript file is packaged as functions, except one line:

```javascript
// holds an instance of XMLHttpRequest
var xmlHttp = createXmlHttpRequestObject();
```

This way we ensure that the xmlHttp variable contains an XMLHttpRequest instance right from the start. The XMLHttpRequest instance is created by calling the createXmlHttpRequestObject function that you encountered a bit earlier.

The process() method gets executed when the onload event fires. The process() method can rely on the xmlHttp object being already initialized, so it only focuses on initializing a server request. The proper error-handling sequence is used to guard against potential problems. The code that initiates the server request is:

```javascript
// initiate reading the async.txt file from the server
xmlHttp.open("GET", "async.txt", true);
```

```
xmlHttp.onreadystatechange = handleRequestStateChange;
xmlHttp.send(null);
```

> Note that you cannot load the script locally, directly from the disk using a `file://`
> resource. Instead, you need to load it through HTTP. To load it locally, you would need
> to mention the complete access path to the `.txt` file, and in that case you may meet a
> security problem that we will deal with later.

Supposing that the HTTP request was successfully initialized and executed asynchronously, the
handleRequestStateChange method will get called every time the state of the request changes. In
real applications we will ignore all states except 4 (which signals the request has completed), but
in this exercise we print a message with each state so you can see the callback method actually
gets executed as advertised.

The code in handleRequestStateChange is not that exciting by itself, but the fact that it's being
called for you is very nice indeed. Instead of waiting for the server to reply with a synchronous
HTTP call, making the request asynchronously allows you to continue doing other tasks until a
response is received.

The handleRequestStateChange function starts by obtaining a reference to the HTML element
called myDivElement, which is used to display the various states the HTTP request is going through:

```
// function that handles the HTTP response
function handleRequestStateChange()
{
  // obtain a reference to the <div> element on the page
  myDiv = document.getElementById("myDivElement");
  // display the status o the request
  if (xmlHttp.readyState == 1)
  {
    myDiv.innerHTML += "Request status: 1 (loading) <br/>";
  }
  else if (xmlHttp.readyState == 2)
  ...
  ...
```

When the status hits the value of 4, we have the typical code that deals with reading the server
response, hidden inside xmlHttp.ResponseText:

```
// when readyState is 4, we also read the server response
else if (xmlHttp.readyState == 4)
{
  // continue only if HTTP status is "OK"
  if (xmlHttp.status == 200)
  {
    try
    {
      // read the message from the server
      response = xmlHttp.responseText;
      // display the message
      myDiv.innerHTML += "Request status: 4 (complete). Server said: <br/>";
      myDiv.innerHTML += response;
    }
    catch(e)
    {
      // display error message
      alert("Error reading the response: " + e.toString());
    }
```

```
    }
    else
    {
      // display status message
      alert("There was a problem retrieving the data:\n" +
          xmlHttp.statusText);
    }
  }
}
```

Apart from the error-handling bits, it's good to notice the `xmlHttp.responseText` method that reads the response from the server. This method has a bigger brother called `xmlHttp.responseXml`, which can be used when the response from the server is in XML format.

> Unless the `responseXml` method of the `XMLHttpRequest` object is used, there's really no XML appearing anywhere, except for the name of that object (the exercise you have just completed is a perfect example of this). A better name for the object would have been `"HttpRequest"`. The XML prefix was probably added by Microsoft because it sounded good at that moment, when XML was a big buzzword as AJAX is nowadays. Don't be surprised if you will see objects called `AjaxRequest` (or similar) in the days to come.

Working with XML Structures

XML documents are similar to HTML documents in that they are text-based, and contain hierarchies of elements. In the last few years, XML has become very popular for packaging and delivering all kinds of data.

Incidentally, XML puts the X in AJAX, and the prefix in `XMLHttpRequest`. However, once again, note that using XML is optional. In the previous exercise, you created a simple application that made an asynchronous call to the server, just to receive a text document; no XML was involved.

> XML is a vast subject, with many complementary technologies. You will hear people talking about DTDs, schemas and namespaces, XSLT and XPath, XLink and XPointer, and more. In this book we will mostly use XML for transmitting simple structures of data. For a quick-start introduction to XML we recommend http://www.xmlnews.org/docs/xml-basics.html. If you don't mind the ads, http://www.w3schools.com/xml/default.asp is a good resource as well. Appendix C available at http://ajaxphp.packtpub.com contains an introduction to XSLT and Xpath.

You can use the DOM to manipulate XML files just as you did for manipulating HTML files. The following exercise is similar to the previous exercise in that you read a static file from the server. The novelty is that the file is XML, and we read it using the DOM.

Time for Action—Making Asynchronous Calls with XMLHttpRequest and XML

1. In the `foundations` folder create a subfolder called `xml`.

2. In the `xml` folder, create a file called `books.xml`, which will contain the XML structure that we will read using JavaScript's DOM. Add the following content to the file:

```
<?xml version="1.0" encoding="UTF-8" standalone="yes"?>
```

```xml
<response>
  <books>
    <book>
      <title>
        Building Reponsive Web Applications with AJAX and PHP
      </title>
      <isbn>
        1-904811-82-5
      </isbn>
    </book>
    <book>
      <title>
        Beginning PHP 5 and MySQL E-Commerce: From Novice to Professional
      </title>
      <isbn>
        1-59059-392-8
      </isbn>
    </book>
  </books>
</response>
```

3. In the same folder create a file called books.html, and add the following code to it:

```html
<!DOCTYPE html PUBLIC "-//W3C//DTD XHTML 1.1//EN"
"http://www.w3.org/TR/xhtml11/DTD/xhtml11.dtd">
<html>
  <head>
    <title>AJAX Foundations: JavaScript and XML</title>
    <script type="text/javascript" src="books.js"></script>
  </head>
  <body onload="process()">
    Server, tell me your favorite books!
    <br/>
    <div id="myDivElement" />
  </body>
</html>
```

4. Finally, create the books.js file:

```javascript
// holds an instance of XMLHttpRequest
var xmlHttp = createXmlHttpRequestObject();

// creates an XMLHttpRequest instance
function createXmlHttpRequestObject()
{
  // will store the reference to the XMLHttpRequest object
  var xmlHttp;
  // this should work for all browsers except IE6 and older
  try
  {
    // try to create XMLHttpRequest object
    xmlHttp = new XMLHttpRequest();
  }
  catch(e)
  {
    // assume IE6 or older
    var xmlHttpVersions = new Array('MSXML2.XMLHTTP.6.0',
                                    'MSXML2.XMLHTTP.5.0',
                                    'MSXML2.XMLHTTP.4.0',
                                    'MSXML2.XMLHTTP.3.0',
                                    'MSXML2.XMLHTTP',
                                    'Microsoft.XMLHTTP');
    // try every prog id until one works
    for (var i=0; i<xmlHttpVersions.length && !xmlHttp; i++)
    {
      try
```

```
        {
          // try to create XMLHttpRequest object
          xmlHttp = new ActiveXObject(XmlHttpVersions[i]);
        }
        catch (e) {}
      }
    }
    // return the created object or display an error message
    if (!xmlHttp)
      alert("Error creating the XMLHttpRequest object.");
    else
      return xmlHttp;
  }

  // read a file from the server
  function process()
  {
    // only continue if xmlHttp isn't void
    if (xmlHttp)
    {
      // try to connect to the server
      try
      {
        // initiate reading a file from the server
        xmlHttp.open("GET", "books.xml", true);
        xmlHttp.onreadystatechange = handleRequestStateChange;
        xmlHttp.send(null);
      }
      // display the error in case of failure
      catch (e)
      {
        alert("Can't connect to server:\n" + e.toString());
      }
    }
  }

  // function called when the state of the HTTP request changes
  function handleRequestStateChange()
  {
    // when readyState is 4, we are ready to read the server response
    if (xmlHttp.readyState == 4)
    {
      // continue only if HTTP status is "OK"
      if (xmlHttp.status == 200)
      {
        try
        {
          // do something with the response from the server
          handleServerResponse();
        }
        catch(e)
        {
          // display error message
          alert("Error reading the response: " + e.toString());
        }
      }
      else
      {
        // display status message
        alert("There was a problem retrieving the data:\n" +
              xmlHttp.statusText);
      }
    }
  }
```

```
// handles the response received from the server
function handleServerResponse()
{
  // read the message from the server
  var xmlResponse = xmlHttp.responseXML;
  // obtain the XML's document element
  xmlRoot = xmlResponse.documentElement;
  // obtain arrays with book titles and ISBNs
  titleArray = xmlRoot.getElementsByTagName("title");
  isbnArray = xmlRoot.getElementsByTagName("isbn");
  // generate HTML output
  var html = "";
  // iterate through the arrays and create an HTML structure
  for (var i=0; i<titleArray.length; i++)
    html += titleArray.item(i).firstChild.data +
            ", " + isbnArray.item(i).firstChild.data + "<br/>";
  // obtain a reference to the <div> element on the page
  myDiv = document.getElementById("myDivElement");
  // display the HTML output
  myDiv.innerHTML = "Server says: <br />" + html;
}
```

5. Load `http://localhost/ajax/foundations/xml/books.html`:

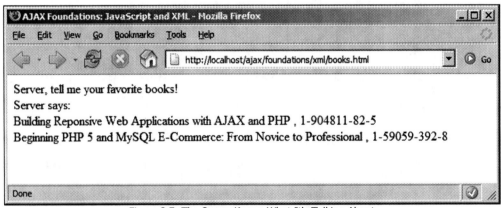

Figure 2.7: The Server Knows What It's Talking About

What Just Happened?

Most of the code will already start looking familiar, as it builds the basic framework we have built so far. The novelty consists in the handleServerResponse function, which is called from handleRequestStateChange when the request is complete.

The handleServerResponse function starts by retrieving the server response in XML format:

```
// handles the response received from the server
function handleServerResponse()
{
  // read the message from the server
  var xmlResponse = xmlHttp.responseXML;
```

The `responsexmL` method of the `XMLHttpRequest` object wraps the received response as a DOM document. If the response isn't a valid XML document, the browser might throw an error. However this depends on the specific browser you're using, because each JavaScript and DOM implementation behaves in its own way.

We will get back to bulletproofing the XML reading code in a minute; for now, let us assume the XML document is valid, and let's see how we read it. As you know, an XML document must have one (and only one) *document element*, which is the root element. In our case this is `<response>`. You will usually need a reference to the document element to start with, as we did in our exercise:

```
// obtain the XML's document element
xmlRoot = xmlResponse.documentElement;
```

The next step was to create two arrays, one with book titles and one with book ISBNs. We did that using the `getElementsByTagName` DOM function, which parses the entire XML file and retrieves the elements with the specified name:

```
// obtain arrays with book titles and ISBNs
titleArray = xmlRoot.getElementsByTagName("title");
isbnArray = xmlRoot.getElementsByTagName("isbn");
```

This is, of course, one of the many ways in which you can read an XML file using the DOM. A much more powerful way is to use XPath, which allows you to define powerful queries on your XML document. .

The two arrays that we generated are arrays of DOM elements. In our case, the text that we want displayed is the first child element of the `title` and `isbn` elements (the first child element is the text element that contains the data we want to display).

```
// generate HTML output
var html = "";
// iterate through the arrays and create an HTML structure
for (var i=0; i<titleArray.length; i++)
  html += titleArray.item(i).firstChild.data +
          ", " + isbnArray.item(i).firstChild.data + "<br/>";
// obtain a reference to the <div> element on the page
myDiv = document.getElementById('myDivElement');
// display the HTML output
myDiv.innerHTML = "Server says: <br />" + html;
}
```

The highlighted bits are used to build an HTML structure that is inserted into the page using the `div` element that is defined in `books.html`.

Handling More Errors and Throwing Exceptions

As highlighted earlier, if the XML document you're trying to read is not valid, each browser reacts in its own way. We have made a simple test by removing the closing `</response>` tag from `books.xml`. Firefox will throw an error to the JavaScript console, but besides that, no error will be shown to the user. This is not good, of course, because not many users browse websites looking at the JavaScript console.

Open the Firefox JavaScript console from Tools | JavaScript Console. Please see Appendix B at http://ajaxphp.packtpub.com for more details about the JavaScript Console and other excellent tools that help with debugging.

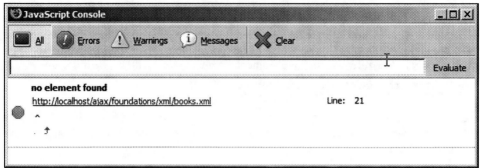

Figure 2.8: The Firefox JavaScript Console is Very Useful

What's really nasty is that all tested browsers except Internet Explorer (all versions) don't catch the error using the try/catch mechanism that exists in place for exactly this kind of errors. Just like Firefox, Mozilla 1.7 doesn't throw any errors, and to make things even worse, it doesn't say anything even in its JavaScript console. It simply ignores everything and behaves like nothing bad happened, as shown in Figure 2.9 (the output is similar to Firefox's).

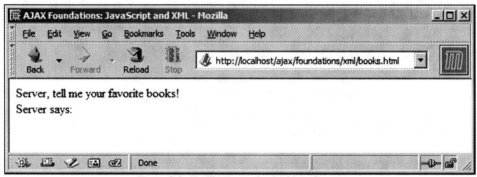

Figure 2.9: Mozilla Keeps the Problem Secret

Opera, on the other hand, is friendlier (if you're the developer, at least). While it completely ignores the try/catch blocks that were supposed to catch the error, it displays a very detailed error message. While this is good for development, for certain you don't want your visitors to see anything like that:

Figure 2.10: Opera Displays the Most Helpful Error Message

For some reason, at the time of writing, Internet Explorer seems to be the only browser where our catch block intercepts the exception, and displays an error message (not a very helpful one, though):

Figure 2.11: Exception Caught by Internet Explorer

Either by design or by default, web browsers don't do very a good job at trapping your errors as we would expect them to. Since certain kinds of errors are not trappable by normal try/catch mechanisms, it is important to find alternative solutions (because, the good news is, there are solutions). You can fix your XML reading code by updating the handleServerResponse function like this:

```
// handles the response received from the server
function handleServerResponse()
{
  // read the message from the server
  var xmlResponse = xmlHttp.responseXML;
  // catching potential errors with IE and Opera
  if (!xmlResponse || !xmlResponse.documentElement)
    throw("Invalid XML structure:\n" + xmlHttp.responseText);
  // catching potential errors with Firefox
  var rootNodeName = xmlResponse.documentElement.nodeName;
  if (rootNodeName == "parsererror")
    throw("Invalid XML structure:\n" + xmlHttp.responseText);
  // obtain the XML's document element
```

```
    xmlRoot = xmlResponse.documentElement;
    // obtain arrays with book titles and ISBNs
    titleArray = xmlRoot.getElementsByTagName("title");
    isbnArray = xmlRoot.getElementsByTagName("isbn");
    // generate HTML output
    var html = "";
    // iterate through the arrays and create an HTML structure
    for (var i=0; i<titleArray.length; i++)
      html += titleArray.item(i).firstChild.data +
              ", " + isbnArray.item(i).firstChild.data + "<br/>";
    // obtain a reference to the <div> element on the page
    myDiv = document.getElementById("myDivElement");
    // display the HTML output
    myDiv.innerHTML = "Server says: <br />" + html;
  }
```

With Internet Explorer and Opera, the documentElement property of xmlResponse object will be null if the underlying XML document is not valid. With Firefox, the XML document will be perfectly valid, but the document itself will be replaced by one containing the error details (yes, an interesting way to report errors); in such cases the document element will be called parsererror.

When we find out there's something wrong with the received XML document, we throw an exception. Throwing an exception means generating a custom-made exception, and is done using the throw keyword in JavaScript. This exception will be caught by the catch block in handleServerResponse, and will get displayed to the visitor:

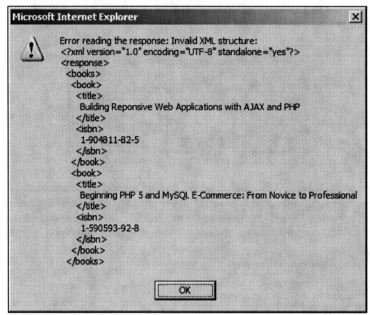

Figure 2.12: Error Message that Gets Displayed by All Tested Browsers

I admit that the following piece of code may have puzzled you:

```
if (!xmlResponse || !xmlResponse.documentElement)
    throw("Invalid XML structure:\n" + xmlHttp.responseText);
```

Apparently, if `xmlResponse` is void, we risk generating another error when trying to read its `documentElement` property. In practice, the JavaScript interpreter only evaluates logical expressions when necessary, and it does so from left to right. In our particular case, if (`!xmlResponse`) is `true`, the second expression isn't evaluated at all, because the end result is `true` anyway. This feature, which is implemented in JavaScript and other languages, is called **short-circuit evaluation** and you can read more about it here: `http://www.webreference.com/javascript/reference/core/expr.html`.

Creating XML Structures

XML and DOM are everywhere. In this chapter, you used the DOM to create HTML elements on the existing DOM object called `document`, and you also learned how to read XML documents received from the server. An important detail that we didn't cover was creating brand new XML documents using JavaScript's DOM. You may need to perform this kind of functionality if you want to create XML documents on the client, and send them for reading on the server.

We won't go through more examples, but we will only show you the missing bits. The trick with creating a brand new XML document is creating the XML document itself. When adding elements to the HTML output, you used the implicit `document` object, but this is not an option when you need to create a new document.

When creating a new DOM object with JavaScript, we're facing the same problem as with creating `XMLHttpRequest` objects; the method of creating the object depends on the browser. The following function is a universal function that returns a new instance of a DOM object:

```
function createDomObject()
{
    // will store reference to the DOM object
    var xmlDoc;
    // create XML document
    if (document.implementation && document.implementation.createDocument)
    {
        xmlDoc = document.implementation.createDocument("", "", null);
    }
    // works for Internet Explorer
    else if (window.ActiveXObject)
    {
        xmlDoc = new ActiveXObject("Microsoft.XMLDOM");
    }
    // returns the created object or displays an error message
    if (!xmlDoc)
        alert("Error creating the DOM object.");
    else
        return xmlDoc;
}
```

After executing this function, you can use the created DOM object to perform whatever actions you want. For more details about creating the DOM object check the following link: `http://www.webreference.com/programming/javascript/domwrapper/index.html`. For details of using the DOM object, refer to the DOM articles mentioned earlier in this chapter.

Summary

This chapter walked you through many fields. Working with HTML, JavaScript, CSS, the DOM, XML, and `XMLHttpRequest` is certainly not easy to start with, especially if some of these technologies are new to you. Where you don't feel confident enough, have a look at the aforementioned resources. When you feel ready, proceed to Chapter 3, where you will learn how to use PHP and MySQL on the server, and make them interact nicely with the AJAX-enabled client.

3
Server-Side Techniques with PHP and MySQL

If AJAX is mainly about building smarter clients, then the servers these clients talk to must be equally smart, otherwise they won't get along very well for too long.

In Chapter 2, you only read static text or XML files from the server. In this chapter, we start putting the server side to work, with PHP to generate dynamic output, and MySQL to manipulate and store the back-end data. In this chapter, you will learn how to:

- Use PHP to perform functionality on the server side
- Let clients communicate with the server by passing parameters
- Use XML on the client and the server
- Use PHP scripts to avoid potential JavaScript security problems
- Perform repetitive tasks in your client
- Work with MySQL databases
- Optimize your application's architecture

PHP and DOM

In Chapter 2, you read data asynchronously from the server. While the mechanism is pretty standard and you will use the same routines many times in this book, what's unusual is that the data passed back from the server was a static file (either text or XML).

In most real-world situations, you will need the server to do some processing, and generate some dynamic output. In this book, we will use PHP to do the server-side part of the job. If your background in PHP isn't strong, an online search for "php tutorial" will generate lots of interesting resources, including the official PHP tutorial at `http://php.net/tut.php`. If you enjoy learning by practicing, you may want to check out one of Cristian Darie and Mihai Bucica's e-commerce books, such as *Beginning PHP 5 and MySQL E-Commerce: From Novice to Professional*.

You can even use the Suggest and Autocomplete application that you will build in Chapter 6, which finds the help page of the PHP functions for you. You will find the application at `http://ajaxphp.packtpub.com/ajax/suggest/`.

In the first exercise for this chapter, you will write a PHP script that uses the PHP's DOM functions to create XML output that will be read by the client. PHP's DOM functionality is similar to JavaScript's DOM functionality, and its official documentation can be found at http://www.php.net/manual/en/ref.dom.php.

The XML document you will create on the server will be almost the same as the XML document you saved as a static XML file in Chapter 2, but this time it will be generated dynamically:

```
<response>
  <books>
    <book>
      <title>Building Reponsive Web Applications with AJAX and PHP</title>
      <isbn>1-904811-82-5</isbn>
    </book>
  </books>
</response>
```

Time for Action—Doing AJAX with PHP

1. In the foundations folder create a subfolder called php.

2. In the php folder create a file named phptest.html, and add the following text to it:

```
<!DOCTYPE html PUBLIC "-//W3C//DTD XHTML 1.1//EN"
"http://www.w3.org/TR/xhtml11/DTD/xhtml11.dtd">
<html>
  <head>
    <title>Practical AJAX: Using the PHP DOM</title>
    <script type="text/javascript" src="phptest.js"></script>
  </head>
  <body onload="process()">
    The AJAX book of 2006 is:
    <br />
    <div id="myDivElement" />
  </body>
</html>
```

3. The client-side code, phptest.js, is almost identical to books.js from the XML exercise in Chapter 2. The changed bits are highlighted:

```
// holds an instance of XMLHttpRequest
var xmlHttp = createXmlHttpRequestObject();

// creates an XMLHttpRequest instance
function createXmlHttpRequestObject()
{
  // will store the reference to the XMLHttpRequest object
  var xmlHttp;
  // this should work for all browsers except IE6 and older
  try
  {
    // try to create XMLHttpRequest object
    xmlHttp = new XMLHttpRequest();
  }
  catch(e)
  {
    // assume IE6 or older
    var XmlHttpVersions = new Array("MSXML2.XMLHTTP.6.0",
                                   "MSXML2.XMLHTTP.5.0",
                                   "MSXML2.XMLHTTP.4.0",
                                   "MSXML2.XMLHTTP.3.0",
                                   "MSXML2.XMLHTTP",
                                   "Microsoft.XMLHTTP");
    // try every prog id until one works
```

```
        for (var i=0; i<xmlHttpVersions.length && !xmlHttp; i++)
        {
          try
          {
            // try to create XMLHttpRequest object
            xmlHttp = new ActiveXObject(xmlHttpVersions[i]);
          }
          catch (e) {}
        }
      }
      // return the created object or display an error message
      if (!xmlHttp)
        alert("Error creating the XMLHttpRequest object.");
      else
        return xmlHttp;
    }

    // read a file from the server
    function process()
    {
      // only continue if xmlHttp isn't void
      if (xmlHttp)
      {
        // try to connect to the server
        try
        {
          // initiate reading a file from the server
          xmlHttp.open("GET", "phptest.php", true);
          xmlHttp.onreadystatechange = handleRequestStateChange;
          xmlHttp.send(null);
        }
        // display the error in case of failure
        catch (e)
        {
          alert("Can't connect to server:\n" + e.toString());
        }
      }
    }


    // function called when the state of the HTTP request changes
    function handleRequestStateChange()
    {
      // when readyState is 4, we are ready to read the server response
      if (xmlHttp.readyState == 4)
      {
        // continue only if HTTP status is "OK"
        if (xmlHttp.status == 200)
        {
          try
          {
            // do something with the response from the server
            handleServerResponse();
          }
          catch(e)
          {
            // display error message
            alert("Error reading the response: " + e.toString());
          }
        }
        else
        {
          // display status message
          alert("There was a problem retrieving the data:\n" +
                xmlHttp.statusText);
```

```
        }
      }
    }

    // handles the response received from the server
    function handleServerResponse()
    {
      // read the message from the server
      var xmlResponse = xmlHttp.responseXML;
      // catching potential errors with IE and Opera
      if (!xmlResponse || !xmlResponse.documentElement)
        throw("Invalid XML structure:\n" + xmlHttp.responseText);
      // catching potential errors with Firefox
      var rootNodeName = xmlResponse.documentElement.nodeName;
      if (rootNodeName == "parsererror") throw("Invalid XML structure");
      // obtain the XML's document element
      xmlRoot = xmlResponse.documentElement;
      // obtain arrays with book titles and ISBNs
      titleArray = xmlRoot.getElementsByTagName("title");
      isbnArray = xmlRoot.getElementsByTagName("isbn");
      // generate HTML output
      var html = "";
      // iterate through the arrays and create an HTML structure
      for (var i=0; i<titleArray.length; i++)
        html += titleArray.item(i).firstChild.data +
                ", " + isbnArray.item(i).firstChild.data + "<br/>";
      // obtain a reference to the <div> element on the page
      myDiv = document.getElementById("myDivElement");
      // display the HTML output
      myDiv.innerHTML = html;
    }
```

4. And finally, the phptest.php file:

```php
<?php
// set the output content type as xml
header('Content-Type: text/xml');
// create the new XML document
$dom = new DOMDocument();

// create the root <response> element
$response = $dom->createElement('response');
$dom->appendChild($response);

// create the <books> element and append it as a child of <response>
$books = $dom->createElement('books');
$response->appendChild($books);

// create the title element for the book
$title = $dom->createElement('title');
$titleText = $dom->createTextNode
      ('Building Reponsive Web Applications with AJAX and PHP');
$title->appendChild($titleText);

// create the isbn element for the book
$isbn = $dom->createElement('isbn');
$isbnText = $dom->createTextNode('1-904811-82-5');
$isbn->appendChild($isbnText);
```

```
// create the <book> element
$book = $dom->createElement('book');
$book->appendChild($title);
$book->appendChild($isbn);

// append <book> as a child of <books>
$books->appendChild($book);

// build the XML structure in a string variable
$xmlString = $dom->saveXML();
// output the XML string
echo $xmlString;
?>
```

5. First let's do a simple test to see what phptest.php returns. Load
   http://localhost/ajax/foundations/php/phptest.php in your web browser to
   ensure it generates a well-formed XML structure:

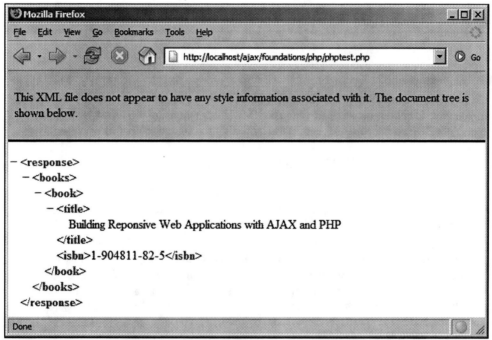

Figure 3.1: Simple XML Structure Generated by PHP

If you don't get the expected result, be sure to check not only the code, but also your PHP
installation. See Appendix A for details about how to correctly set up your machine.

6. Once you know the server gives back the right response, you can test the whole solution by loading `http://localhost/ajax/foundations/php/phptest.html`:

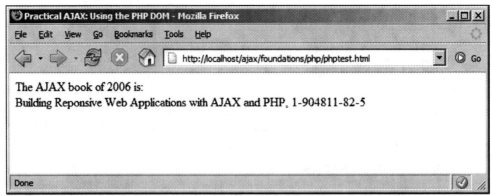

Figure 3.2: AJAX with PHP

What Just Happened?

When it comes to generating XML structures, not only on the client side but on the server side as well, you have to choose between creating the XML document using the DOM, or by joining strings. Your PHP script, `phptest.php`, starts by setting the content output to `text/xml`:

```php
<?php
// set the output content type as xml
header('Content-Type: text/xml');
```

The PHP documentation for `header` is `http://www.php.net/manual/en/function.header.php` (remember, you can simply search for 'header' in the Suggest application, and it will direct you to the help page).

> While in JavaScript files we use double quotes for strings, in PHP we will always try to use single quotes. They are processed faster, they are more secure, and they are less likely to cause programming errors. Learn more about PHP strings at `http://php.net/types.string`. You can find two useful articles on PHP strings at `http://www.sitepoint.com/print/quick-php-tips` and `http://www.jeroenmulder.com/weblog/2005/04/php_single_and_double_quotes.php`.

The PHP DOM, not very surprisingly, looks a lot like the JavaScript DOM. It all begins by creating a DOM document object, which in PHP is represented by the DOMDocument class:

```php
// create the new XML document
$dom = new DOMDocument();
```

Then you continue by creating the XML structure using methods such as `createElement`, `createTextNode`, `appendChild`, and so on:

```
// create the root <response> element
$response = $dom->createElement('response');
$dom->appendChild($response);

// create the <books> element and append it as a child of <response>
$books = $dom->createElement('books');
$response->appendChild($books);
...
```

In the end, we save the whole XML structure as a string, using the saveXML function, and echo the string to the output.

```
$xmlString = $dom->saveXML();
// output the XML string
echo $xmlString;
?>
```

The XML document is then read and displayed at the client side using techniques that you came across in Chapter 2.

> In most cases, you will generate XML documents on the server, and will read them on the client, but of course you can do it the other way round. In Chapter 2, you saw how to create XML documents and elements using JavaScript's DOM. You can then pass these structures to PHP (using GET or POST as you will see in the following exercise). To read XML structures from PHP you can also use the DOM, or you can use an easier-to-use API called **SimpleXML**. You will practice using SimpleXML in Chapter 9, when building your RSS Reader application.

Passing Parameters and Handling PHP Errors

The previous exercise with PHP ignores two very common aspects of writing PHP scripts:

- You usually need to send parameters to your server-side (PHP) script.
- Now that the client side is quite well protected, you should implement some error-handling technique on the server side as well.

You can send parameters to the PHP script using either GET or POST. Handling PHP errors is done with a PHP-specific technique. In the following exercise, you will pass parameters to a PHP script, and implement an error-handling mechanism that you will test by supplying bogus values. The application will look as shown in Figure 3.3.

This page will make an asynchronous call to a server, asking the server to divide two numbers for you. The server, when everything works well, will return the result as an XML structure that looks like this:

```
<?xml version="1.0"?>
<response>1.5</response>
```

In the case of a PHP error, instead of generating an XML string, the server script returns a plain text error message, which is intercepted by the client (after doing the exercise, you will understand why).

Time for Action—Passing PHP Parameters and Error Handling

1. In the `foundations` folder, create a new folder called `morephp`.

2. In the `morephp` folder, create a file named `morephp.html`:

```
<!DOCTYPE html PUBLIC "-//W3C//DTD XHTML 1.1//EN"
"http://www.w3.org/TR/xhtml11/DTD/xhtml11.dtd">
<html>
  <head>
    <title>Practical AJAX: PHP Parameters and Error Handling</title>
    <script type="text/javascript" src="morephp.js"></script>
  </head>
  <body>
    Ask server to divide
    <input type="text" id="firstNumber" />
    by
    <input type="text" id="secondNumber" />
    <input type="button" value="Send" onclick="process()" />
    <div id="myDivElement" />
  </body>
</html>
```

3. Create a new file named `morephp.js`:

```
// holds an instance of XMLHttpRequest
var xmlHttp = createXmlHttpRequestObject();

// creates an XMLHttpRequest instance
function createXmlHttpRequestObject()
{
  // will store the reference to the XMLHttpRequest object
  var xmlHttp;
  // this should work for all browsers except IE6 and older
  try
  {
    // try to create XMLHttpRequest object
    xmlHttp = new XMLHttpRequest();
  }
  catch(e)
  {
    // assume IE6 or older
    var XmlHttpVersions = new Array("MSXML2.XMLHTTP.6.0",
                                    "MSXML2.XMLHTTP.5.0",
                                    "MSXML2.XMLHTTP.4.0",
                                    "MSXML2.XMLHTTP.3.0",
                                    "MSXML2.XMLHTTP",
                                    "Microsoft.XMLHTTP");
    // try every prog id until one works
    for (var i=0; i<XmlHttpVersions.length && !xmlHttp; i++)
    {
      try
      {
        // try to create XMLHttpRequest object
        xmlHttp = new ActiveXObject(XmlHttpVersions[i]);
      }
      catch (e) {}
    }
  }
  // return the created object or display an error message
  if (!xmlHttp)
    alert("Error creating the XMLHttpRequest object.");
  else
    return xmlHttp;
}
```

```javascript
// read a file from the server
function process()
{
  // only continue if xmlHttp isn't void
  if (xmlHttp)
  {
    // try to connect to the server
    try
    {
      // get the two values entered by the user
      var firstNumber = document.getElementById("firstNumber").value;
      var secondNumber = document.getElementById("secondNumber").value;
      // create the params string
      var params = "firstNumber=" + firstNumber +
                   "&secondNumber=" + secondNumber;
      // initiate the asynchronous HTTP request
      xmlHttp.open("GET", "morephp.php?" + params, true);
      xmlHttp.onreadystatechange = handleRequestStateChange;
      xmlHttp.send(null);
    }
    // display the error in case of failure
    catch (e)
    {
      alert("Can't connect to server:\n" + e.toString());
    }
  }
}

// function called when the state of the HTTP request changes
function handleRequestStateChange()
{
  // when readyState is 4, we are ready to read the server response
  if (xmlHttp.readyState == 4)
  {
    // continue only if HTTP status is "OK"
    if (xmlHttp.status == 200)
    {
      try
      {
        // do something with the response from the server
        handleServerResponse();
      }
      catch(e)
      {
        // display error message
        alert("Error reading the response: " + e.toString());
      }
    }
    else
    {
      // display status message
      alert("There was a problem retrieving the data:\n" +
            xmlHttp.statusText);
    }
  }
}

// handles the response received from the server
function handleServerResponse()
{
  // retrieve the server's response packaged as an XML DOM object
  var xmlResponse = xmlHttp.responseXML;
  // catching potential errors with IE and Opera
  if (!xmlResponse || !xmlResponse.documentElement)
    throw("Invalid XML structure:\n" + xmlHttp.responseText);
```

```
    // catching potential errors with Firefox
    var rootNodeName = xmlResponse.documentElement.nodeName;
    if (rootNodeName == "parsererror")
      throw("Invalid XML structure:\n" + xmlHttp.responseText);
    // getting the root element (the document element)
    xmlRoot = xmlResponse.documentElement;
    // testing that we received the XML document we expect
    if (rootNodeName != "response" || !xmlRoot.firstChild)
      throw("Invalid XML structure:\n" + xmlHttp.responseText);
    // the value we need to display is the child of the root <response>
element
    responseText = xmlRoot.firstChild.data;
    // display the user message
    myDiv = document.getElementById("myDivElement");
    myDiv.innerHTML = "Server says the answer is: " + responseText;
}
```

4. Create a file called morephp.php:

```php
<?php
// load the error handling module
require_once('error_handler.php');
// specify that we're outputting an XML document
header('Content-Type: text/xml');
// calculate the result
$firstNumber = $_GET['firstNumber'];
$secondNumber = $_GET['secondNumber'];
$result = $firstNumber / $secondNumber;
// create a new XML document
$dom = new DOMDocument();
// create the root <response> element and add it to the document
$response = $dom->createElement('response');
$dom->appendChild($response);
// add the calculated sqrt value as a text node child of <response>
$responseText = $dom->createTextNode($result);
$response->appendChild($responseText);
// build the XML structure in a string variable
$xmlString = $dom->saveXML();
// output the XML string
echo $xmlString;
?>
```

5. Finally, create the error-handler file, error_handler.php:

```php
<?php
// set the user error handler method to be error_handler
set_error_handler('error_handler', E_ALL);
// error handler function
function error_handler($errNo, $errStr, $errFile, $errLine)
{
    // clear any output that has already been generated
    if(ob_get_length()) ob_clean();
    // output the error message
    $error_message = 'ERRNO: ' . $errNo . chr(10) .
                     'TEXT: ' . $errStr . chr(10) .
                     'LOCATION: ' . $errFile .
                     ', line ' . $errLine;
    echo $error_message;
    // prevent processing any more PHP scripts
    exit;
}
?>
```

6. Load http://localhost/ajax/foundations/morephp/morephp.html and play
    with it.

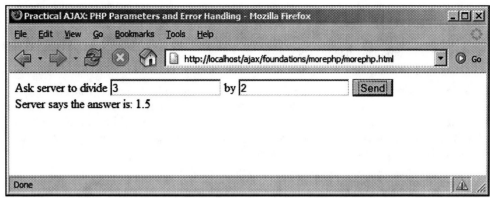

Figure 3.3: PHP Parameters and Error Handling

What Just Happened?

You must be familiar with almost all the code on the client side by now, so let's focus on the server side, where we have two files: morephp.php and error_handler.php.

The morephp.php file is expected to output the XML structure with the results of the number division. However, it starts by loading the error-handling routine. This routine is expected to catch any errors, create a better error message than the default one, and send the message back to the client.

```php
<?php
// load the error handling module
require_once('error_handler.php');
```

PHP 5 does support exceptions like the other OOP languages. However, with PHP 5, you are limited to using exception objects that you throw and catch yourself, and they can help when building a large architecture where they can improve your code. PHP's core doesn't generate exceptions when something bad happens. Probably because of backward compatibility reasons, when a problem happens, instead of throwing exceptions, PHP 5 generates **errors**, which represent a much more primitive way to handle run-time problems. For example, you can't catch an error, deal with it locally, and then let the script continue normally, as you can do with exceptions. Instead, to deal with errors, the best you can do is to specify a function to execute automatically; this function is called before the script dies, and offers you a last chance to do some final processing, such as logging the error, closing database connections, or telling your visitor something "friendly".

In our code, the error_handler.php script is instructed to handle errors. It simply receives the error, and transforms the error message into something easier to read than the default error message. However, note that error_handler.php catches most errors, but not all! Fatal errors cannot be trapped with PHP code, and they generate output that is out of the control of your program. For example, parse errors, which can happen when you forget to write the $ symbol in the front of a variable name, are intercepted before the PHP code is executed; so they cannot be caught with PHP code, but they are logged in the Apache error log file.

> It is important to keep an eye on the Apache error log when your PHP script behaves strangely. The default location and name of this file is Apache2\logs\error.log, and it can save you from many headaches.

After setting the error-handling routine, we set the content type to XML, and divide the first received number by the second number. Note the usage of $_GET to read the variables sent using GET. If you sent your variables using POST you should have used $_POST. Alternatively, you can use $_REQUEST, which finds variables sent with any method (including cookies); but it is generally recommended to avoid using it because it is a bit slower than the others.

```
// specify that we are outputting an XML document
header('Content-Type: text/xml');
// calculate the result
$firstNumber = $_GET['firstNumber'];
$secondNumber = $_GET['secondNumber'];
$result = $firstNumber / $secondNumber;
```

The division operation will generate an error if $secondNumber is 0. In this case, we expect the error-handler script to intercept the error. Note that in a real-world the situation, the professional way would be to check the value of the variable before calculating the division, but in this case we are interested in checking the error-handling script.

After calculating the value, you package it into a nice XML document and output it, just as in the previous exercise:

```
// create a new XML document
$dom = new DOMDocument();
// create the root <response> element and add it to the document
$response = $dom->createElement('response');
$dom->appendChild($response);
// add the calculated sqrt value as a text node child of <response>
$responseText = $dom->createTextNode($result);
$response->appendChild($responseText);
// build the XML structure in a string variable
$xmlString = $dom->saveXML();
// output the XML string
echo $xmlString;
?>
```

Let's now have a look at the error-handling script—error_handler.php. This file has the role of intercepting any error messages generated by PHP, and outputting an error message that makes sense, and can be displayed by your JavaScript code:

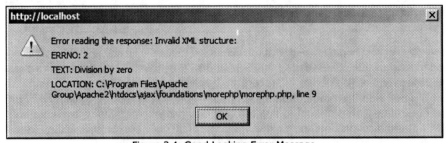

Figure 3.4: Good Looking Error Message

Without the customized error handler, the error message you will get would be:

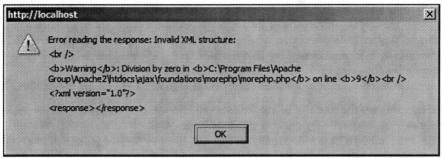

Figure 3.5: Bad Looking Error Message

The error message will look like Figure 3.5 if the `display_errors` option in `php.ini` is on. By default, that option is `off` and the errors are logged just in the Apache error log, but while writing code it may help to make them be displayed as well. If the code was production code, both error messages would have been inappropriate. You should never show such debugging information to your end users.

So what happens in `error_handler.php`? First, the file uses the `set_error_handler` function to establish a new error-handling function:

```php
<?php
// set the user error handler method to be error_handler
set_error_handler('error_handler', E_ALL);
```

When an error happens, we first call `ob_clean()` to erase any output that has already been generated—such as the `<response></response>` bit from Figure 3.5:

```php
// error handler function
function error_handler($errNo, $errStr, $errFile, $errLine)
{
    // clear any output that has already been generated
    if(ob_get_length()) ob_clean();
```

Of course, if you prefer to decide to keep those bits when doing certain debugging things, you can comment out the `ob_clean()` call. The actual error message is built using the system variables $errNo, $errStr, $errFile, and $errLine, and the carriage return is generated using the `chr` function.

```php
    // output the error message
    $error_message = 'ERRNO: ' . $errNo . chr(10) .
                     'TEXT: ' . $errStr . chr(10) .
                     'LOCATION: ' . $errFile .
                     ', line ' . $errLine;
    echo $error_message;
    // prevent processing any more PHP scripts
    exit;
}
?>
```

> The error-handling scheme presented is indeed quite simplistic, and it is only appropriate while writing and debugging your code. In a production solution, you need to show your end user a friendly message without any technical details. If you want to package the error details as an XML document to be read on the client, keep in mind that parse and fatal errors will not be processed by your function, and will behave as set up in PHP's configuration file (`php.ini`).

This case also presents the scenario where the user can attempt to make several server requests at the same time (you can do this by clicking the Send button multiple times quickly enough). If you try to make a request on a busy XMLHttpRequest object, its open method generates an exception. The code is well protected with try/catch constructs, but the error message doesn't look very user-friendly as shown in Figure 3.6.

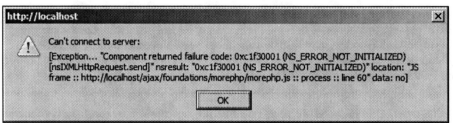

Figure 3.6: Request on a Busy XMLHttpRequest

This message might be just what you need, but in certain circumstances you may prefer to react differently to this kind of error than with other kinds of errors. For example, in a production scenario, you may prefer to display a note on the page, or display a friendly "*please try again later*" message, by modifying the process() function as shown in the following code snippet:

```
// read a file from the server
function process()
{
  // only continue if xmlHttp isn't void
  if (!xmlHttp) return;
  // don't try to make server requests if the XMLHttpObject is busy
  if !(xmlHttp.readyState == 0 || xmlHttp.readyState == 4)
    alert("Can't connect to server, please try again later.");
  else
  {
    // try to connect to the server
    try
    {
      // get the two values entered by the user
      var firstNumber = document.getElementById("firstNumber").value;
      var secondNumber = document.getElementById("secondNumber").value;
      // create the params string
      var params = "firstNumber=" + firstNumber +
                   "&secondNumber=" + secondNumber;
      // initiate the asynchronous HTTP request
      xmlHttp.open("GET", "morephp.php?" + params, true);
      xmlHttp.onreadystatechange = handleRequestStateChange;
      xmlHttp.send(null);
    }
```

```
        // display the error in case of failure
        catch (e)
        {
          alert("Can't connect to server:\n" + e.toString());
        }
      }
    }
  }
```

The exact way you handle these errors can vary depending on the scenario. During the course of this book, you will see more solutions in action:

- Sometimes you may prefer to simply ignore these errors.

- Other times you will display a custom error message as shown in the code above.

In most cases you will try to avoid getting the errors in the first place—it is always better to prevent a problem than to handle it after it happened. For example, there are several ways to avoid getting "connection busy"-type errors, which happen when you try to make a server request using an XMLHttpRequest object that is still busy processing a previous request:

- You could open a new connection (create a new XMLHttpRequest object) for every message you need to send to the server. This method is easy to implement and it can be helpful in many scenarios, but we'll generally try to avoid it because it can affect the server's performance (your script continues to open connections and initiate requests even if the server hasn't finished answering older requests), and it doesn't guarantee that you receive the responses in the same order as you made the calls (especially if the server is busy or the network is slow).

- You could record the message in a *queue* and send it later when the connection becomes available (you will see this method in action in several exercises of this book, including the AJAX Form Validation, and the AJAX Chat).

- You can ignore the message altogether if you can implement the code in such a way that it would not attempt to make multiple requests over the same connection, and use the existing error-handling code.

Connecting to Remote Servers and JavaScript Security

You may be surprised to find out that the PHP exercises you have just completed worked smoothly because the server (PHP) scripts you called asynchronously were running on the same server from which the HTML file was loaded.

Web browsers have very strict (and different) ways to control what resources you can access from the JavaScript code. If you want to access another server from your JavaScript code, it is safe to say that you are in trouble. And this is what we will do in the exercise that follows; but before that, let's learn a bit of theory first.

So, the JavaScript code runs under the security privileges of its parent HTML file. By default, when you load an HTML page from a server, the JavaScript code in that HTML page will be allowed to make HTTP requests only to that server. Any other server is a potential enemy, and (unfortunately) these enemies are handled differently by each browser.

Internet Explorer is a friendly kind of web browser; which means that is arguably less secure, but more functional. It has a security model based on **zones**. The four zones are Internet, Local intranet, Trusted sites, and Restricted sites. Each zone has different security settings, which you can change going to Tools | Internet Options | Security. When accessing a web resource, it will be automatically assigned to one of the security zones, and the specific security options will be applied.

The default security options may vary depending on your system. By default, Internet Explorer will give full privileges to scripts loaded from a local file resource (not through a web server, not even the local web server). So if you try to load `c:\ajax\...` the script will run smoothly (before execution, you may be warned that the script you are loading has full privileges). If the JavaScript code was loaded through HTTP (say, `http://localhost/ajax/..../ping.html`), and that JavaScript code tries to make an HTTP request to another server, Internet Explorer will automatically display a confirmation box, where the user is asked to give permission for that action.

Firefox and Mozilla-based browsers have a more restrictive and more complicated security model, based on **privileges**. These browsers don't display a confirmation window automatically; instead, your JavaScript code must use a Mozilla specific API to ask about performing the required actions. If you are lucky the browser will display a confirmation box to the user, and depending on user's input, it will give the permission (or not) to your JavaScript code. If you aren't lucky, the Mozilla-based browser will ignore your code request completely. By default, Mozilla-based browsers will listen to privilege requests asked from local (`file:///`) resources, and will ignore completely requests from scripts loaded through HTTP, unless these scripts are signed (these are the default settings that can be changed manually, though). Learn more about signing scripts for Mozilla browsers at `http://www.mozilla.org/projects/security/components/signed-scripts.html`.

In the next exercise, you'll create a JavaScript program that reads random numbers from the online service `http://www.random.org`. This site provides an online web service that generates *truly random numbers*. The page that explains how to access the server through HTTP is located at `http://www.random.org/http.html`. When writing programs for this purpose, you should check the guidelines mentioned at: `http://www.random.org/guidelines.html`. Finally, to get a feeling about what random numbers look like, feel free to load `http://www.random.org/cgi-bin/randnum` in your web browser (when called with no options, by default it generates 100 random numbers between 1 and 100). Our client will ask for one random number between 1 and 100 at a time, by making a request to `http://www.random.org/cgibin/randnum?num=1&min=1&max=100`.

Figure 3.7: Connecting to Remote Servers

Time for Action—Connecting to Remote Servers

1. Start by creating a new subfolder of the foundations folder, called ping.

2. In the ping folder, create a new file named ping.html with the following contents:

```
<!DOCTYPE html PUBLIC "-//W3C//DTD XHTML 1.1//EN"
"http://www.w3.org/TR/xhtml11/DTD/xhtml11.dtd">
<html>
  <head>
    <title>Practical AJAX: Connecting to Remote Servers</title>
    <script type="text/javascript" src="ping.js"></script>
  </head>
  <body onload="process()">
    Server, tell me a random number!<br/>
    <div id="myDivElement" />
  </body>
</html>
```

3. Create a new file named ping.js with the following code:

```
// holds an instance of XMLHttpRequest
var xmlHttp = createXmlHttpRequestObject();
// holds the remote server address and parameters
var serverAddress = "http://www.random.org/cgi-bin/randnum";
var serverParams = "num=1" + // how many random numbers to generate
                   "&min=1" + // the min number to generate
                   "&max=100"; // the max number to generate

// creates an XMLHttpRequest instance
function createXmlHttpRequestObject()
{
  // will store the reference to the XMLHttpRequest object
  var xmlHttp;
  // this should work for all browsers except IE6 and older
  try
  {
    // try to create XMLHttpRequest object
    xmlHttp = new XMLHttpRequest();
  }
  catch(e)
  {
```

```
      // assume IE6 or older
      var XmlHttpVersions = new Array("MSXML2.XMLHTTP.6.0",
                                      "MSXML2.XMLHTTP.5.0",
                                      "MSXML2.XMLHTTP.4.0",
                                      "MSXML2.XMLHTTP.3.0",
                                      "MSXML2.XMLHTTP",
                                      "Microsoft.XMLHTTP");
      // try every prog id until one works
      for (var i=0; i<XmlHttpVersions.length && !xmlHttp; i++)
      {
        try
        {
          // try to create XMLHttpRequest object
          xmlHttp = new ActiveXObject(XmlHttpVersions[i]);
        }
        catch (e) {}
      }
    }
    // return the created object or display an error message
    if (!xmlHttp)
      alert("Error creating the XMLHttpRequest object.");
    else
      return xmlHttp;
}

// call server asynchronously
function process()
{
    // only continue if xmlHttp isn't void
    if (xmlHttp)
    {
      // try to connect to the server
      try
      {
        // ask for permission to call remote server, for Mozilla-based browsers
        try
        {
          // this generates an error (that we ignore) if the browser is not
          // Mozilla

netscape.security.PrivilegeManager.enablePrivilege('UniversalBrowserRead')
;
        }
        catch(e) {} // ignore error
        // initiate server access
        xmlHttp.open("GET", serverAddress + "?" + serverParams, true);
        xmlHttp.onreadystatechange = handleRequestStateChange;
        xmlHttp.send(null);
      }
      // display the error in case of failure
      catch (e)
      {
        alert("Can't connect to server:\n" + e.toString());
      }
    }
}

// function called when the state of the HTTP request changes
function handleRequestStateChange()
{
    // when readyState is 4, we are ready to read the server response
    if (xmlHttp.readyState == 4)
    {
```

```
         // continue only if HTTP status is "OK"
         if (xmlHttp.status == 200)
         {
           try
           {
             // do something with the response from the server
             handleServerResponse();
           }
           catch(e)
           {
             // display error message
             alert("Error reading the response: " + e.toString());
           }
         }
         else
         {
           // display status message
           alert("There was a problem retrieving the data:\n" +
                 xmlHttp.statusText);
         }
       }
     }
}

// handles the response received from the server
function handleServerResponse()
{
   // retrieve the server's response
   var response = xmlHttp.responseText;
   // obtain a reference to the <div> element on the page
   myDiv = document.getElementById('myDivElement');
   // display the HTML output
   myDiv.innerHTML = "New random number retrieved from server: "
                     + response + "<br/>";
}
```

4. Load `http://localhost/ajax/foundations/ping/ping.html`. If you are using
    Internet Explorer with the default options, you will be asked whether you will allow
    the script to connect to a remote server as shown in Figure 3.8. If you are using
    Firefox or Opera with the default options, you will get security errors like the ones
    shown in Figure 3.9 and Figure 3.10, respectively.

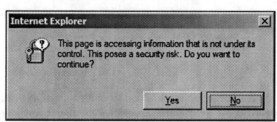

Figure 3.8: Internet Explorer Asking for Permission

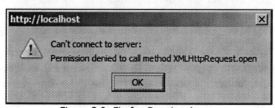

Figure 3.9: Firefox Denying Access

Figure 3.10: Opera Denying Access

5. Now try to load the very same HTML file but directly from the file system. The path to the file should be like `file:///C:/Apache2/htdocs/ajax/foundations/ping/ping.html`. With the default options, Internet Explorer will run with no problems, because the page is located in a trusted zone. Firefox will ask for a confirmation as shown in Figure 3.11. Opera will display the very same error message that you saw in Figure 3.10.

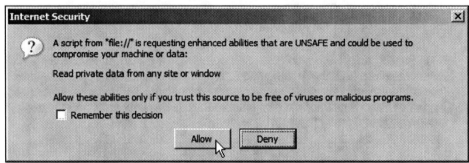

Figure 3.11: Firefox Asking for Permission

What Just Happened?

Opera is indeed the safest browser in the world. You have no way of convincing Opera 8.5 to allow the JavaScript code to access a different server than the one it was loaded from.

Internet Explorer behaves as instructed by the zones settings. By default, it will make your life easy enough, by giving maximum trust to local files, and by asking for confirmation when scripts loaded from the Internet try to do potentially dangerous actions.

Firefox has to be asked politely if you want to have things happen. The problem is that by default it won't even listen for your polite request unless the script is signed, or loaded from a local `file://` location. However, requesting your visitor to change browser settings isn't a real option in most scenarios.

You can make Firefox listen to all requests, even those coming from unsigned scripts, by typing about:config in the address bar, and changing the value of signed.applets.codebase_principal_support to true.

The following is the code that asks Firefox for permission to access a remote server:

```
// ask for permission to call remote server, for Mozilla-based browsers
try
{
  // this generates an error (that we ignore) if the browser is not
  // Mozilla

netscape.security.PrivilegeManager.enablePrivilege('UniversalBrowserRead');
}
catch(e) {}
// ignore error
```

Any errors in this code are ignored using the try/catch construct because the code is Mozilla-specific, and it will generate an exception on the other browsers.

Using a Proxy Server Script

It is quite clear that unless you are building a solution where you can control the environment, such as ensuring that your users use Internet Explorer or Firefox (in which case you would need to sign your scripts or configure the browsers manually to be more permissive), accessing remote servers from your JavaScript code is not an option.

The very good news is that the workaround is simple; instead of having the JavaScript access the remote server directly you can have a PHP script on your server that will access the remote server on behalf of the client. This technique is described in the following figure:

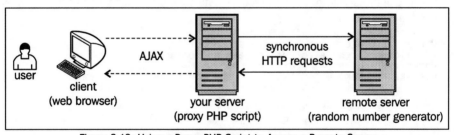

Figure 3.12: Using a Proxy PHP Script to Access a Remote Server

To read data from a remote server with PHP we will use the file_get_contents function, whose documentation can be found at http://www.php.net/manual/en/function.file-get-contents.php.

A popular (and more powerful) alternative to using `file_get_contents` is a library called **Client URL Library (CURL)**. You can find more details about CURL from `http://curl.haxx.se`, `http://www.php.net/curl` and `http://www.zend.com/zend/tut/tutorial-thome3.php`. For basic needs though, `file_get_contents` gets the job done nicely and easily.

Let's try this out with some code. The functionality we want to implement is the same as in the previous exercise (get a random number and display it), but this time it will work with all browsers.

Time for Action—Using a Proxy Server Script to Access Remote Servers

1. In the `foundations` folder, create a subfolder named `proxyping`.

2. In the `proxyping` folder, create `proxyping.html`:

    ```
    <!DOCTYPE html PUBLIC "-//W3C//DTD XHTML 1.1//EN"
    "http://www.w3.org/TR/xhtml11/DTD/xhtml11.dtd">
    <html>
      <head>
        <title>Practical AJAX: Accessing Remote Server through Proxy PHP
    Script</title>
        <script type="text/javascript" src="proxyping.js"></script>
      </head>
      <body onload="process()">
        Server, tell me a random number!<br/>
        <div id="myDivElement" />
      </body>
    </html>
    ```

3. In the same folder create `proxyping.js`. Note that this file is similar to `ping.js`, and the new bits are highlighted. (We removed the bits that handle Mozilla security from `process()`, changed the server address in the header, removed the `num` parameter because in this scenario we'll only request one number at a time, and added an error-handling measure.)

    ```
    // holds an instance of XMLHttpRequest
    var xmlHttp = createXmlHttpRequestObject();
    // holds the remote server address and parameters
    var serverAddress = "proxyping.php";
    var serverParams = "&min=1" + // the min number to generate
                       "&max=100"; // the max number to generate

    // creates an XMLHttpRequest instance
    function createXmlHttpRequestObject()
    {
      // will store the reference to the XMLHttpRequest object
      var xmlHttp;
      // this should work for all browsers except IE6 and older
      try
      {
        // try to create XMLHttpRequest object
        xmlHttp = new XMLHttpRequest();
      }
      catch(e)
      {
        // assume IE6 or older
        var XmlHttpVersions = new Array("MSXML2.XMLHTTP.6.0",
                                       "MSXML2.XMLHTTP.5.0",
    ```

```
                                    "MSXML2.XMLHTTP.4.0",
                                    "MSXML2.XMLHTTP.3.0",
                                    "MSXML2.XMLHTTP",
                                    "Microsoft.XMLHTTP");
    // try every prog id until one works
    for (var i=0; i<xmlHttpVersions.length && !xmlHttp; i++)
    {
      try
      {
        // try to create XMLHttpRequest object
        xmlHttp = new ActiveXObject(xmlHttpVersions[i]);
      }
      catch (e) {}
    }
  }
  // return the created object or display an error message
  if (!xmlHttp)
    alert("Error creating the XMLHttpRequest object.");
  else
    return xmlHttp;
}

// call server asynchronously
function process()
{
  // only continue if xmlHttp isn't void
  if (xmlHttp)
  {
    // try to connect to the server
    try
    {
      // initiate server access
      xmlHttp.open("GET", serverAddress + "?" + serverParams, true);
      xmlHttp.onreadystatechange = handleRequestStateChange;
      xmlHttp.send(null);
    }
    // display the error in case of failure
    catch (e)
    {
      alert("Can't connect to server:\n" + e.toString());
    }
  }
}

// function called when the state of the HTTP request changes
function handleRequestStateChange()
{
  // when readyState is 4, we are ready to read the server response
  if (xmlHttp.readyState == 4)
  {
    // continue only if HTTP status is "OK"
    if (xmlHttp.status == 200)
    {
      try
      {
        // do something with the response from the server
        handleServerResponse();
      }
      catch(e)
      {
        // display error message
        alert("Error reading the response: " + e.toString());
      }
    }
    else
```

```
        {
            // display status message
            alert("There was a problem retrieving the data:\n" +
                xmlHttp.statusText);
        }
    }
}

// handles the response received from the server
function handleServerResponse()
{
    // retrieve the server's response
    var response = xmlHttp.responseText;
    // if the response is longer than 3 characters, or if it is void, we
    // assume we just received a server-side error report
    if(response.length > 3 || response.length == 0)
        throw(response.length == 0 ? "Server error" : response);
    // obtain a reference to the <div> element on the page
    myDiv = document.getElementById("myDivElement");
    // display the HTML output
    myDiv.innerHTML = "Server says: " + response + "<br/>";
}
```

4. Build the hero proxy PHP script, `proxyping.php`:

```php
<?php
// load the error handling module
require_once('error_handler.php');
// make sure the user's browser doesn't cache the result
header('Expires: Wed, 23 Dec 1980 00:30:00 GMT');
header('Last-Modified: ' . gmdate('D, d M Y H:i:s') . ' GMT');
header('Cache-Control: no-cache, must-revalidate');
header('Pragma: no-cache');
// retrieve the parameters
$num = 1; // this is hardcoded on the server
$min = $_GET['min'];
$max = $_GET['max'];
// holds the remote server address and parameters
$serverAddress = 'http://www.random.org/cgi-bin/randnum';
$serverParams = 'num=' . $num . // how many random numbers to generate
                '&min=' . $min . // the min number to generate
                '&max=' . $max; // the max number to generate
// retrieve the random number from foreign server
$randomNumber = file_get_contents($serverAddress . '?' . $serverParams);
// output the random number
echo $randomNumber;
?>
```

5. Finally, add the error-handler function. Yes, it's a bit more to type, but it does good things to your solution (you can copy and paste it from other examples, because it is not going to change). Create a new file named `error_handler.php`, and write this code:

```php
<?php
// set the user error handler method to be error_handler
set_error_handler('error_handler', E_ALL);
// error handler function
function error_handler($errNo, $errStr, $errFile, $errLine)
{
    // clear any output that has already been generated
    if(ob_get_length()) ob_clean();
    // output the error message
    $error_message = 'ERRNO: ' . $errNo . chr(10) .
```

```
                              'TEXT: '  . $errStr . chr(10) .
                              'LOCATION: '  . $errFile .
                              ', line '  . $errLine;
            echo $error_message;
            // prevent processing any more PHP scripts
            exit;
        }
    ?>
```

6. Load `http://localhost/ajax/foundations/proxyping/proxyping.html` with your favorite web browser (yes, even with Opera), and admire the random number you get.

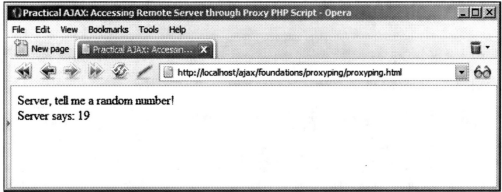

Figure 3.13: Using a Proxy PHP Script to Access the Remote Server

What Just Happened?

The JavaScript code is allowed to access the server it was loaded from. We placed a script on the server, called `proxyping.php`, which accesses the random number generator server on the behalf of the client.

In order for the client to still have complete control over what kind of number to receive, we pass the `min` and `max` parameters to the PHP script, and the PHP script passes them in its turn to the random number generator server. We don't pass the `num` parameter from the client because now we don't want to give the client the option to ask for more than one number at a time. In this example, if the response is larger than 3 characters, we assume we received a server error report:

```
// handles the response received from the server
function handleServerResponse()
{
  // retrieve the server's response
  var response = xmlHttp.responseText;
  // if the response is longer than 3 characters, or if it is void, we assume
  // we just received a server-side error report
  if(response.length > 3 || response.length == 0)
    throw(response.length == 0 ? "Server error" : response);
```

Errors can happen on the client side, or on the server side. We made efforts to have the client protected by implementing a try/catch mechanism in key portions of the code. On the other hand, when an error happens on the server, that error doesn't propagate to the client as a client error. Instead, on the client we must manually analyze the input received from the server, and if it doesn't look like what we expected, we generate an error manually using throw.

If the display_errors setting in php.ini is set to off, when a PHP parse or fatal error happens, the error is logged only to the Apache error log file (Apache/logs/error.log), and the script's output will be void. So if we receive a void response, we also assume that something bad happened on the server, and we build a generic error message on the client.

For example, if you try to load the page when no internet connection is available (so the remote server isn't reachable), then it should result in the following error being displayed (the error message will look differently if display_errors is set to off in php.ini):

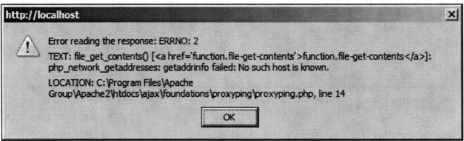

Figure 3.14: An Error Message When No Internet Connection is Available

The code in proxyping.php simply uses the parameters received though GET to access the random number generator server. One interesting detail to note in this script is the way we set the **page expiration** headers. Setting page expiration is important because the server is always called using the same URL and query string, and the client browser may decide to cache the result—and we don't want that, because the results wouldn't be exactly random any more.

```php
<?php
// load the error handling module
require_once('error_handler.php');
// make sure the user's browser doesn't cache the result
header('Expires: Wed, 23 Dec 1980 00:30:00 GMT');
header('Last-Modified: ' . gmdate('D, d M Y H:i:s') . ' GMT');
header('Cache-Control: no-cache, must-revalidate');
header('Pragma: no-cache');
```

You can find an excellent article on *page caching* and PHP at http://www.sitepoint.com/article/php-anthology-2-5-caching. The remainder of proxyping.php simply uses the file_get_contents function to retrieve a response from the random number generator service, and output it for the client.

```
// retrieve the parameters
$num = 1; // this is hardcoded on the server
$min = $_GET['min'];
$max = $_GET['max'];
// holds the remote server address and parameters
$serverAddress = 'http://www.random.org/cgi-bin/randnum';
$serverParams = 'num=' . $num . // how many random numbers to generate
                '&min=' . $min . // the min number to generate
                '&max=' . $max; // the max number to generate
// retrieve the random number from foreign server
$randomNumber = file_get_contents($serverAddress . '?' . $serverParams);
// output the random number
echo $randomNumber;
?>
```

A Framework for Making Repetitive Asynchronous Requests

Quite frequently when building AJAX applications, you will need your client script to retrieve data from the server at regular intervals. There are numerous example scenarios, and you will meet many in this book, and perhaps many more in your real-world projects.

JavaScript offers four functions that can help achieving repetitive (or scheduled) functionality: setTimeout, setInterval, clearTimeout, and clearInterval, which can be used like this:

```
// using setTimeout and clearTimeout
timerId = window.setTimeout("function()", interval_in_milliseconds);
window.clearTimeout(timeId);
// using setInterval and clearInterval
timerId = window.setInterval("function()", interval_in_milliseconds);
window.clearInterval(timeId);
```

setTimeout causes the function to be executed once, after the specified time period. setInterval executes the function repeatedly, at the mentioned interval, until clearInterval is used. In most AJAX scenarios we prefer using setTimeout because it offers more flexibility in controlling when the server is accessed.

For a quick demonstration, we will extend the client that reads random numbers by making the following improvements:

- When making a server request, we wait until the response containing the random number is received, and then we use setTimeout to restart the sequence (to make a new server request) after one second. This way, the interval between two requests is one second plus the time it takes to retrieve the random number. If you want to make the requests at exact periods, you must use setInterval, but in that case you need to check that the XMLHttpRequest object isn't busy waiting to complete the previous request (which can happen if the network is slow, or the server busy).

- In this new example, we will also check for the server's availability from time to time. The random number generator service has a buffer of random numbers, which is used to serve the requests, and anyone can check the buffer's level at http://www.random.org/cgi-bin/checkbuf. Our program will check this page every 10 requests, and will request new random numbers only if the buffer level is at least 50%.

The web application will look like Figure 3.15:

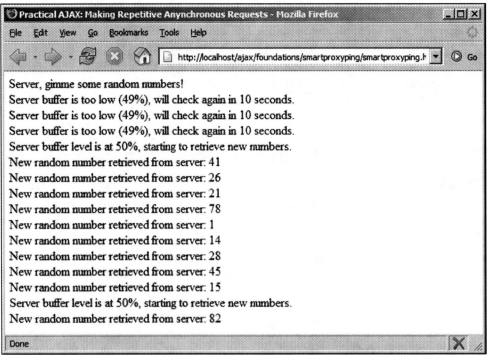

Figure 3.15: Making Repetitive Asynchronous Requests

This repetitive task must start somewhere. In our application, everything starts with process().
There, we decide what kind of server request to make; we can either ask for a new random
number, or we can check for the buffer level of the random number generator server. We check for
the buffer level every 10 requests, and by default we don't ask for new random numbers unless the
buffer is higher than 50%. The process is described in the flowchart given opposite:

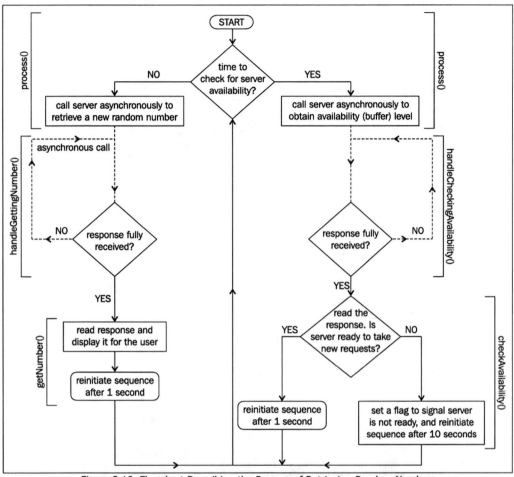

Figure 3.16: Flowchart Describing the Process of Retrieving Random Numbers

With the default code, setTimeout is only called to restart the process after successful HTTP requests; there is no setTimeout in the catch blocks. (Depending on your particular solution, you may want to try calling the server again after a while even if an error happens.)

Time for Action—Implementing Repetitive Tasks

1. In the foundations folder, create a new folder named smartproxyping.

2. In the smartproxyping folder, create a file named smartproxyping.html:

```
<!DOCTYPE html PUBLIC "-//W3C//DTD XHTML 1.1//EN"
"http://www.w3.org/TR/xhtml11/DTD/xhtml11.dtd">
<html>
  <head>
    <title>Practical AJAX: Making Repetitive Asynchronous Requests</title>
    <script type="text/javascript" src="smartproxyping.js"></script>
  </head>
  <body onload="process()">
```

```
     Server, gimme some random numbers!<br/>
     <div id="myDivElement" />
   </body>
</html>
```

3. In the same folder, create `smartproxyping.js`:

```javascript
// holds an instance of XMLHttpRequest
var xmlHttp = createXmlHttpRequestObject();
// holds the remote server address and parameters
var serverAddress = "smartproxyping.php";
var getNumberParams = "action=GetNumber" + // get a new random number
                     "&min=1" + // the min number to generate
                     "&max=100"; // the max number to generate
var checkAvailabilityParams = "action=CheckAvailability";
// variables used to check for server availability
var requestsCounter = 0; // counts how many numbers have been retrieved
var checkInterval = 10; // counts interval for checking server
availability
var updateInterval = 1; // how many seconds to wait to get a new number
var updateIntervalIfServerBusy = 10; // seconds to wait when server busy
var minServerBufferLevel = 50; // what buffer level is considered acceptable

// creates an XMLHttpRequest instance
function createXmlHttpRequestObject()
{
  // will store the reference to the XMLHttpRequest object
  var xmlHttp;
  // this should work for all browsers except IE6 and older
  try
  {
    // try to create XMLHttpRequest object
    xmlHttp = new XMLHttpRequest();
  }
  catch(e)
  {
    // assume IE6 or older
    var XmlHttpVersions = new Array("MSXML2.XMLHTTP.6.0",
                                    "MSXML2.XMLHTTP.5.0",
                                    "MSXML2.XMLHTTP.4.0",
                                    "MSXML2.XMLHTTP.3.0",
                                    "MSXML2.XMLHTTP",
                                    "Microsoft.XMLHTTP");
    // try every prog id until one works
    for (var i=0; i<XmlHttpVersions.length && !xmlHttp; i++)
    {
      try
      {
        // try to create XMLHttpRequest object
        xmlHttp = new ActiveXObject(XmlHttpVersions[i]);
      }
      catch (e) {}
    }
  }
  // return the created object or display an error message
  if (!xmlHttp)
    alert("Error creating the XMLHttpRequest object.");
  else
    return xmlHttp;
}

// call server asynchronously
function process()
{
```

```
    // only continue if xmlHttp isn't void
    if (xmlHttp)
    {
      // try to connect to the server
      try
      {
        // if just starting, or if we hit the specified number of requests,
        // check for server availability, otherwise ask for a new random number
        if (requestsCounter % checkInterval == 0)
        {
          // check if server is available
          xmlHttp.open("GET", serverAddress + "?" +
                                        checkAvailabilityParams, true);
          xmlHttp.onreadystatechange = handleCheckingAvailability;
          xmlHttp.send(null);
        }
        else
        {
          // get new random number
          xmlHttp.open("GET", serverAddress + "?" + getNumberParams, true);
          xmlHttp.onreadystatechange = handleGettingNumber;
          xmlHttp.send(null);
        }
      }
      catch(e)
      {
        alert("Can't connect to server:\n" + e.toString());
      }
    }
  }

  // function called when the state of the HTTP request changes
  function handleCheckingAvailability()
  {
    // when readyState is 4, we are ready to read the server response
    if (xmlHttp.readyState == 4)
    {
      // continue only if HTTP status is "OK"
      if (xmlHttp.status == 200)
      {
        try
        {
          // do something with the response from the server
          checkAvailability();
        }
        catch(e)
        {
          // display error message
          alert("Error reading server availability:\n" + e.toString());
        }
      }
      else
      {
        // display status message
        alert("Error reading server availability:\n" + xmlHttp.statusText);
      }
    }
  }

  // handles the response received from the server
  function checkAvailability()
  {
    // retrieve the server's response
    var response = xmlHttp.responseText;
```

```
// if the response is long enough, or if it is void, we assume we just
// received a server-side error report
if(response.length > 5 || response.length == 0)
  throw(response.length == 0 ? "Server error" : response);
// obtain a reference to the <div> element on the page
myDiv = document.getElementById("myDivElement");
// display the HTML output
if (response >= minServerBufferLevel)
{
  // display new message to user
  myDiv.innerHTML += "Server buffer level is at " + response + "%, "
                    + "starting to retrieve new numbers. <br/>";
  // increases counter to start retrieving new numbers
  requestsCounter++;
  // reinitiate sequence
  setTimeout("process();", updateInterval * 1000);
}
else
{
  // display new message to user
  myDiv.innerHTML += "Server buffer is too low (" + response + "%), "
                    + "will check again in " + updateIntervalIfServerBusy
                    + " seconds. <br/>";
  // reinitiate sequence
  setTimeout("process();", updateIntervalIfServerBusy * 1000);
}
}

// function called when the state of the HTTP request changes
function handleGettingNumber()
{
  // when readyState is 4, we are ready to read the server response
  if (xmlHttp.readyState == 4)
  {
    // continue only if HTTP status is "OK"
    if (xmlHttp.status == 200)
    {
      try
      {
        // do something with the response from the server
        getNumber();
      }
      catch(e)
      {
        // display error message
        alert("Error receiving new number:\n" + e.toString());
      }
    }
    else
    {
      // display status message
      alert("Error receiving new number:\n" + xmlHttp.statusText);
    }
  }
}

// handles the response received from the server
function getNumber()
{
  // retrieve the server's response
  var response = xmlHttp.responseText;
  // if the response is long enough, or if it is void, we assume we just
  // received a server-side error report
  if(response.length > 5 || response.length == 0)
```

```
       throw(response.length == 0 ? "Server error" : response);
       // obtain a reference to the <div> element on the page
       myDiv = document.getElementById("myDivElement");
       // display the HTML output
       myDiv.innerHTML += "New random number retrieved from server: "
                          + response + "<br/>";
       // increase requests count
       requestsCounter++;
       // reinitiate sequences
       setTimeout("process();", updateInterval * 1000);
     }
```

4. In the same folder, create `smartproxyping.php`:

```php
<?php
// load the error handling module
require_once('error_handler.php');
// make sure the user's browser doesn't cache the result
header('Expires: Wed, 23 Dec 1980 00:30:00 GMT'); // time in the past
header('Last-Modified: ' . gmdate('D, d M Y H:i:s') . ' GMT');
header('Cache-Control: no-cache, must-revalidate');
header('Pragma: no-cache');
// retrieve the action parameter
$action = $_GET['action'];
// check availability or get new random number?
if ($action == 'GetNumber')
{
  $num = 1; // value is hardcoded because client can't deal with more numbers
  $min = $_GET['min'];
  $max = $_GET['max'];
  // holds the remote server address and parameters
  $serverAddress = 'http://www.random.org/cgi-bin/randnum';
  $serverParams = 'num=' . $num . // how many random numbers to generate
                  '&min=' . $min . // the min number to generate
                  '&max=' . $max; // the max number to generate
  // retrieve the random number from foreign server
  $randomNumber = file_get_contents($serverAddress . '?' . $serverParams);
  // output the random number
  echo $randomNumber;
}
elseif ($action == 'CheckAvailability')
{
  // address of page that returns buffer level
  $serverAddress = 'http://www.random.org/cgi-bin/checkbuf';
  // received buffer level is in form 'x%'
  $bufferPercent = file_get_contents($serverAddress);
  // extract the number
  $buffer = substr($bufferPercent, 0, strlen($bufferPercent) - 2);
  // echo the number
  echo $buffer;
}
else
{
  echo 'Error talking to the server.';
}
?>
```

5. In the same folder, create the `error_handler.php` file, which should be identical to its version from the previous exercises:

```php
<?php
// set the user error handler method to be error_handler
set_error_handler('error_handler', E_ALL);
// error handler function
```

```
function error_handler($errNo, $errStr, $errFile, $errLine)
{
    // clear any output that has already been generated
    if(ob_get_length()) ob_clean();
    // output the error message
    $error_message = 'ERRNO: ' . $errNo . chr(10) .
                     'TEXT: ' . $errStr . chr(10) .
                     'LOCATION: ' . $errFile .
                     ', line ' . $errLine;
    echo $error_message;
    // prevent processing any more PHP scripts
    exit;
}
?>
```

6. Load `http://localhost/ajax/foundations/smartproxyping/`
    `smartproxyping.html`. The output should look like the one in Figure 3.15.

What Just Happened?

Our client, in this example, knows how to check from time to time if the server is available. The random number generator service provides the page `http://www.random.org/cgi-bin/checkbuf` —which you can use to check its buffer level.

The JavaScript code in `smartproxyping.js` starts by defining a number of global variables that you use to control the program's behavior:

```
// holds the remote server address and parameters
var serverAddress = "smartproxyping.php";
var getNumberParams = "action=GetNumber" + // get a new random number
                      "&min=1" + // the min number to generate
                      "&max=100"; // the max number to generate
var checkAvailabilityParams = "action=CheckAvailability";

// variables used to check for server availability
var requestsCounter = 0; // counts how many numbers have been retrieved
var checkInterval = 10; // counts interval for checking server availability
var updateInterval = 1; // how many seconds to wait to get a new number
var updateIntervalIfServerBusy = 10; // seconds to wait when server busy
var minServerBufferLevel = 50; // what buffer level is considered acceptable
```

These variables contain the data required to make server requests. `getNumberParams` contains the query string parameters needed to request a new random number, and `checkAvailabilityParams` contains the parameters used to check the server's buffer level. The other variables are used to control the intervals for making the asynchronous requests.

A novelty in this exercise compared to the previous ones is that you have two functions that handle server responses—`handleCheckingAvailability` and `handleGettingNumber`. The roots of this happen to be in the `process()` function, which assigns one of these callback functions depending on the server action it requests.

In this program, `process()` is not called only once as in other exercises; instead, it is called multiple times, and each time it must decide what action to make—should it ask for a new random number, or should it check the server's buffer level? The `requestsCounter` variable, which keeps a track of how many times we have retrieved a new random number since the last buffer check, helps us make a decision:

```
function process()
{
  // ...
      if (requestsCounter % checkInterval == 0)
      {
        // check if server is available
        xmlHttp.open("GET", serverAddress + "?" +
                                      checkAvailabilityParams, true);
        xmlHttp.onreadystatechange = handleCheckingAvailability;
        xmlHttp.send(null);
      }
      else
      {
        // get new random number
        xmlHttp.open("GET", serverAddress + "?" + getNumberParams, true);
        xmlHttp.onreadystatechange = handleGettingNumber;
        xmlHttp.send(null);
      }
  // ...
}
```

The handleCheckingAvailability and handleGettingNumber functions are similar; they both are specialized versions of the handleRequestStateChange function you know from the previous exercises. Their role is to wait until the response has successfully been received from the server, and call a helper function (checkAvailability and getNumber) to deal with the response as soon as the response is in.

Notice the action query string parameter, which is used to tell the PHP script what kind of remote server request to make. On the server side, in smartproxyping.php, after loading the error-handling module, we read that action parameter and decide what to do depending on its value:

```
<?php
// load the error handling module
require_once('error_handler.php');
// retrieve the action parameter
$action = $_GET['action'];
// check availability or get new random number?
if ($action == 'GetNumber')
{
  // ...
```

If the action is GetNumber then we use the file_get_contents PHP function to read a new random number from the remote server:

```
if ($action == 'GetNumber')
{
  $num = 1; // value is hardcoded because client can't deal with more numbers
  $min = $_GET['min'];
  $max = $_GET['max'];
  // holds the remote server address and parameters
  $serverAddress = 'http://www.random.org/cgi-bin/randnum';
  $serverParams = 'num=' . $num . // how many random numbers to generate
                  '&min=' . $min . // the min number to generate
                  '&max=' . $max; // the max number to generate
  // retrieve the random number from foreign server
  $randomNumber = file_get_contents($serverAddress . '?' . $serverParams);
  // output the random number
  echo $randomNumber;
}
```

If the action is `CheckAvailability` we call

```
elseif ($action == 'CheckAvailability')
{
    // address of page that returns buffer level
    $serverAddress = 'http://www.random.org/cgi-bin/checkbuf';
    // received buffer level is in form 'x%'
    $bufferPercent = file_get_contents($serverAddress);
    // extract the number
    $buffer = substr($bufferPercent, 0, strlen($bufferPercent) - 2);
    // echo the number
    echo $buffer;
}
```

Note that the `file_get_contents` calls are not asynchronous, and they don't need to be. The PHP script isn't in direct connection with the user, and it can take as long as needed to complete. On the client side, the `checkAvailability` and `getNumber` functions receive these responses we are generating from the PHP script. The functions start by reading the response, and checking its size:

```
// handles the response received from the server
function getNumber()
{
    // retrieve the server's response
    var response = xmlHttp.responseText;
    // if the response is long enough, or if it is void, we assume we just
    // received a server-side error report
    if(response.length > 5 || response.length == 0)
        throw(response.length == 0 ? "Server error" : response);
```

> This is a method to check whether the PHP script executed successfully. Deciding whether the execution was successful depending on the size of the response is quite a primitive, but yet an efficient, method. The fact that PHP throws those fatal errors that can't be caught and dealt with makes it hard to implement a generic, powerful error-handling mechanism.
>
> Apart from detecting the error, in a commercial implementation you will also need to think very seriously what to do with it—and the options are endless, depending on your circumstances. Keep in mind that *users don't care about the technical details of the error*. In our scenario, for example, we could simply output a message such as "The server is temporarily unavailable, please try later."
>
> However, if you want to output the exact error message, consider that your custom-made errors use the \n new line character, while PHP's fatal errors output HTML formatted message. If you intend to display that message in a JavaScript box, you need to format it somehow.

After updating the client display, we reinitiate the sequence by using `setTimeout`:

```
    // reinitiate sequences
    setTimeout('process();', updateInterval * 1000);
}
```

Working with MySQL

A back-end data store is necessary when you implement any kind of application that is expected to generate some useful dynamic output. The most common ways to store the application's data are in **Relational Database Management Systems (RDBMS)**, which are very powerful tools that can store and manage our data.

Much like the other ingredients, the database is not a part of AJAX, but it's not likely that you'll be able to build real web applications without a database to support them. In this book, we'll present simple applications that don't have impressive data needs, but still require a database nevertheless. For the examples in this book we chose MySQL, which is a very popular database among PHP developers. However, because the database functionality is very generic, you can port it to other database systems with very little effort.

To build an application that uses databases you need to know the basics of:

1. Creating database tables that can hold your data
2. Writing SQL queries to manipulate that data
3. Connecting to your MySQL database using PHP code
4. Sending SQL queries to the database, and retrieving the results

> Once again, we'll only be able to cover the very basics of working with PHP and MySQL databases here. The PHP and MySQL online free manuals are quite well written, so you may find them useful along the way.

Creating Database Tables

To create a data table you need to know the basic concepts of the structure of a relational database. A data table is made up of columns (**fields**), and rows (**records**). When creating a data table you need to define its fields, which can have various properties. Here we will discuss:

- Primary Keys
- Data Types
- NULL and NOT NULL columns
- Default column values
- auto_increment columns
- Indexes

The **primary key** is a special column (or set of columns) in a table that makes each row uniquely identifiable. The primary key column doesn't allow repeating values, so every value will be unique. When the primary key is formed of more than one column, then the set of columns (and not each column separately) must be unique. Technically, PRIMARY KEY is a constraint (a rule) that you apply to a column, but for convenience, when saying "primary key", we usually refer to the column that has the PRIMARY KEY constraint. When creating a PRIMARY KEY constraint, a unique index is also created on that column, significantly improving searching performance.

Each column has a **data type**, which describes its size and behavior. There are three important categories of data types (*numerical types*, *character and string types*, and *date and time types*), and each category contains many data types. For complete details on this subject refer to the official MySQL 5 documentation at http://dev.mysql.com/doc/refman/5.0/en/data-types.html.

When creating a new data table you must decide which values are mandatory, and mark them with the **NOT NULL** property, which says the column isn't allowed to store NULL values. The definition of NULL is *undefined*. When reading the contents of the table you see NULL, it means a value has not been specified for that field. Note that an empty string, or a string containing spaces, or a value of "0" (for numerical columns) are real (non-NULL) values. The primary key field can't allow NULLs.

Sometimes instead of (or complementary to) disallowing NULLs for a certain field, you may want to specify a **default value**. In that case, when a new record is created, if a value isn't specified for that field, the default value will be used. For the default value you can also specify a function that will be executed to retrieve the value when needed.

A different way of letting the system generate values for you is by using auto_increment columns. This is an option you will often use for primary key columns, which represent IDs that you prefer to be auto-generated for you. You can set auto_increment only for numerical columns, and the newly generated values will be automatically incremented so no value will be generated twice.

Indexes are database objects used to improve the performance of database operations. An index is a structure that greatly improves *searches* on the field (or fields) it is set on, but it slows down the update and insert operations (because the index must be updated as well on these operations). A well-chosen combination of indexes can make a huge difference in the speed of your application. In the examples in this book, we will rely on the indexes that we build on the primary key columns.

You can create data tables using SQL code, or using a visual interface. Here's an example of a SQL command that creates a simple data table:

```
CREATE TABLE users
(
 user_id INT UNSIGNED NOT NULL AUTO_INCREMENT,
 user_name VARCHAR(32) NOT NULL,
 PRIMARY KEY (user_id)
);
```

In case you don't like how you created the table, you have the option to alter it using ALTER TABLE, or to drop (delete) it altogether using DROP TABLE. You can use TRUNCATE TABLE to rapidly drop and recreate the table (it has the same effect as deleting all the records, but it's much faster and also clears the auto-increment index).

For each exercise, we will give you the SQL code that builds the necessary data tables. You can execute this code by using a program such as phpMyAdmin (Appendix A describes the installation procedure). To execute SQL code using phpMyAdmin, you need to connect to a database by selecting its name in the Database list, and clicking the SQL tab on the main panel, as shown in Figure 3.17.

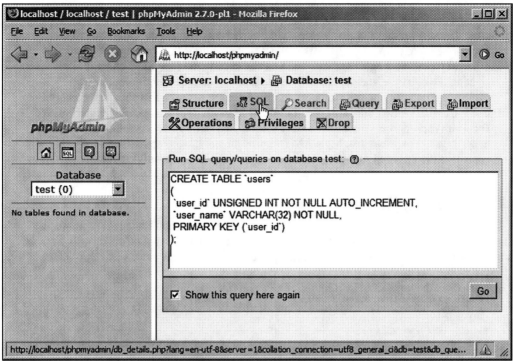

Figure 3.17: Executing SQL Code Using phpMyAdmin

phpMyAdmin also gives you the possibility to create the tables visually, using forms as shown in Figure 3.18.

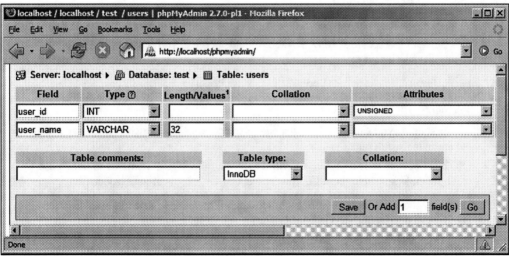

Figure 3.18: Creating a New Table Using the phpMyAdmin Designer

> If you were wondering about the Table type option, read on. MySQL is different than other database products in that it ships with several database engines, the two most popular being **MyISAM** and **InnoDB**. What's interesting is that you can have tables of different types in a single database, and you can specify the type for each table when creating it (otherwise, the default will be used, which on most configurations is MyISAM). Each engine has strengths and weaknesses, but probably the most powerful one is InnoDB, which fully supports the **ACID (Atomicity, Consistency, Isolation, and Durability)** properties of transactions, *row-level locking*, foreign keys and referential integrity, and other features. MyISAM's significant strength compared to the other engines is the included support for full-text searching, and (arguably) speed.

Manipulating Data

You can manipulate your data using SQL's DML (Data Manipulation Language) commands, SELECT, INSERT, UPDATE, and DELETE, used to retrieve, add, modify, and delete records from data tables. These commands are very powerful, and flexible. Their basic syntax is:

```
SELECT <column list>
FROM <table name(s)>
[WHERE <restrictive condition(s)>]

INSERT INTO <table name> [(column list)]
VALUES (column values)

UPDATE   <table name>
SET <column name> = <new value> [, <column name> = <new value> ... ]
[WHERE <restrictive condition>]

DELETE FROM <table name>
[WHERE <restrictive condition>]
```

A few basic things to keep in mind:

- The SQL code can be written in one or more lines, however you feel it looks nicer.

- If you want to execute several SQL commands at once, you must separate them using the semicolon (;).

- The values written between square brackets in the syntax are optional. (Be careful with the DELETE statement though; if you don't specify a restrictive condition, *all* elements will be deleted.)

- With SELECT, you can specify *, instead of the column list, which includes all the existing table columns.

- SQL is not case sensitive, but we will try to write the SQL statements in uppercase, and the table and field names in lowercase. Consistency is always good.

You can test how these commands work by practicing on the users table that was described earlier. Feel free to open a SQL tab in phpMyAdmin and execute commands such as:

```
INSERT INTO users (user_name) VALUES ('john');
INSERT INTO users (user_name) VALUES ('sam');
INSERT INTO users (user_name) VALUES ('ajax');
```

```
SELECT user_id, user_name FROM users;

UPDATE users SET user_name='cristian' WHERE user_id=1;

SELECT user_id, user_name FROM users;

DELETE FROM users WHERE user_id=3;

SELECT * FROM users WHERE user_id>1;
```

During the course of this book, you will meet much more complicated query examples, which will be explained as necessary. Please remember that SQL is a big subject, so you will likely need additional resources if you haven't written much SQL code so far.

Connecting to Your Database and Executing Queries

In our examples, the code that connects to the database will be written in PHP. As Figure 3.19 shows, the database will never be accessed directly by the client, but only by the business logic written in the PHP code on the server.

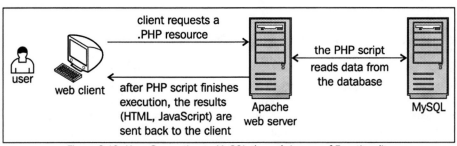

Figure 3.19: User Connecting to MySQL through Layers of Functionality

To get to the necessary data, your PHP code will need to authenticate to the database.

Database security—as with any other kind of security system—involves two important concepts: **authentication** and **authorization**. Authentication is the process in which the user is uniquely identified using some sort of login mechanism (usually by entering a username and password). Authorization refers to the resources that can be accessed (and actions that can be performed) by the authenticated user.

If you configured MySQL security as shown in Appendix A, you will connect to your local MySQL server, to the database called ajax, with a user called **ajaxuser**, with the password **practical**. These details will be kept in a configuration file called config.php, which can be easily updated when necessary. The config.php script will look like this:

```php
<?
// defines database connection data
define('DB_HOST', 'localhost');
define('DB_USER', 'ajaxuser');
define('DB_PASSWORD', 'practical');
define('DB_DATABASE', 'ajax');
?>
```

This data will be used when performing database operations. Any database operation consists of three mandatory steps:

1. Opening the database connection
2. Executing the SQL queries and reading the results
3. Closing the database connection

It's a good practice to open the database connection as late as possible, and close it as soon as possible, because open database connections consume server resources. The following code snippet shows a simple PHP script that opens a connection, reads some data from the database, and closes the connection:

```
// connect to the database
$mysqli = new mysqli(DB_HOST, DB_USER, DB_PASSWORD, DB_DATABASE);
// what SQL query you want executed?
$query = 'SELECT user_id, user_name FROM users';
// execute the query
$result = $mysqli->query($query);
// do something with the results...
// ...
// close the input stream
$result->close();
// close the database connection
$mysqli->close();
```

> Note that we use the mysqli library to access MySQL. This is a newer and improved version of the mysql library, which provides both object-oriented and procedural interfaces to MySQL, and can access more advanced features of MySQL. If you have older versions of MySQL or PHP that don't support mysqli, use mysql instead.

The exercise that follows doesn't contain AJAX-specific functionality; it is just a simple example of accessing a MySQL database from PHP code.

Time for Action—Working with PHP and MySQL

1. Connect to the ajax database, and create a table named users with the following code:

```
CREATE TABLE users
(
 user_id INT UNSIGNED NOT NULL AUTO_INCREMENT,
 user_name VARCHAR(32) NOT NULL,
 PRIMARY KEY (user_id)
);
```

2. Execute the following INSERT commands to populate your users table with some sample data:

```
INSERT INTO users (user_name) VALUES ('bogdan');
INSERT INTO users (user_name) VALUES ('filip');
INSERT INTO users (user_name) VALUES ('mihai');
INSERT INTO users (user_name) VALUES ('emilian');
INSERT INTO users (user_name) VALUES ('paula');
INSERT INTO users (user_name) VALUES ('cristian');
```

> Because user_id is an auto_increment column, its values will be generated by the database.

3. In your `foundations` folder, create a new folder named `mysql`.

4. In the `mysql` folder, create a file named `config.php`, and add the database configuration code to it (change these values to match your configuration):

```php
<?php
// defines database connection data
define('DB_HOST', 'localhost');
define('DB_USER', 'ajaxuser');
define('DB_PASSWORD', 'practical');
define('DB_DATABASE', 'ajax');
?>
```

5. Now add the standard error-handling file, `error_handler.php`. Feel free to copy this file from the previous exercises:

```php
<?php
// set the user error handler method to be error_handler
set_error_handler('error_handler', E_ALL);
// error handler function
function error_handler($errNo, $errStr, $errFile, $errLine)
{
  // clear any output that has already been generated
  if(ob_get_length()) ob_clean();
  // output the error message
  $error_message = 'ERRNO: ' . $errNo . chr(10) .
                   'TEXT: ' . $errStr . chr(10) .
                   'LOCATION: ' . $errFile .
                   ', line ' . $errLine;
  echo $error_message;
  // prevent processing any more PHP scripts
  exit;
}
?>
```

6. Create a new file named `index.php`, and add this code to it:

```php
<!DOCTYPE html PUBLIC "-//W3C//DTD XHTML 1.1//EN"
"http://www.w3.org/TR/xhtml11/DTD/xhtml11.dtd">
<html>
  <head>
    <title>Practical AJAX: Working with PHP and MySQL</title>
  </head>
  <body>

<?php
// load configuration file
require_once('error_handler.php');
require_once('config.php');
// connect to the database
$mysqli = new mysqli(DB_HOST, DB_USER, DB_PASSWORD, DB_DATABASE);
// the SQL query to execute
$query = 'SELECT user_id, user_name FROM users';
// execute the query
$result = $mysqli->query($query);
// loop through the results
while ($row = $result->fetch_array(MYSQLI_ASSOC))
{
  // extract user id and name
  $user_id = $row['user_id'];
  $user_name = $row['user_name'];
  // do something with the data (here we output it)
  echo 'Name of user #' . $user_id . ' is ' . $user_name . '<br/>';
}
// close the input stream
```

```
        $result->close();
        // close the database connection
        $mysqli->close();
    ?>

    </body>
</html>
```

7. Test your script by loading
   `http://localhost/ajax/foundations/mysql/index.php` with a web browser.

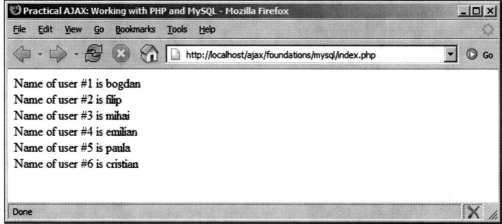

Figure 3.20: These User Names are Read from the Database

What Just Happened?

First of all, note that there is no AJAX going on here; the example is demonstrating plain PHP data access functionality. All the interesting things happen in `index.php`. The real functionality starts by loading the error handler, and the configuration scripts:

```
<?php
// load configuration file
require_once('error_handler.php');
require_once('config.php');
```

Then, just as mentioned, we create a new database connection:

```
// connect to the database
$mysqli = new mysqli(DB_HOST, DB_USER, DB_PASSWORD, DB_DATABASE);
```

Note that a database connection contains a reference to a specific database inside the database server, not to the database server itself. The database we connect to is ajax, which contains the users table that you created earlier. When performing queries on the created connection, you can count on having access to the users table:

```
// the SQL query to execute
$query = 'SELECT user_id, user_name FROM users';
// execute the query
$result = $mysqli->query($query);
```

After these commands execute, the `$result` variable contains a pointer to the results stream, which we read line by line using the `fetch_array` method. This method returns an array with the fields of the current result row, and moves the pointer to the next result row. We parse the results row by row in a `while` loop until reaching the end of the stream, and for each row we read its individual fields:

```
// loop through the results
while ($row = $result->fetch_array(MYSQLI_ASSOC))
{
  // extract user id and name
  $user_id = $row['user_id'];
  $user_name = $row['user_name'];
  // do something with the data (here we output it)
  echo 'Name of user #' . $user_id . ' is ' . $user_name . '<br/>';
}
```

At the end, we close the open database objects so we don't consume any resources unnecessarily, and we don't keep any database locks that could hurt the activity of other queries running at the same time:

```
// close the input stream
$result->close();
// close the database connection
$mysqli->close();
?>
```

Wrapping Things Up and Laying Out the Structure

In this final section of the chapter, we are establishing the scheme of a basic code structure, which we will use in all the following case studies. Most of the basic building blocks have already been presented, except for separating the sever-side business logic in a separate class, which will be demonstrated in a new exercise.

So far, the server-side code was always built as a single PHP file. In order to achieve better flexibility and a more powerful design, we will split the server-side PHP functionality in two files:

- One script, called `appname.php` (where `appname` is the name of your application) will be the main access point for the client-side JavaScript code. It will deal with the input parameters received through POST and GET, and will make decisions based on these parameters.

- The second script, called `appname.class.php`, will contain a helper class named `Appname`, which encapsulates the real functionality that needs to be processed. The methods of this class will be called by `appname.php` depending on the requested action.

To fully understand the code you need to know the basics of OOP, and how this works with PHP. We don't cover these aspects in this book, but here are a few major things to keep in mind:

- OOP is based on the notion of classes, which are the blueprints for objects. Classes are formed of class members, which include methods (functions inside a class), the constructor, the destructor, and class fields (other OOP languages include even more class member types). Class fields are just like variables, but they have a class-wide scope.

- In classes, you can implement two special methods called the *constructor* and *destructor*. The constructor is called __construct(), and is executed automatically when you create new instances of a class. The constructor is useful when you have code that initializes various class members, because you can rely on it always executing as soon as a new object of the class is created.

- The destructor is named __destruct(), and is called automatically when the object is destroyed. Destructors are very useful for doing housekeeping work. In most examples, we will close the database connection in the destructor, ensuring that we don't leave any database connections open, consuming unnecessary resources.

- It is true that it may be a bit better for performance to create the database connection just before needing it, instead of the class constructor, and to close it right after using it, instead of the class destructor. However, we choose to use the constructor and destructor because we get cleaner code where we are less likely to cause errors by forgetting to close the connection, for example.

When referring to any class member, you must specify the object it is a part of. If you want to access a local class member, you must use the special $this object, that refers to the current class instance.

The *public interface* of a class consists of its *public members*, which are accessible from the outside, and can be used by programs that create instances of the class. Class members can be *public*, *private*, or *protected*. Private members can be used only internally by the class, and protected members can be used by derived classes.

Separating the various layers of functionality of an application is important, because it allows you to build flexible and extensible applications that can be easily updated when necessary. In Cristian Darie and Mihai Bucica's PHP e-commerce books, you even learn how to use a templating engine called Smarty that allows you to further separate presentation logic from the HTML template, so that designers are not bothered with the programming part of the site.

> When preparing the design of your code, keep in mind is that the power, flexibility, and scalability of the architecture is directly proportional to the time you invest in designing it and writing the foundation code. Reference to these issues is available for free download at http:// ajaxphp.packtpub.com/ajax/

For this final exercise, we will build a simple but complete AJAX application called **friendly**, that implements many of the practices and techniques shown so far. The application will have a standard structure, composed of these files:

- index.html is the file loaded initially by the user. It contains the JavaScript code that makes asynchronous requests to friendly.php.

- friendly.css is the file containing the CSS styles to be used in the application.

- friendly.js is the JavaScript file loaded together with index.html on the client side. It makes asynchronous requests to a PHP script called friendly.php to perform various functionality required to support the rich client interface.

- `friendly.php` is a PHP script residing on the same server as `index.html`, and it offers the server-side functionality requested asynchronously by the JavaScript code in `index.html`. Remember that it is important for these files to reside on the same server, because the JavaScript code, when executed by the client, may not be allowed to access other servers. In most cases, `friendly.php` will make use of the functionality of yet another PHP file, named `friendly.class.php`, to perform its duties.

- `friendly.class.php` is a PHP script that contains a class called `Friendly`, which contains the business logic and database operations to support the functionality of `friendly.php`.

- `config.php` will be used to store global configuration options for your application, such as database connection data, etc.

- `error_handler.php` contains the error-handling mechanism that changes the text of an error message into a human-readable format.

The Friendly application, at configurable intervals (by default, of 5 seconds), reads two random records from the `users` table that you have created at the MySQL exercise, and reads a random number from the random number generator service that you have also met earlier in this chapter. Using this data, the server composes a message like "User paula works with user emilian at project #33", which is read by the client and displayed as shown in Figure 3.21.

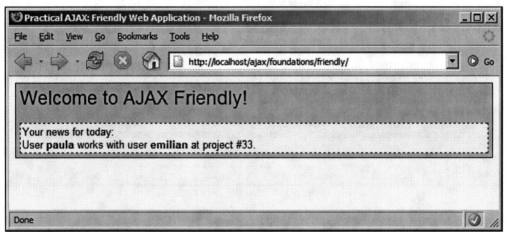

Figure 3.21: Friendly Web Application

The application will display "Reading the new message from server..." while making the asynchronous request (you get to read this message because the server adds an artificial delay to simulate some more complex server-side functionality).

In the case of an error, the application can be configured to display a detailed error message (useful when debugging), as shown in Figure 3.22, or a more user friendly error message as shown in Figure 3.23.

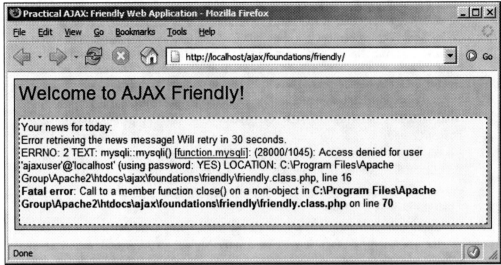

Figure 3.22: What Happens When you Lose the Database Password—A Detailed Error Page

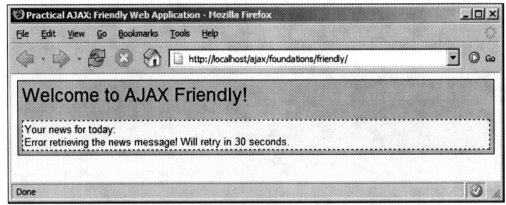

Figure 3.23: A Friendlier Error Page

Now that you know what we are up to, it's time for action…

Time for Action—Building the Friendly Application

1. This exercise makes use of the users table that is created in the previous exercise. If you haven't already, please follow steps 1 and 2 of the *Working with PHP and MySQL* exercise.

2. Create a new folder named friendly as a child of the foundations folder.

3. Create a new file named index.html with this code in it:
    ```
    <!DOCTYPE html PUBLIC "-//W3C//DTD XHTML 1.1//EN"
    "http://www.w3.org/TR/xhtml11/DTD/xhtml11.dtd">
    <html>
      <head>
        <title>Practical AJAX: Friendly Web Application</title>
    ```

```html
      <link href="friendly.css" rel="stylesheet" type="text/css"/>
      <script type="text/javascript" src="friendly.js"></script>
    </head>
    <body onload="process()">
      <noscript>
        <strong>
          This example requires a JavaScript-enabled browser!<br/><br/>
        </strong>
      </noscript>
      <div class="project">
        <span class="title">Welcome to AJAX Friendly!</span>
        <br/><br/>
        <div class="news">
          Your news for today:
          <div id="myDivElement" />
        </div>
      </div>
    </body>
</html>
```

4. Add a new file named friendly.css:

```css
body
{
  font-family: Arial, Helvetica, sans-serif;
  font-size: small;
  background-color: #fffccc;
}

input
{
  margin-bottom: 3px;
  border: #000099 1px solid;
}

.title
{
  font-size: x-large;
}

div.project
{
  background-color: #99ccff;
  padding: 5px;
  border: #000099 1px solid;
}

div.news
{
  background-color: #fffbb8;
  padding: 2px;
  border: 1px dashed;
}
```

5. Now add the JavaScript source file, friendly.js:

```javascript
// holds an instance of XMLHttpRequest
var xmlHttp = createXmlHttpRequestObject();
// holds the remote server address and parameters
var serverAddress = "friendly.php?action=GetNews";
// variables that establish how often to access the server
var updateInterval = 5; // how many seconds to wait to get new message
var errorRetryInterval = 30; // seconds to wait after server error
// when set to true, display detailed error messages
var debugMode = true;
```

```javascript
// creates an XMLHttpRequest instance
function createXmlHttpRequestObject()
{
  // will store the reference to the XMLHttpRequest object
  var xmlHttp;
  // this should work for all browsers except IE6 and older
  try
  {
    // try to create XMLHttpRequest object
    xmlHttp = new XMLHttpRequest();
  }
  catch(e)
  {
    // assume IE6 or older
    var XmlHttpVersions = new Array("MSXML2.XMLHTTP.6.0",
                                    "MSXML2.XMLHTTP.5.0",
                                    "MSXML2.XMLHTTP.4.0",
                                    "MSXML2.XMLHTTP.3.0",
                                    "MSXML2.XMLHTTP",
                                    "Microsoft.XMLHTTP");
    // try every prog id until one works
    for (var i=0; i<XmlHttpVersions.length && !xmlHttp; i++)
    {
      try
      {
        // try to create XMLHttpRequest object
        xmlHttp = new ActiveXObject(XmlHttpVersions[i]);
      }
      catch (e) {}
    }
  }
  // return the created object or display an error message
  if (!xmlHttp)
    alert("Error creating the XMLHttpRequest object.");
  else
    return xmlHttp;
}

// function that displays a new message on the page
function display($message)
{
  // obtain a reference to the <div> element on the page
  myDiv = document.getElementById("myDivElement");
  // display message
  myDiv.innerHTML = $message + "<br/>";
}

// function that displays an error message
function displayError($message)
{
  // display error message, with more technical details if debugMode is true
  display("Error retrieving the news message! Will retry in " +
          errorRetryInterval + " seconds." +
          (debugMode ? "<br/>" + $message : ""));
  // restart sequence
  setTimeout("process();", errorRetryInterval * 1000);
}

// call server asynchronously
function process()
{
  // only continue if xmlHttp isn't void
  if (xmlHttp)
  {
```

```
        // try to connect to the server
        try
        {
          // remove this line if you don't like the 'Receiving...' message
          display("Receiving new message from server...")
          // make asynchronous HTTP request to retrieve new message
          xmlHttp.open("GET", serverAddress, true);
          xmlHttp.onreadystatechange = handleGettingNews;
          xmlHttp.send(null);
        }
        catch(e)
        {
          displayError(e.toString());
        }
      }
    }

    // function called when the state of the HTTP request changes
    function handleGettingNews()
    {
      // when readyState is 4, we are ready to read the server response
      if (xmlHttp.readyState == 4)
      {
        // continue only if HTTP status is "OK"
        if (xmlHttp.status == 200)
        {
          try
          {
            // do something with the response from the server
            getNews();
          }
          catch(e)
          {
            // display error message
            displayError(e.toString());
          }
        }
        else
        {
          // display error message
          displayError(xmlHttp.statusText);
        }
      }
    }

    // handles the response received from the server
    function getNews()
    {
      // retrieve the server's response
      var response = xmlHttp.responseText;
      // server error?
      if (response.indexOf("ERRNO") >= 0
          || response.indexOf("error") >= 0
          || response.length == 0)
        throw(response.length == 0 ? "Server error." : response);
      // display the message
      display(response);
      // restart sequence
      setTimeout("process();", updateInterval * 1000);
    }
```

6. It's time to write the server-side scripts now. Start by creating friendly.php:

```php
<?php
// load the error handling module
require_once('error_handler.php');
require_once('friendly.class.php');
```

```php
// make sure the user's browser doesn't cache the result
header('Expires: Wed, 23 Dec 1980 00:30:00 GMT'); // time in the past
header('Last-Modified: ' . gmdate('D, d M Y H:i:s') . ' GMT');
header('Cache-Control: no-cache, must-revalidate');
header('Pragma: no-cache');
// read the action parameter
$action = $_GET['action'];
// get news
if ($action == 'GetNews')
{
  // create new instance of the Friendly class
  $friendly = new Friendly();
  // use Friendly functionality to retrieve the news message
  $news = $friendly->getNews();
  // echo the message to be read by the client
  echo $news;
}
else
{
  echo 'Communication error: server doesn\'t understand command.';
}
?>
```

7. Create the friendly.class.php script with the following contents:

```php
<?php
// load error handling sequence
require_once ('error_handler.php');
// load configuration
require_once ('config.php');

// class stores Friendly web application functionality
class Friendly
{
  // stores the database connection
  private $mMysqli;

  // constructor opens database connection
  function __construct()
  {
    $this->mMysqli = new mysqli(DB_HOST, DB_USER, DB_PASSWORD,
                                              DB_DATABASE);
  }

  // generate news message
  public function getNews()
  {
    // this will store the news line
    $news = 'No news for today.';
    // SQL that selects two random users from the database.
    $query = 'SELECT user_name FROM users ' .
             'ORDER BY RAND() ' .
             'LIMIT 2';
    // execute the query
    $result = $this->mMysqli->query($query);
    // retrieve the user rows
    $row1 = $result->fetch_array(MYSQLI_ASSOC);
    $row2 = $result->fetch_array(MYSQLI_ASSOC);
    // close the input stream
    $result->close();
    // generate the news
    if (!$row1 || !$row2)
    {
      $news = 'The project needs more users!';
    }
    else
    {
```

```
                // create HTML-formatted news message
                $name1 = '<b>' . $row1['user_name'] . '</b>';
                $name2 = '<b>' . $row2['user_name'] . '</b>';
                $randNum = $this->getRandomNumber();
                $news = 'User ' . $name1 . ' works with user ' . $name2 .
                        ' at project #' . $randNum . '.';
            }
            // output the news line
            return $news;
        }

        // returns a random number between 1 and 100
        private function getRandomNumber()
        {
            // delays execution for quarter of a second
            usleep(250000);
            // holds the remote server address and parameters
            $serverAddress = 'http://www.random.org/cgi-bin/randnum';
            $serverParams = 'num=1&min=1&max=100';
            // retrieve the random number from remote server
            $randomNumber = file_get_contents($serverAddress . '?' .
                                                         $serverParams);

            // output the random number
            return trim($randomNumber);
        }

        // destructor closes database connection
        function __destruct()
        {
            $this->mMysqli->close();
        }
    }
?>
```

8. Add the configuration file, config.php:

```
<?php
// defines database connection data
define('DB_HOST', 'localhost');
define('DB_USER', 'ajaxuser');
define('DB_PASSWORD', 'practical');
define('DB_DATABASE', 'ajax');
?>
```

9. Finally, add the error-handler script, error_handler.php:

```
<?php
// set the user error handler method to be error_handler
set_error_handler('error_handler', E_ALL);
// error handler function
function error_handler($errNo, $errStr, $errFile, $errLine)
{
    // clear any output that has already been generated
    if(ob_get_length()) ob_clean();
    // output the error message
    $error_message = 'ERRNO: ' . $errNo . chr(10) .
                     'TEXT: ' . $errStr . chr(10) .
                     'LOCATION: ' . $errFile .
                     ', line ' . $errLine;
    echo $error_message;
    // prevent processing any more PHP scripts
    exit;
}
?>
```

10. Load http://localhost/ajax/foundations/friendly/.

What Just Happened?

Most of the principles implemented in the application were covered earlier in the book, so we will quickly analyze what's new here, starting from the client-side code. The novelty in index.html consists in using the <noscript> element to offer a minimal support for browsers that don't support JavaScript, or for ones whose JavaScript support has been disabled:

```
<body onload="process()">
  <noscript>
    <strong>
      This example requires a JavaScript-enabled browser!<br/><br/>
    </strong>
  </noscript>
```

Browsers that have JavaScript enabled will ignore everything between <noscript> and </noscript>, while the others will parse and display that HTML code.

The client-side JavaScript file, friendly.js has a few surprises of its own:

- We grouped common functionality that handles displaying user messages into the display and displayError functions. Both receive as parameter the message to be displayed, but displayError displays the message only if debugMode is true (this variable is defined at the beginning of the file).

- displayError is called in the catch blocks after an exception has been thrown somewhere, and it uses setTimeout to restart the sequence that makes server requests. You can set how much time the script should wait before attempting a new server request when an error happens by modifying the value of the errorRetryInterval variable.

- You can change how often the news message should be displayed by changing the updateInterval variable.

- In getNews(), we have a simplistic mechanism that checks whether the text received from the server was a server-side error instead of the message we are waiting for. This mechanism verifies if the response contains "ERRNO" (which is generated by our server-side custom error handler), or "error" (which is generated automatically by PHP in the case of fatal errors or parse errors), or if the response is empty (if the displayErrors option is set to off in php.ini, no error text is generated). In any of these cases, we throw an error manually, which is then received by our error-handling mechanism that informs the users that an error has happened.

At the server side, everything starts in friendly.php, which is called from the client. The most important part of friendly.php is the one where it creates a new instance of the Friendly class (defined in friendly.class.php), and calls its getNews method:

```php
// read the action parameter
$action = $_GET['action'];
// get news
if ($action == 'GetNews')
{
    // create new instance of the Friendly class
    $friendly = new Friendly();
    // use Friendly functionality to retrieve the news message
    $news = $friendly->getNews();
    // echo the message to be read by the client
    echo $news;
}
```

On the server side, all the interesting things happen in friendly.class.php, which is called from friendly.php to do the interesting part of the work. In friendly.class.php you can find the Friendly class, which has the following four members:

- $mMysqli: A private field that stores an open database connection during the life of the object.

- __construct(): The class constructor initializes $mMysqli by opening a database connection. Because the constructor is executed automatically when an instance of the class is created, you can safely assume to have the connection available in all methods of the class.

- __destruct(): The class destructor closes the database connection. The destructor is executed automatically when the class instance is destroyed.

- getRandomNumber(): This is a private helper method that returns a random number. Private methods can't be called from programs that create instances of the class, and are meant to provide internal functionality only. The code in getRandomNumber is familiar from the previous exercises, as it calls the external random.org server to retrieve new random numbers. The usleep PHP function is used to artificially add a quarter of a second delay, so that you can admire the "Receiving new message from server..." message on the client for a little longer.

- getNews(): This is a public method that an external program can access to get a new "news" message. The method gets two random user names from the database, uses the getRandomNumber method to retrieve a random number, and composes a message such as "User x works with user y at project #z". (Yes that's not very imaginative but we couldn't think of anything more interesting—sorry!) Note the $this special object that is used to access $mMysqli and getRandomNumber(). Class members can only be accessed using an instance of the class and in PHP $this refers to the current class instance.

Summary

Hopefully, you have enjoyed the little examples of this chapter, because many more will follow! This chapter walked you through the technologies that live at the server side of a typical AJAX application. We have done a few exercises that involved simple server functionality, and PHP did a wonderful job at delivering that functionality. You have also learned the basics of working with databases, and simple database operations with the first table created in this book.

In the following chapters, you'll meet even more interesting examples that use more advanced code to implement their functionality. In Chapter 4, you'll build an AJAX-enabled form validation page, which is safe to work even if the client doesn't support JavaScript and AJAX.

4
AJAX Form Validation

Validating input data is an essential requirement for quality and secure software applications. In the case of web applications, validation is an even more sensitive area, because your application is widely reachable by many users with varying skill sets and intentions.

Validation is not something to play with, because invalid data has the potential to harm the application's functionality, and even corrupt the application's most sensitive area: the database.

Input data validation means checking whether the data entered by the user complies with previously defined rules, which are established according to the business rules of your application. For example, if you require dates to be entered in the YYYY-MM-DD format, then a date of "February 28" would be considered invalid. Email addresses and phone numbers are other examples of data that should be checked against valid formats.

> Carefully define the input data validation rules in the software requirements document of the application you're developing, and then use them consistently to validate your data!

Historically, web form validation was implemented mostly at the server side, after the form was submitted. In some cases, there was also some JavaScript code on the client that performed simple validation such as checking whether the email address was valid, or if a user name had been entered.

The problems encountered with traditional web form validation techniques are:

- Server-side form validation meets the limits of the HTTP protocol, which is a stateless protocol. Unless special code is written to deal with this issue, after submitting a page containing invalid data, the user is shown back an empty form that has to be filled from scratch.

- When submitting the page, the user needs to wait for a full page reload. For every mistake that is made when filling the form, a new page reload happens.

In this chapter, we will create a form-validation application that implements the good old traditional techniques and adds an AJAX flavor, thereby making the form more user-friendly and responsive.

Even if you implement AJAX validation, server-side validation is mandatory, because the server is the last line of defense against invalid data. The JavaScript code that gets to the client can not only be disabled permanently from the browser's settings, but it also can be easily modified or bypassed.

The code in this chapter can be verified online at `http://ajaxphp.packtpub.com`.

Implementing AJAX Form Validation

The form-validation application we will build in this chapter validates the form at the server side on the classic form submit, and also implements AJAX validation while the user navigates through the form. The final validation is performed at the server, as shown in Figure 4.1.

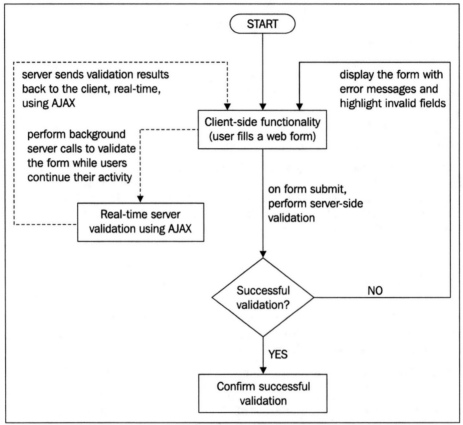

Figure 4.1: Validation Being Performed Seamlessly while Users Continue Their Activity

Doing a final server-side validation when the form is submitted is always a must. If someone disables JavaScript in the browser settings, AJAX validation on the client side won't work, exposing sensitive data, and thereby allowing an evil-intended visitor to harm important data back on the server (e.g. through SQL injection).

Always validate user input on the server.

The application you are about to build validates a registration form, as shown in Figure 4.2, using both AJAX validation (client side) and typical server-side validation:

- AJAX-style—when each form field loses focus (onblur). The field's value is sent to the server, which validates the data and returns a result (0 for failure, 1 for success). If validation fails, an error message will unobtrusively show up and notify the user about the failed validation as shown in Figure 4.3.

- PHP-style—when the entire form is submitted. This is the usual validation you would do on the server, by checking user input against certain rules. If no errors are found and the input data is valid, the browser is redirected to a success page as shown in Figure 4.4. If validation fails, however, the user is sent back to the form page with the invalid fields highlighted as shown in Figure 4.3.

Both AJAX validation and PHP validation check the entered data against these rules:

- Username must not already exist in the database
- Name field cannot be empty
- A gender must be selected
- Month of Birth must be selected
- Birthday must be a valid date (between 1-31)
- Year of birth must be a valid year (between 1900-2000)
- The date must exist taking into consideration the number of days for each month
- Email address must be written in a valid email format, such as filip@yahoo.co.uk or cristian@subdomain.domain.com
- Phone number must be written in standard US form: xxx-xxx-xxxx
- "I've read the Terms of Use" must be checked

Watch the application in action in the following screenshots:

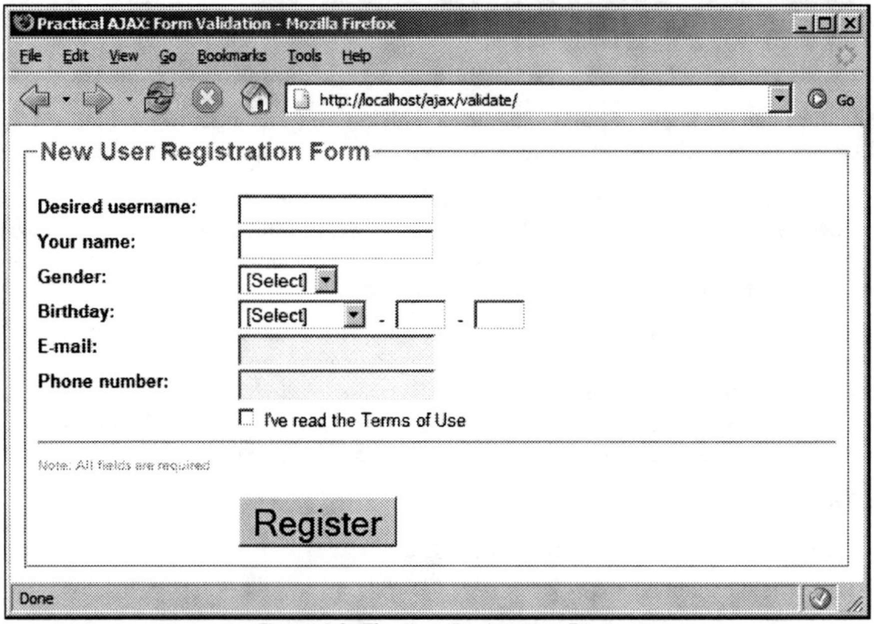

Figure 4.2: The User Registration Form

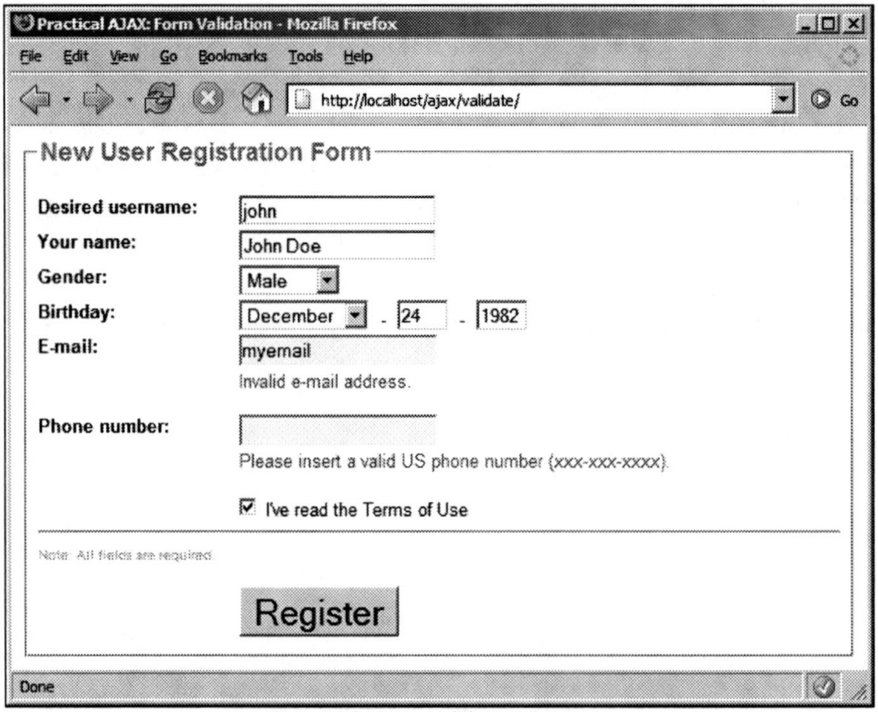

Figure 4.3: Form Validation in Action

Figure 4.4: Successful Submission

Thread-Safe AJAX

A piece of code is thread-safe if it functions correctly during simultaneous execution by multiple threads. This chapter contains the first example where an external factor—the user—directly influences the AJAX requests. We need to make an asynchronous request to the server to validate the entered data every time the user leaves an input box or changes a selection.

The hidden danger behind this technique is only revealed if the user moves very quickly through the input fields, or the server connection is slow; in these cases, the web application would attempt to make new server requests through an XMLHttpRequest object that is still busy waiting for the response to a previous request (this would generate an error and the application would stop functioning properly).

Depending on the circumstances at hand, the ideal solution to this problem may be:

- Create a new XMLHttpRequest instance for every message you need to send to the server. This method is easy to implement, but it can degrade server's performance if multiple requests are sent at the same time, and it doesn't guarantee for the order in which you receive the responses.

- Record the message in a *queue* and send it later when the XMLHttpRequest object is able to make new requests. The requests are made in the expected order. Using a queue is particularly important in applications where the order of the messages is important.

- Schedule to automatically retry making the request after a specified amount of time. This method is similar to the one with the queue in that you don't make more than one server request at a time, but it doesn't guarantee for either the order in which the requests are made, or for the order in which the responses are received.

- Ignore the message.

In this chapter, for the first time in the book, we'll choose to implement a message queue. When the user leaves an input element, a message to validate its value is added to the queue. When the XMLHttpRequest object is clear to make a new request, it takes the first message from the queue.

The queue is a **First-In**, **First-Out (FIFO)** structure, which guarantees that the messages are sent in the proper order. To get a feeling about how this works, go to the demo page for this chapter (or implement the code), and press tab quickly multiple times, and then wait to see how the validation responses show up one by one.

125

Note that dealing with these problems only makes sense in scenarios where elements outside your control can trigger the server requests. Otherwise, in scenarios such as the Friendly application from Chapter 3, where you initiated new requests only after the response was received, implementing thread-safe code doesn't make a huge difference.

It's time to code.

Time for Action—AJAX Form Validation

If you have read the previous chapter then you should already have the users table set up. If you do, you may skip steps 1 and 2.

1. Connect to the ajax database, and create a table named users with the following code:

```
CREATE TABLE users
(
 user_id INT UNSIGNED NOT NULL AUTO_INCREMENT,
 user_name VARCHAR(32) NOT NULL,
 PRIMARY KEY (user_id)
);
```

2. Execute the following INSERT commands to populate your users table with some sample data (because user_id is an auto_increment column, its values will be generated by the database):

```
INSERT INTO users (user_name) VALUES ('bogdan');
INSERT INTO users (user_name) VALUES ('filip');
INSERT INTO users (user_name) VALUES ('mihai');
INSERT INTO users (user_name) VALUES ('emilian');
INSERT INTO users (user_name) VALUES ('paula');
INSERT INTO users (user_name) VALUES ('cristian');
```

3. In your ajax folder, create a new folder named validate.

4. Let's start writing the code with the presentation tier. Create a file named validate.css, and add the following code to it:

```
body
{
    font-family: Arial, Helvetica, sans-serif;
    font-size: 0.8em;
    color: #000000;
}

label
{
    float: left;
    width: 150px;
    font-weight: bold;
}

input, select
{
    margin-bottom: 3px;
}

.button
{
    font-size: 2em;
}
```

```css
.left
{
  margin-left: 150px;
}

.txtFormLegend
{
  color: #777777;
  font-weight: bold;
  font-size: large;
}

.txtSmall
{
  color: #999999;
  font-size: smaller;
}

.hidden
{
  display: none;
}

.error
{
  display: block;
  margin-left: 150px;
  color: #ff0000;
}
```

5. Now create a new file named index_top.php, and add the following code. This script will be loaded from the main page index.php.

```php
<?php
// enable PHP session
session_start();

// Build HTML <option> tags
function buildOptions($options, $selectedOption)
{
  foreach ($options as $value => $text)
  {
    if ($value == $selectedOption)
    {
      echo '<option value="' . $value .
          '" selected="selected">' . $text . '</option>';
    }
    else
    {
      echo '<option value="' . $value . '">' . $text . '</option>';
    }
  }
}

// initialize gender options array
$genderOptions = array("0" => "[Select]",
                       "1" => "Male",
                       "2" => "Female");

// initialize month options array
$monthOptions = array("0" => "[Select]",
                      "1" => "January",
                      "2" => "February",
```

```
                                  "3"  => "March",
                                  "4"  => "April",
                                  "5"  => "May",
                                  "6"  => "June",
                                  "7"  => "July",
                                  "8"  => "August",
                                  "9"  => "September",
                                  "10" => "October",
                                  "11" => "November",
                                  "12" => "December");

    // initialize some session variables to prevent PHP throwing Notices
    if (!isset($_SESSION['values']))
    {
      $_SESSION['values']['txtUsername'] = '';
      $_SESSION['values']['txtName'] = '';
      $_SESSION['values']['selGender'] = '';
      $_SESSION['values']['selBthMonth'] = '';
      $_SESSION['values']['txtBthDay'] = '';
      $_SESSION['values']['txtBthYear'] = '';
      $_SESSION['values']['txtEmail'] = '';
      $_SESSION['values']['txtPhone'] = '';
      $_SESSION['values']['chkReadTerms'] = '';
    }
    if (!isset($_SESSION['errors']))
    {
      $_SESSION['errors']['txtUsername'] = 'hidden';
      $_SESSION['errors']['txtName'] = 'hidden';
      $_SESSION['errors']['selGender'] = 'hidden';
      $_SESSION['errors']['selBthMonth'] = 'hidden';
      $_SESSION['errors']['txtBthDay'] = 'hidden';
      $_SESSION['errors']['txtBthYear'] = 'hidden';
      $_SESSION['errors']['txtEmail'] = 'hidden';
      $_SESSION['errors']['txtPhone'] = 'hidden';
      $_SESSION['errors']['chkReadTerms'] = 'hidden';
    }
    ?>
```

6. Now create index.php, and add this code to it:

```
<?php
require_once ('index_top.php');
?>

<!DOCTYPE html PUBLIC "-//W3C//DTD XHTML 1.1//EN"
"http://www.w3.org/TR/xhtml11/DTD/xhtml11.dtd">
<html xmlns="http://www.w3.org/1999/xhtml">
  <head>
    <title>Practical AJAX: Form Validation</title>
    <meta http-equiv="Content-Type" content="text/html; charset=utf-8" />
    <link href="validate.css" rel="stylesheet" type="text/css" />
    <script type="text/javascript" src="validate.js"></script>
  </head>

  <body onload="setFocus();">
    <fieldset>
      <legend class="txtFormLegend">New User Registration Form</legend>
      <br />
      <form name="frmRegistration" method="post"
            action="validate.php?validationType=php">

        <!-- Username -->
        <label for="txtUsername">Desired username:</label>
        <input id="txtUsername" name="txtUsername" type="text"
               onblur="validate(this.value, this.id)"
```

```
            value="<?php echo $_SESSION['values']['txtUsername'] ?>" />
<span id="txtUsernameFailed"
     class="<?php echo $_SESSION['errors']['txtUsername'] ?>">
   This username is in use, or empty username field.
</span>
<br />

<!-- Name -->
<label for="txtName">Your name:</label>
<input id="txtName" name="txtName" type="text"
     onblur="validate(this.value, this.id)"
     value="<?php echo $_SESSION['values']['txtName'] ?>" />
<span id="txtNameFailed"
     class="<?php echo $_SESSION['errors']['txtName'] ?>">
   Please enter your name.
</span>
<br />

<!-- Gender -->
<label for="selGender">Gender:</label>
<select name="selGender" id="selGender"
     onblur="validate(this.value, this.id)">
   <?php buildOptions($genderOptions,
                    $_SESSION['values']['selGender']); ?>
</select>
<span id="selGenderFailed"
     class="<?php echo $_SESSION['errors']['selGender'] ?>">
   Please select your gender.
</span>
<br />

<!-- Birthday -->
<label for="selBthMonth">Birthday:</label>

<!-- Month -->
<select name="selBthMonth" id="selBthMonth"
     onblur="validate(this.value, this.id)">
   <?php buildOptions($monthOptions,
                    $_SESSION['values']['selBthMonth']); ?>
</select>
 - 
<!-- Day -->
<input type="text" name="txtBthDay" id="txtBthDay" maxlength="2"
     size="2"
     onblur="validate(this.value, this.id)"
     value="<?php echo $_SESSION['values']['txtBthDay'] ?>" />
 - 
<!-- Year -->
<input type="text" name="txtBthYear" id="txtBthYear" maxlength="4"
     size="2"
onblur="validate(document.getElementById('selBthMonth').options[document.g
etElementById('selBthMonth').selectedIndex].value + '#' +
document.getElementById('txtBthDay').value + '#' + this.value, this.id)"
     value="<?php echo $_SESSION['values']['txtBthYear'] ?>" />

<!-- Month, Day, Year validation -->
<span id="selBthMonthFailed"
     class="<?php echo $_SESSION['errors']['selBthMonth'] ?>">
   Please select your birth month.
</span>
<span id="txtBthDayFailed"
     class="<?php echo $_SESSION['errors']['txtBthDay'] ?>">
   Please enter your birth day.
</span>
<span id="txtBthYearFailed"
```

```
                    class="<?php echo $_SESSION['errors']['txtBthYear'] ?>">
            Please enter a valid date.
          </span>
          <br />

          <!-- Email -->
          <label for="txtEmail">E-mail:</label>
          <input id="txtEmail" name="txtEmail" type="text"
                 onblur="validate(this.value, this.id)"
                 value="<?php echo $_SESSION['values']['txtEmail'] ?>" />
          <span id="txtEmailFailed"
                class="<?php echo $_SESSION['errors']['txtEmail'] ?>">
            Invalid e-mail address.
          </span>
          <br />

          <!-- Phone number -->
          <label for="txtPhone">Phone number:</label>
          <input id="txtPhone" name="txtPhone" type="text"
                 onblur="validate(this.value, this.id)"
                 value="<?php echo $_SESSION['values']['txtPhone'] ?>" />
          <span id="txtPhoneFailed"
                class="<?php echo $_SESSION['errors']['txtPhone'] ?>">
            Please insert a valid US phone number (xxx-xxx-xxxx).
          </span>
          <br />

          <!-- Read terms checkbox -->
          <input type="checkbox" id="chkReadTerms" name="chkReadTerms"
                 class="left"
                 onblur="validate(this.checked, this.id)"
                 <?php if ($_SESSION['values']['chkReadTerms'] == 'on')
                       echo 'checked="checked"' ?> />
          I've read the Terms of Use
          <span id="chkReadTermsFailed"
                class="<?php echo $_SESSION['errors']['chkReadTerms'] ?>">
            Please make sure you read the Terms of Use.
          </span>

          <!-- End of form -->
          <hr />
          <span class="txtSmall">Note: All fields are required.</span>
          <br /><br />
          <input type="submit" name="submitbutton" value="Register"
                 class="left button" />
        </form>
      </fieldset>
    </body>
</html>
```

7. Create a new file named allok.php, and add the following code to it:

```php
<?php
  // clear any data saved in the session
  session_start();
  session_destroy();
?>
<!DOCTYPE html PUBLIC "-//W3C//DTD XHTML 1.1//EN"
"http://www.w3.org/TR/xhtml11/DTD/xhtml11.dtd">
<html xmlns="http://www.w3.org/1999/xhtml">
  <head>
    <title>AJAX Form Validation</title>
    <meta http-equiv="Content-Type" content="text/html; charset=utf-8" />
    <link href="validate.css" rel="stylesheet" type="text/css" />
  </head>
```

```
    <body>
      Registration Successful!<br />
      <a href="index.php" title="Go back">&lt;&lt; Go back</a>
    </body>
</html>
```

8. Create a file named validate.js. This file performs the client-side functionality, including the AJAX requests:

```
// holds an instance of XMLHttpRequest
var xmlHttp = createXmlHttpRequestObject();
// holds the remote server address
var serverAddress = "validate.php";
// when set to true, display detailed error messages
var showErrors = true;
// initialize the validation requests cache
var cache = new Array();

// creates an XMLHttpRequest instance
function createXmlHttpRequestObject()
{
  // will store the reference to the XMLHttpRequest object
  var xmlHttp;
  // this should work for all browsers except IE6 and older
  try
  {
    // try to create XMLHttpRequest object
    xmlHttp = new XMLHttpRequest();
  }
  catch(e)
  {
    // assume IE6 or older
    var XmlHttpVersions = new Array("MSXML2.XMLHTTP.6.0",
                                    "MSXML2.XMLHTTP.5.0",
                                    "MSXML2.XMLHTTP.4.0",
                                    "MSXML2.XMLHTTP.3.0",
                                    "MSXML2.XMLHTTP",
                                    "Microsoft.XMLHTTP");
    // try every id until one works
    for (var i=0; i<XmlHttpVersions.length && !xmlHttp; i++)
    {
      try
      {
        // try to create XMLHttpRequest object
        xmlHttp = new ActiveXObject(XmlHttpVersions[i]);
      }
      catch (e) {} // ignore potential error
    }
  }
  // return the created object or display an error message
  if (!xmlHttp)
    displayError("Error creating the XMLHttpRequest object.");
  else
    return xmlHttp;
}

// function that displays an error message
function displayError($message)
{
  // ignore errors if showErrors is false
  if (showErrors)
  {
    // turn error displaying off
    showErrors = false;
    // display error message
```

```
        alert("Error encountered: \n" + $message);
        // retry validation after 10 seconds
        setTimeout("validate();", 10000);
    }
}

// the function handles the validation for any form field
function validate(inputValue, fieldID)
{
    // only continue if xmlHttp isn't void
    if (xmlHttp)
    {
        // if we received non-null parameters, we add them to cache in the
        // form of the query string to be sent to the server for validation
        if (fieldID)
        {
            // encode values for safely adding them to an HTTP request query string
            inputValue = encodeURIComponent(inputValue);
            fieldID = encodeURIComponent(fieldID);
            // add the values to the queue
            cache.push("inputValue=" + inputValue + "&fieldID=" + fieldID);
        }
        // try to connect to the server
        try
        {
            // continue only if the XMLHttpRequest object isn't busy
            // and the cache is not empty
            if ((xmlHttp.readyState == 4 || xmlHttp.readyState == 0)
                && cache.length > 0)
            {
                // get a new set of parameters from the cache
                var cacheEntry = cache.shift();
                // make a server request to validate the extracted data
                xmlHttp.open("POST", serverAddress, true);
                xmlHttp.setRequestHeader("Content-Type",
                                         "application/x-www-form-urlencoded");
                xmlHttp.onreadystatechange = handleRequestStateChange;
                xmlHttp.send(cacheEntry);
            }
        }
        catch (e)
        {
            // display an error when failing to connect to the server
            displayError(e.toString());
        }
    }
}

// function that handles the HTTP response
function handleRequestStateChange()
{
    // when readyState is 4, we read the server response
    if (xmlHttp.readyState == 4)
    {
        // continue only if HTTP status is "OK"
        if (xmlHttp.status == 200)
        {
            try
            {
                // read the response from the server
                readResponse();
            }
            catch(e)
```

```
        {
          // display error message
          displayError(e.toString());
        }
      }
      else
      {
        // display error message
        displayError(xmlHttp.statusText);
      }
    }
  }

  // read server's response
  function readResponse()
  {
    // retrieve the server's response
    var response = xmlHttp.responseText;
    // server error?
    if (response.indexOf("ERRNO") >= 0
        || response.indexOf("error:") >= 0
        || response.length == 0)
      throw(response.length == 0 ? "Server error." : response);
    // get response in XML format (assume the response is valid XML)
    responseXml = xmlHttp.responseXML;
    // get the document element
    xmlDoc = responseXml.documentElement;
    result = xmlDoc.getElementsByTagName("result")[0].firstChild.data;
    fieldID = xmlDoc.getElementsByTagName("fieldid")[0].firstChild.data;
    // find the HTML element that displays the error
    message = document.getElementById(fieldID + "Failed");
    // show the error or hide the error
    message.className = (result == "0") ? "error" : "hidden";
    // call validate() again, in case there are values left in the cache
    setTimeout("validate();", 500);
  }

  // sets focus on the first field of the form
  function setFocus()
  {
    document.getElementById("txtUsername").focus();
  }
```

9. It's time to add the business logic now. Start by creating config.php, with this code in it:

```php
<?php
// defines database connection data
define('DB_HOST', 'localhost');
define('DB_USER', 'ajaxuser');
define('DB_PASSWORD', 'practical');
define('DB_DATABASE', 'ajax');
?>
```

10. Now create the error handler code in a file named error_handler.php:

```php
<?php
// set the user error handler method to be error_handler
set_error_handler('error_handler', E_ALL);

// error handler function
function error_handler($errNo, $errStr, $errFile, $errLine)
{
  // clear any output that has already been generated
  if(ob_get_length()) ob_clean();
```

```
            // output the error message
            $error_message = 'ERRNO: ' . $errNo . chr(10) .
                             'TEXT: ' . $errStr . chr(10) .
                             'LOCATION: ' . $errFile .
                             ', line ' . $errLine;
            echo $error_message;
            // prevent processing any more PHP scripts
            exit;
        }
?>
```

11. The PHP script that handles the client's AJAX calls, and also handles the validation on form submit, is validate.php:

```php
<?php
// start PHP session
session_start();
// load error handling script and validation class
require_once ('error_handler.php');
require_once ('validate.class.php');

// Create new validator object
$validator = new Validate();

// read validation type (PHP or AJAX?)
$validationType = '';
if (isset($_GET['validationType']))
{
    $validationType = $_GET['validationType'];
}

// AJAX validation or PHP validation?
if ($validationType == 'php')
{
    // PHP validation is performed by the ValidatePHP method, which returns
    // the page the visitor should be redirected to (which is allok.php if
    // all the data is valid, or back to index.php if not)
    header("Location:" . $validator->ValidatePHP());
}
else
{
    // AJAX validation is performed by the ValidateAJAX method. The results
    // are used to form an XML document that is sent back to the client
    $response =
    '<?xml version="1.0" encoding="UTF-8" standalone="yes"?>' .
    '<response>' .
      '<result>' .
        $validator->ValidateAJAX($_POST['inputValue'], $_POST['fieldID']) .
      '</result>' .
      '<fieldid>' .
        $_POST['fieldID'] .
      '</fieldid>' .
    '</response>';
    // generate the response
    if(ob_get_length()) ob_clean();
    header('Content-Type: text/xml');
    echo $response;
}
?>
```

12. The class that supports the validation functionality is called validate, and it is hosted in a script file called validate.class.php, which looks like this:

```php
<?php
// load error handler and database configuration
```

```php
require_once ('config.php');

// Class supports AJAX and PHP web form validation
class Validate
{
  // stored database connection
  private $mMysqli;

  // constructor opens database connection
  function __construct()
  {
    $this->mMysqli = new mysqli(DB_HOST, DB_USER, DB_PASSWORD, DB_DATABASE);
  }

  // destructor closes database connection
  function __destruct()
  {
    $this->mMysqli->close();
  }

  // supports AJAX validation, verifies a single value
  public function ValidateAJAX($inputValue, $fieldID)
  {
    // check which field is being validated and perform validation
    switch($fieldID)
    {
      // Check if the username is valid
      case 'txtUsername':
        return $this->validateUserName($inputValue);
        break;

      // Check if the name is valid
      case 'txtName':
        return $this->validateName($inputValue);
        break;

      // Check if a gender was selected
      case 'selGender':
        return $this->validateGender($inputValue);
        break;

      // Check if birth month is valid
      case 'selBthMonth':
        return $this->validateBirthMonth($inputValue);
        break;

      // Check if birth day is valid
      case 'txtBthDay':
        return $this->validateBirthDay($inputValue);
        break;

      // Check if birth year is valid
      case 'txtBthYear':
        return $this->validateBirthYear($inputValue);
        break;

      // Check if email is valid
      case 'txtEmail':
        return $this->validateEmail($inputValue);
        break;

      // Check if phone is valid
      case 'txtPhone':
        return $this->validatePhone($inputValue);
```

```
          break;

        // Check if "I have read the terms" checkbox has been checked
        case 'chkReadTerms':
          return $this->validateReadTerms($inputValue);
          break;
    }
}

// validates all form fields on form submit
public function ValidatePHP()
{
    // error flag, becomes 1 when errors are found.
    $errorsExist = 0;
    // clears the errors session flag
    if (isset($_SESSION['errors']))
      unset($_SESSION['errors']);
    // By default all fields are considered valid
    $_SESSION['errors']['txtUsername'] = 'hidden';
    $_SESSION['errors']['txtName'] = 'hidden';
    $_SESSION['errors']['selGender'] = 'hidden';
    $_SESSION['errors']['selBthMonth'] = 'hidden';
    $_SESSION['errors']['txtBthDay'] = 'hidden';
    $_SESSION['errors']['txtBthYear'] = 'hidden';
    $_SESSION['errors']['txtEmail'] = 'hidden';
    $_SESSION['errors']['txtPhone'] = 'hidden';
    $_SESSION['errors']['chkReadTerms'] = 'hidden';

    // Validate username
    if (!$this->validateUserName($_POST['txtUsername']))
    {
      $_SESSION['errors']['txtUsername'] = 'error';
      $errorsExist = 1;
    }

    // Validate name
    if (!$this->validateName($_POST['txtName']))
    {
      $_SESSION['errors']['txtName'] = 'error';
      $errorsExist = 1;
    }

    // Validate gender
    if (!$this->validateGender($_POST['selGender']))
    {
      $_SESSION['errors']['selGender'] = 'error';
      $errorsExist = 1;
    }

    // Validate birth month
    if (!$this->validateBirthMonth($_POST['selBthMonth']))
    {
      $_SESSION['errors']['selBthMonth'] = 'error';
      $errorsExist = 1;
    }

    // Validate birth day
    if (!$this->validateBirthDay($_POST['txtBthDay']))
    {
      $_SESSION['errors']['txtBthDay'] = 'error';
      $errorsExist = 1;
    }

    // Validate birth year and date
    if (!$this->validateBirthYear($_POST['selBthMonth'] . '#' .
```

```
                                     $_POST['txtBthDay'] . '#' .
                                     $_POST['txtBthYear']))
    {
      $_SESSION['errors']['txtBthYear'] = 'error';
      $errorsExist = 1;
    }

    // Validate email
    if (!$this->validateEmail($_POST['txtEmail']))
    {
      $_SESSION['errors']['txtEmail'] = 'error';
      $errorsExist = 1;
    }

    // Validate phone
    if (!$this->validatePhone($_POST['txtPhone']))
    {
      $_SESSION['errors']['txtPhone'] = 'error';
      $errorsExist = 1;
    }

    // Validate read terms
    if (!isset($_POST['chkReadTerms']) ||
        !$this->validateReadTerms($_POST['chkReadTerms']))
    {
      $_SESSION['errors']['chkReadTerms'] = 'error';
      $_SESSION['values']['chkReadTerms'] = '';
      $errorsExist = 1;
    }

    // If no errors are found, point to a successful validation page
    if ($errorsExist == 0)
    {
      return 'allok.php';
    }
    else
    {
      // If errors are found, save current user input
      foreach ($_POST as $key => $value)
      {
        $_SESSION['values'][$key] = $_POST[$key];
      }
      return 'index.php';
    }
}

// validate user name (must be empty, and must not be already registered)
private function validateUserName($value)
{
    // trim and escape input value
    $value = $this->mMysqli->real_escape_string(trim($value));
    // empty user name is not valid
    if ($value == null)
      return 0; // not valid
    // check if the username exists in the database
    $query = $this->mMysqli->query('SELECT user_name FROM users ' .
                                   'WHERE user_name="' . $value . '"');
    if ($this->mMysqli->affected_rows > 0)
      return '0'; // not valid
    else
      return '1'; // valid
}

// validate name
```

```php
      private function validateName($value)
      {
        // trim and escape input value
        $value = trim($value);
        // empty user name is not valid
        if ($value)
          return 1; // valid
        else
          return 0; // not valid
      }

      // validate gender
      private function validateGender($value)
      {
        // user must have a gender
        return ($value == '0') ? 0 : 1;
      }

      // validate birth month
      private function validateBirthMonth($value)
      {
        // month must be non-null, and between 1 and 12
        return ($value == '' || $value > 12 || $value < 1) ? 0 : 1;
      }
      // validate birth day
      private function validateBirthDay($value)
      {
        // day must be non-null, and between 1 and 31
        return ($value == '' || $value > 31 || $value < 1) ? 0 : 1;
      }

      // validate birth year and the whole date
      private function validateBirthYear($value)
      {
        // valid birth year is between 1900 and 2000
        // get whole date (mm#dd#yyyy)
        $date = explode('#', $value);
        // date can't be valid if there is no day, month, or year
        if (!$date[0]) return 0;
        if (!$date[1] || !is_numeric($date[1])) return 0;
        if (!$date[2] || !is_numeric($date[2])) return 0;
        // check the date
        return (checkdate($date[0], $date[1], $date[2])) ? 1 : 0;
      }

      // validate email
      private function validateEmail($value)
      {
        // valid email formats: *@*.*, *@*.*.*, *.*@*.*, *.*@*.*.*
        return (!eregi('^[_a-z0-9-]+(\.[_a-z0-9-]+)*@[a-z0-9-]+(\.[a-z0-9-
]+)*(\.[a-z]{2,3})$', $value)) ? 0 : 1;
      }

      // validate phone
      private function validatePhone($value)
      {
        // valid phone format: ###-###-####
        return (!eregi('^[0-9]{3}-*[0-9]{3}-*[0-9]{4}$', $value)) ? 0 : 1;
      }

      // check the user has read the terms of use
      private function validateReadTerms($value)
      {
        // valid value is 'true'
```

```
                return ($value == 'true' || $value == 'on') ? 1 : 0;
        }
    }
    ?>
```

13. Test your script by loading `http://localhost/ajax/validate/index.php` in a web browser.

What Just Happened?

The AJAX validation technique allows us to validate form fields and at the same time inform users if there were any validation errors. But the cherry on the top of the cake is that we are doing all of this without interrupting the user's activity! This is called unobtrusive form validation.

The unobtrusive validation is combined with a pure server-side PHP validation that happens when submitting the form. At the server, both validation types are supported by a PHP script called `validate.php`, with the help of another PHP script called `validate.class.php`.

Let us examine the code, starting with the script that handles client-side validation, `index.php`. In this validation example, the client page is not a simple HTML file, but a PHP file instead, so portions of it will be still dynamically generated at the server side. This is necessary because we want to retain the form field values when the form is submitted and server-side validation fails. Without the help of the PHP code, when the index page is reloaded, all its fields would become empty.

`index.php` starts with loading a helper script named `index_top.php`, which starts the session by calling `session_start()`, defines some variables and a function that will be used later in `index.php`, and initializes some session variables (`$_SESSION['values']` and `$_SESSION['errors']`) that we will be using to avoid PHP sending notices about variables that are not initialized.

Notice the `onload` event of the body tag in `index.php`. It calls the `setFocus()` function defined in `validate.js`, which sets the input cursor on the first form field.

Later in `index.php`, you will see the following sequence of code repeating itself, with only small changes:

```html
<!-- Username -->
<label for="txtUsername">Desired username:</label>
<input id="txtUsername" name="txtUsername" type="text"
        onblur="validate(this.value, this.id)"
        value="<?php echo $_SESSION['values']['txtUsername'] ?>" />
<span id="txtUsernameFailed"
        class="<?php echo $_SESSION['errors']['txtUsername'] ?>">
    This username is in use, or empty username field.
</span>
<br />
```

This is the code that displays a form field with its label and displays an error message underneath it if a validation has been performed and has failed.

> In this example, we display an error message right under the validated field, but you can customize the position and appearance of these error messages in `validate.css` by changing the properties of the `error` CSS class.

The onblur event of the input element, which is generated when the user leaves an input element, triggers the validate() JavaScript function with two parameters: the field's value and the field's ID. This function will handle AJAX validation, by making an asynchronous HTTP request to the validate.php script. The server script needs to know which field we need to validate and what the input value is.

The value attribute should be empty on first page load, but after submitting the form it will hold the input value, in case the form is reloaded as a result of a validation error. We use session variables to save user input on form submit, in case validation fails and the form is re-displayed.

The span element that follows contains an error message that gets displayed on failed validation. This span is initially hidden using the hidden CSS class, but we change its CSS class into error, if validation fails.

Inside validate.js, the validate function sends an AJAX request to the server, by calling validate.php with two parameters, the field's value and the field's ID.

Remember that XMLHttpRequest cannot make two HTTP requests at the same time, so if the object is busy processing a previous request, we save the details of the current request for later. This is particularly useful when the connection to the network or the Internet is slow. The request details are saved using a cache system with the properties of a FIFO structure. Luckily, the JavaScript's Array class offers the exact functionality we need (through its push and shift methods) and hence we use it for caching purposes:

```
var cache = new Array();
```

So validate() starts by adding the data to validate to the cache (if the function received any).

```
// the function handles the validation for any form field
function validate(inputValue, fieldID)
{
  // only continue if xmlHttp isn't void
  if (xmlHttp)
  {
    // if we received non-null parameters, we add them to cache
    // in the form of the query string to be sent to the server for validation
    if (fieldID)
    {
      // encode values for safely adding them to an HTTP request query string
      inputValue = encodeURIComponent(inputValue);
      fieldID = encodeURIComponent(fieldID);
      // add the values to the queue
      cache.push("inputValue=" + inputValue + "&fieldID=" + fieldID);
    }
```

This adds a new element at the end of our cache array. The cache entry is composed of two parts, the value and the ID of the field to be validated, separated by '&'. Note that the new element is added only if fieldID is not null. The value of fieldID is null when the function is called just to check if the cache contains any pending validations to be made, without adding new entries to the cache.

> The field ID and value retrieved from the cache will be sent to the server for validation. To make sure they arrive at the destination successfully and unaltered, they are escaped using JavaScript's encodeURIComponent function. This enables safely transmitting any characters to the server, including characters such as "&" which otherwise would cause problems. For more details, please read an excellent article on JavaScript's escaping functions at http://xkr.us/articles/javascript/encode-compare/.

If the XMLHttpRequest object is free to initiate new HTTP requests, we use shift() to get a new value from the cache to validate (this function also removes the entry from the cache array, which is perfect for our purposes). Note that this value may not be the one just added using push—in FIFO scenarios, the oldest (pending) record is retrieved first.

```
// try to connect to the server
try
{
  // continue only if the XMLHttpRequest object isn't busy
  // and the cache is not empty
  if ((xmlHttp.readyState == 4 || xmlHttp.readyState == 0)
      && cache.length>0)
  {
    //
    var cacheEntry = cache.shift();
```

If the XMLHttpRequest object's status is 0 or 4 it means that there are no active requests and we can send a new request. When sending the new request, we use the data read from the cache, which already contains the formatted query string:

```
// make a server request to validate the extracted data
xmlHttp.open("POST", serverAddress, true);
xmlHttp.setRequestHeader("Content-Type",
                    "application/x-www-form-urlencoded");
xmlHttp.onreadystatechange = handleRequestStateChange;
xmlHttp.send(cacheEntry);
}
```

The function that handles the server's response is called handleRequestStateChange, and in turn calls readResponse() once the response is fully received from the server. This method starts by checking if what we received from the server is the report of a server-side error:

```
// read server's response
function readResponse()
{
  // retrieve the server's response
  var response = xmlHttp.responseText;
  // server error?
  if (response.indexOf("ERRNO") >= 0
      || response.indexOf("error:") >= 0
      || response.length == 0)
    throw(response.length == 0 ? "Server error." : response);
```

After this basic check is done, we read the server's response, which tells us if the value is valid or not:

```
// get response in XML format (assume the response is valid XML)
responseXml = xmlHttp.responseXML;
// get the document element
xmlDoc = responseXml.documentElement;
result = xmlDoc.getElementsByTagName("result")[0].firstChild.data;
fieldID = xmlDoc.getElementsByTagName("fieldid")[0].firstChild.data;
```

Depending on the result, we change the CSS class of the error message associated with the tested element to hidden (if the validation was successful), or to error (if the validation failed). You change the element's CSS class using its className property:

```
// find the HTML element that displays the error
message = document.getElementById(fieldID + "Failed");
// show the error or hide the error
message.className = (result == "0") ? "error" : "hidden";
// call validate() again, in case there are values left in the cache
setTimeout("validate();", 500);
}
```

The PHP script that handles server-side processing is validate.php. It starts by loading the error handling script (error_handler.php) and the validate class that handles data validation (validate.class.php). Then, it looks for a GET variable named validationType. This only exists when the form is submitted, as the form's action attribute is validate.php?validationType=php.

```
// read validation type (PHP or AJAX?)
$validationType = '';
if (isset($_GET['validationType']))
{
    $validationType = $_GET['validationType'];
}
```

Then, based on the value of $validationType, we perform either AJAX validation or PHP validation.

```
// AJAX validation or PHP validation?
if ($validationType == 'php')
{
    // PHP validation is performed by the ValidatePHP method, which returns
    // the page the visitor should be redirected to (which is allok.php if
    // all the data is valid, or back to index.php if not)
    header("Location:" . $validator->ValidatePHP());
}
else
{
    // AJAX validation is performed by the ValidateAJAX method. The results
    // are used to form an XML document that is sent back to the client
    $response =
      '<?xml version="1.0" encoding="UTF-8" standalone="yes"?>' .
      '<response>' .
        '<result>' .
          $validator->ValidateAJAX($_POST['inputValue'], $_POST['fieldID']) .
        '</result>' .
        '<fieldid>' .
          $_POST['fieldID'] .
        '</fieldid>' .
      '</response>';
    // generate the response
    if(ob_get_length()) ob_clean();
    header('Content-Type: text/xml');
    echo $response;
}
?>
```

If we are dealing with classic server-side validation, we call the validatePHP() method, which returns the name of the page the browser should be redirected to (which will be allok.php if the validation was successful, or index.php if not). The validation results for each field are stored in the session and if it gets reloaded, index.php will show the fields that didn't pass the test.

In the case of AJAX calls, the server composes a response that specifies if the field is valid. The response is a short XML document that looks like this:

```xml
<?xml version="1.0" encoding="UTF-8" standalone="yes"?>
<response>
  <result>0</result>
  <fieldid>txtUsername</fieldid>
</response>
```

If the result is 0, then txtUsername isn't valid and should be marked accordingly. If the result is 1, the field's value is valid.

Next, let's look into validate.class.php. The class constructor creates a connection to the database and the destructor closes that connection. We then have two public methods: validateAJAX (handles AJAX validation) and validatePHP (handles typical server-side validation).

AJAX validation requires two parameters, one that holds the value to be validated ($inputvalue) and one that holds the form field's ID ($fieldID). A switch block loads specific validation for each form field. This function will return 0 if validation fails or 1 if validation is successful.

The PHP validation function takes no parameters, as it will always validate the entire form (after form submit). First we initialize the $errorsExist flag to 0. Whenever validation fails for a field, this flag will be set to 1 and we will know validation has failed. Then we need to make sure that older session variables are unset in order to ensure that older errors are cleared.

We then check each form field against a set of custom-created rules. If validation fails, we raise the flag ($errorsExist = 1) and set the session variable that sets the CSS class for error message to error. If, in the end, the $errorsExist flag is still set to 0, it means that the whole validation has been successful and we return the name of the success page, thus redirecting the browser to that page.

If errors are found, we save current user input into session variables, which will be used by index.php to fill the form (remember that by default, when loading the page, all fields are empty). This is how we save current user input:

```php
foreach ($_POST as $key => $value)
{
    $_SESSION['values'][$key] = $_POST[$key];
}
```

$_POST is an array holding the names and values of all form elements, and it can be walked through with foreach. This means that for each element inside the $_POST array, we create a new element inside the $_SESSION['values'] array.

There's nothing special to mention about validate.css. The success page (allok.php) is very simple as well—it just displays a successful submission confirmation.

Summary

While we don't claim to have built the perfect validation technique, we provided a working proof of concept; a working application that takes care of user input and ensures its validity.

You cannot do that only with JavaScript nor would you want to wait for the field to be validated only on form submit.

The reason we used AJAX for pseudo client-side validation instead of simple JavaScript validation is that in many scenarios form fields need to be checked against a database (like the username field in this case). Also, in most cases it's more professional to have all the business logic (including the validation) stored in a central place on the server.

AJAX can be so handy, don't you think?

5
AJAX Chat

We are living in a world where communication has become very important; there's a real need to be able to communicate quickly and easily with others. Email, phone texting, postal letters, and online chat offer media through which people can exchange ideas in the form of written words. An important aspect when communicating is the responsiveness factor. While emails and letters don't offer a live feedback from the other participants, phone and online chat offer a more dynamic way to communicate. In this chapter, we will build an AJAX-enabled online chat solution.

Introducing AJAX Chat

Most of the communication that takes place through the computer is done via desktop applications. These applications communicate with each other in a decentralized way using **Peer to Peer (P2P)** systems. However, these may not be viable options if you are inside a company whose security policy prevents users from opening connections on other ports than the HTTP port 80. If that is the case, you are facing a real problem.

There are numerous audio and video web chat solutions out there, most of them based on Java applets. Applets are known for their common security problems across browsers and sometimes they don't even use port 80 for communication. So, they are not a solution for getting in touch with your friends outside the company either.

This is where AJAX comes into play and brings one answer for our problem. With a little effort one can even integrate into a browser an **Internet Relay Chat (IRC)** client or you can develop your own web chat solution such as the one you'll build later.

Are you getting tired of being told that you cannot install or use your favorite messenger when you are at work, or when you are in an Internet Café? You might well have found yourself in such a situation before. This is the right time to see how we can break out of this unfortunate situation by using AJAX chat solution.

AJAX Chat Solutions

Probably the most impressive solution available today is `www.meebo.com`. We are pretty sure that some of you have heard about it, and if you haven't, it is time to have a look at it. The first and the most important feature is that it allows you to log in into your favorite instant messaging system by using only a web interface. See Meebo's login screen in Figure 5.1.

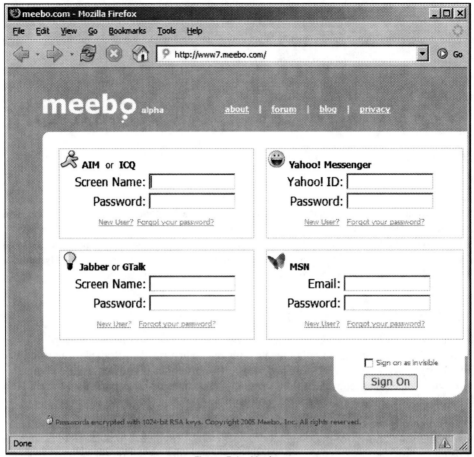

Figure 5.1: Meebo

Meebo offers access to all these services from a single start web page with a user friendly interface, with no pop-up windows, Java applets and so on. By using a solution based on AJAX you can forget about all the problems mentioned in the beginning.

Meebo isn't the only web application that offers chat functionality. Even if AJAX is very young, you can already find several other online chat applications and even solutions based on it:

- `http://www.plasticshore.com/projects/chat/index.html`
- `http://treehouse.ofb.net/chat/?lang=en.`
- `http://www.chategory.org`
- `http://www.socket7.net/lace/`
- `http://drupal.org/node/27689.`

It's time to get to work. In the rest of the chapter, we'll implement our own online chat application.

Implementing AJAX Chat

We'll keep the application simple, modular, and extensible. For this we won't implement a login module, chat rooms, the online users list, etc. By keeping it simple we try to focus on what the goal of this chapter is—AJAX Chat. We will implement the basic chat functions: posting and retrieving messages without causing any page reloads. We'll also let the user pick a color for her or his messages, because this involves an AJAX mechanism that will be another good exercise.

Starting from the following application that will be presented in this chapter, we can easily extend it by implementing any other modules that can be found in the solutions presented above and that are not presented here. Take this part as homework for those of you who are interested in it.

> In order to have these example working you need the **GD library**. The installation
> instructions in Appendix A include support for the GD library.

The chat application can be tested online at `http://ajaxphp.packtpub.com`, and it looks like in Figure 5.2.

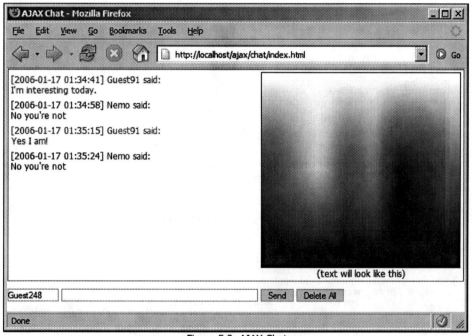

Figure 5.2: AJAX Chat

A novelty in this chapter is that you will have two XMLHttpRequest objects. The first one will handle updating the chat window and the second will handle the color picker (when you click on the image, the coordinates are sent to the server, and the server replies with the color code).

The messages for the AJAX Chat are saved in a queue (a FIFO structure), such as you learned about in Chapter 4, so that messages are not lost even if the server is slow, and they always get to the server in the same order as you sent them. Unlike with other patterns you can find on Internet these days, we also ensure we don't load the server with any more requests until the current one is finished.

Time for Action—Ajax Chat

1. Connect to the `ajax` database, and create a table named `chat` with the following code:

```
CREATE TABLE chat
(
    chat_id int(11) NOT NULL auto_increment,
    posted_on datetime NOT NULL,
    user_name varchar(255) NOT NULL,
    message text NOT NULL,
    color char(7) default '#000000',
    PRIMARY KEY (chat_id)
);
```

2. In your `ajax` folder, create a new folder named `chat`.

3. Copy the `palette.png` file from the code download to the `chat` folder.

4. We will create the application starting with the server functionality. In the `chat` folder, create a file named `config.php`, and add the database configuration code to it (change these values to match your configuration):

```php
<?php
// defines database connection data
define('DB_HOST', 'localhost');
define('DB_USER', 'ajaxuser');
define('DB_PASSWORD', 'practical');
define('DB_DATABASE', 'ajax');
?>
```

5. Now add the standard error handling file, `error_handler.php`:

```php
<?php
// set the user error handler method to be error_handler
set_error_handler('error_handler', E_ALL);
// error handler function
function error_handler($errNo, $errStr, $errFile, $errLine)
{
    // clear any output that has already been generated
    if(ob_get_length()) ob_clean();
    // output the error message
    $error_message = 'ERRNO: '  . $errNo . chr(10) .
                     'TEXT: '   . $errStr . chr(10) .
                     'LOCATION: '  . $errFile .
                     ', line '  . $errLine;
    echo $error_message;
    // prevent processing any more PHP scripts
    exit;
}
?>
```

6. Create another file named `chat.php` and add this code to it:

```php
<?php
// reference the file containing the Chat class
require_once("chat.class.php");
// retrieve the operation to be performed
$mode = $_POST['mode'];
```

```php
// default the last id to 0
$id = 0;
// create a new Chat instance
$chat = new Chat();
// if the operation is SendAndRetrieve
if($mode == 'SendAndRetrieveNew')
{
  // retrieve the action parameters used to add a new message
  $name = $_POST['name'];
  $message = $_POST['message'];
  $color = $_POST['color'];
  $id = $_POST['id'];

  // check if we have valid values
  if ($name != '' && $message != '' && $color != '')
  {
    // post the message to the database
    $chat->postMessage($name, $message, $color);
  }
}
// if the operation is DeleteAndRetrieve
elseif($mode == 'DeleteAndRetrieveNew')
{
  // delete all existing messages
  $chat->deleteMessages();
}
// if the operation is Retrieve
elseif($mode == 'RetrieveNew')
{
  // get the id of the last message retrieved by the client
  $id = $_POST['id'];
}
// Clear the output
if(ob_get_length()) ob_clean();
// Headers are sent to prevent browsers from caching
header('Expires: Mon, 26 Jul 1997 05:00:00 GMT');
header('Last-Modified: ' . gmdate('D, d M Y H:i:s') . 'GMT');
header('Cache-Control: no-cache, must-revalidate');
header('Pragma: no-cache');
header('Content-Type: text/xml');
// retrieve new messages from the server
echo $chat->retrieveNewMessages($id);
?>
```

7. Create another file named chat.class.php, and add this code to it:

```php
<?php
// load configuration file
require_once('config.php');
// load error handling module
require_once('error_handler.php');

// class that contains server-side chat functionality
class Chat
{
  // database handler
  private $mMysqli;

  // constructor opens database connection
  function __construct()
  {
    // connect to the database
    $this->mMysqli = new mysqli(DB_HOST, DB_USER, DB_PASSWORD,
                                                   DB_DATABASE);
  }
```

```php
   // destructor closes database connection
   public function __destruct()
   {
     $this->mMysqli->close();
   }

   // truncates the table containing the messages
   public function deleteMessages()
   {
     // build the SQL query that adds a new message to the server
     $query = 'TRUNCATE TABLE chat';
     // execute the SQL query
     $result = $this->mMysqli->query($query);
   }

   /*
   The postMessages method inserts a message into the database
    - $name represents the name of the user that posted the message
    - $messsage is the posted message
    - $color contains the color chosen by the user
   */
   public function postMessage($name, $message, $color)
   {
     // escape the variable data for safely adding them to the database
     $name = $this->mMysqli->real_escape_string($name);
     $message = $this->mMysqli->real_escape_string($message);
     $color = $this->mMysqli->real_escape_string($color);
     // build the SQL query that adds a new message to the server
     $query = 'INSERT INTO chat(posted_on, user_name, message, color) ' .
              'VALUES (NOW(), "' . $name . '" , "' . $message .
              '","' . $color . '")';
     // execute the SQL query
     $result = $this->mMysqli->query($query);
   }

   /*
   The retrieveNewMessages method retrieves the new messages that have
   been posted to the server.
    - the $id parameter is sent by the client and it
   represents the id of the last message received by the client. Messages
   more recent by $id will be fetched from the database and returned to
   the client in XML format.
   */
   public function retrieveNewMessages($id=0)
   {
     // escape the variable data
     $id = $this->mMysqli->real_escape_string($id);
     // compose the SQL query that retrieves new messages
     if($id>0)
     {
       // retrieve messages newer than $id
       $query =
       'SELECT chat_id, user_name, message, color, ' .
       '       DATE_FORMAT(posted_on, "%Y-%m-%d %H:%i:%s") ' .
       '       AS posted_on ' .
       ' FROM chat WHERE chat_id > ' . $id .
       ' ORDER BY chat_id ASC';
     }
     else
     {
       // on the first load only retrieve the last 50 messages from server
       $query =
       ' SELECT chat_id, user_name, message, color, posted_on FROM ' .
       '     (SELECT chat_id, user_name, message, color, ' .
```

```
'            DATE_FORMAT(posted_on, "%Y-%m-%d %H:%i:%s") AS posted_on ' .
'        FROM chat ' .
'        ORDER BY chat_id DESC ' .
'          LIMIT 50) AS Last50' .
'  ORDER BY chat_id ASC';
}
// execute the query
$result = $this->mMysqli->query($query);

// build the XML response
$response = '<?xml version="1.0" encoding="UTF-8" standalone="yes"?>';
$response .= '<response>';
// output the clear flag
$response .= $this->isDatabaseCleared($id);
// check to see if we have any results
if($result->num_rows)
{
    // loop through all the fetched messages to build the result message
    while ($row = $result->fetch_array(MYSQLI_ASSOC))
    {
        $id = $row['chat_id'];
        $color = $row['color'];
        $userName = $row['user_name'];
        $time = $row['posted_on'];
        $message = $row['message'];
        $response .= '<id>' . $id . '</id>' .
                     '<color>' . $color . '</color>' .
                     '<time>' . $time . '</time>' .
                     '<name>' . $userName . '</name>' .
                     '<message>' . $message . '</message>';
    }
    // close the database connection as soon as possible
    $result->close();
}

// finish the XML response and return it
$response = $response . '</response>';
return $response;
}

/*
  The isDatabaseCleared method checks to see if the database has been
  cleared since last call to the server
  -    the $id parameter contains the id of the last message received by
  the client
*/
private function isDatabaseCleared($id)
{
    if($id>0)
    {
        // by checking the number of rows with ids smaller than the client's
        // last id we check to see if a truncate operation was performed in
        // the meantime
        $check_clear = 'SELECT count(*) old FROM chat where chat_id<=' . $id;
        $result = $this->mMysqli->query($check_clear);
        $row = $result->fetch_array(MYSQLI_ASSOC);

        // if a truncate operation occured the whiteboard needs to be reset
        if($row['old']==0)
            return '<clear>true</clear>';
    }
    return '<clear>false</clear>';
```

```
    }
  }
?>
```

8. Create another file named `get_color.php` and add this code to it:

```php
<?php
// the name of the image file
$imgfile='palette.png';
// load the image file
$img=imagecreatefrompng($imgfile);
// obtain the coordinates of the point clicked by the user
$offsetx=$_GET['offsetx'];
$offsety=$_GET['offsety'];
// get the clicked color
$rgb = ImageColorAt($img, $offsetx, $offsety);
$r = ($rgb >> 16) & 0xFF;
$g = ($rgb >> 8) & 0xFF;
$b = $rgb & 0xFF;
// return the color code
printf('#%02s%02s%02s', dechex($r), dechex($g), dechex($b));
?>
```

9. Let's deal with the client now. Start by creating `chat.css` and adding this code to it:

```css
body
{
  font-family: Tahoma, Helvetica, sans-serif;
  margin: 1px;
  font-size: 12px;
  text-align: left
}

#content
{
  border: DarkGreen 1px solid;
  margin-bottom: 10px
}

input
{
  border: #999 1px solid;
  font-size: 10px
}

#scroll
{
  position: relative;
  width: 340px;
  height: 270px;
  overflow: auto
}

.item
{
  margin-bottom: 6px
}

#colorpicker
{
  text-align:center
}
```

10. Create a new file named `index.html`, and add this code to it:

```
<!DOCTYPE html PUBLIC "-//W3C//DTD XHTML 1.0 Transitional//EN"
"http://www.w3.org/TR/xhtml1/DTD/xhtml1-transitional.dtd">
<html xmlns="http://www.w3.org/1999/xhtml" xml:lang="en" lang="en">
<head>
  <title>AJAX Chat</title>
  <meta http-equiv="Content-Type" content="text/html; charset=UTF-8" />
  <link href="chat.css" rel="stylesheet" type="text/css" />
  <script type="text/javascript" src="chat.js" ></script>
</head>
  <body onload="init();">
    <noscript>
      Your browser does not support JavaScript!!
    </noscript>
    <table id="content">
      <tr>
        <td>
          <div id="scroll">
          </div>
        </td>
        <td id="colorpicker">
          <img src="palette.png" id="palette" alt="Color
               Palette" border="1" onclick="getColor(event);"/>
          <br />
          <input id="color" type="hidden" readonly="true" value="#000000" />
          <span id="sampleText">
            (text will look like this)
          </span>
        </td>
      </tr>
    </table>
    <div>
      <input type="text" id="userName" maxlength="10" size="10"
onblur="checkUsername();"/>
      <input type="text" id="messageBox" maxlength="2000" size="50"
             onkeydown="handleKey(event)"/>
      <input type="button" value="Send" onclick="sendMessage();" />
      <input type="button" value="Delete All" onclick="deleteMessages();" />
    </div>
  </body>
</html>
```

11. Create another file named chat.js and add this code to it:

```
/* chatURL - URL for updating chat messages */
var chatURL = "chat.php";
/* getColorURL - URL for retrieving the chosen RGB color */
var getColorURL = "get_color.php";
/* create XMLHttpRequest objects for updating the chat messages and
getting the selected color */
var xmlHttpGetMessages = createXmlHttpRequestObject();
var xmlHttpGetColor = createXmlHttpRequestObject();
/* variables that establish how often to access the server */
var updateInterval = 1000; // how many miliseconds to wait to get new
message
// when set to true, display detailed error messages
var debugMode = true;
/* initialize the messages cache */
var cache = new Array();
/* lastMessageID - the ID of the most recent chat message */
var lastMessageID = -1;
/* mouseX, mouseY - the event's mouse coordinates */
var mouseX,mouseY;
```

```
/* creates an XMLHttpRequest instance */
function createXmlHttpRequestObject()
{
  // will store the reference to the XMLHttpRequest object
  var xmlHttp;
  // this should work for all browsers except IE6 and older
  try
  {
    // try to create XMLHttpRequest object
    xmlHttp = new XMLHttpRequest();
  }
  catch(e)
  {
    // assume IE6 or older
    var XmlHttpVersions = new Array("MSXML2.XMLHTTP.6.0",
                                    "MSXML2.XMLHTTP.5.0",
                                    "MSXML2.XMLHTTP.4.0",
                                    "MSXML2.XMLHTTP.3.0",
                                    "MSXML2.XMLHTTP",
                                    "Microsoft.XMLHTTP");
    // try every prog id until one works
    for (var i=0; i<XmlHttpVersions.length && !xmlHttp; i++)
    {
      try
      {
        // try to create XMLHttpRequest object
        xmlHttp = new ActiveXObject(XmlHttpVersions[i]);
      }
      catch (e) {}
    }
  }
  // return the created object or display an error message
  if (!xmlHttp)
    alert("Error creating the XMLHttpRequest object.");
  else
    return xmlHttp;
}

/* this function initiates the chat; it executes when the chat page loads
*/
function init()
{
  // get a reference to the text box where the user writes new messages
  var oMessageBox = document.getElementById("messageBox");
  // prevents the autofill function from starting
  oMessageBox.setAttribute("autocomplete", "off");
  // references the "Text will look like this" message
  var oSampleText = document.getElementById("sampleText");
  // set the default color to black
  oSampleText.style.color = "black";
  // ensures our user has a default random name when the form loads
  checkUsername();
  // initiates updating the chat window
  requestNewMessages();
}

// function that ensures that the username is never empty and if so
// a random name is generated
function checkUsername()
{
  // ensures our user has a default random name when the form loads
  var oUser=document.getElementById("userName");
  if(oUser.value == "")
    oUser.value = "Guest" + Math.floor(Math.random() * 1000);
}
```

```
/* function called when the Send button is pressed */
function sendMessage()
{
    // save the message to a local variable and clear the text box
    var oCurrentMessage = document.getElementById("messageBox");
    var currentUser = document.getElementById("userName").value;
    var currentColor = document.getElementById("color").value;
    // don't send void messages
    if (trim(oCurrentMessage.value) != "" &&
        trim(currentUser) != "" && trim (currentColor) != "")
    {
        // if we need to send and retrieve messages
        params =  "mode=SendAndRetrieveNew" +
                  "&id=" + encodeURIComponent(lastMessageID) +
                  "&color=" + encodeURIComponent(currentColor) +
                  "&name=" + encodeURIComponent(currentUser) +
                  "&message=" + encodeURIComponent(oCurrentMessage.value);
        // add the message to the queue
        cache.push(params);
        // clear the text box
        oCurrentMessage.value = "";
    }
}

/* function called when the Delete Messages button is pressed */
function deleteMessages()
{
    // set the flag that specifies we're deleting the messages
    params = "mode=DeleteAndRetrieveNew";
    // add the message to the queue
    cache.push(params);
}

/* makes asynchronous request to retrieve new messages, post new messages,
delete messages */
function requestNewMessages()
{
    // retrieve the username and color from the page
    var currentUser = document.getElementById("userName").value;
    var currentColor = document.getElementById("color").value;
    // only continue if xmlHttpGetMessages isn't void
    if(xmlHttpGetMessages)
    {
        try
        {
            // don't start another server operation if such an operation
            //    is already in progress
            if (xmlHttpGetMessages.readyState == 4 ||
                xmlHttpGetMessages.readyState == 0)
            {
                // we will store the parameters used to make the server request
                var params = "";
                // if there are requests stored in queue, take the oldest one
                if (cache.length>0)
                    params = cache.shift();
                // if the cache is empty, just retrieve new messages
                else
                    params = "mode=RetrieveNew" +
                             "&id=" +lastMessageID;
                // call the server page to execute the server-side operation
                xmlHttpGetMessages.open("POST", chatURL, true);
                xmlHttpGetMessages.setRequestHeader("Content-Type",
                                        "application/x-www-form-urlencoded");
                xmlHttpGetMessages.onreadystatechange = handleReceivingMessages;
```

```
          xmlHttpGetMessages.send(params);
      }
      else
      {
        // we will check again for new messages
        setTimeout("requestNewMessages();", updateInterval);
      }
    }
    catch(e)
    {
      displayError(e.toString());
    }
  }
}

/* function that handles the http response when updating messages */
function handleReceivingMessages()
{
  // continue if the process is completed
  if (xmlHttpGetMessages.readyState == 4)
  {
    // continue only if HTTP status is "OK"
    if (xmlHttpGetMessages.status == 200)
    {
      try
      {
        // process the server's response
        readMessages();
      }
      catch(e)
      {
        // display the error message
        displayError(e.toString());
      }
    }
    else
    {
      // display the error message
      displayError(xmlHttpGetMessages.statusText);
    }
  }
}

/* function that processes the server's response when updating messages */
function readMessages()
{
  // retrieve the server's response
  var response = xmlHttpGetMessages.responseText;
  // server error?
  if (response.indexOf("ERRNO") >= 0
      || response.indexOf("error:") >= 0
      || response.length == 0)
    throw(response.length == 0 ? "Void server response." : response);
  // retrieve the document element
  response = xmlHttpGetMessages.responseXML.documentElement;
  // retrieve the flag that says if the chat window has been cleared or not
  clearChat =
          response.getElementsByTagName("clear").item(0).firstChild.data;
  // if the flag is set to true, we need to clear the chat window
  if(clearChat == "true")
  {
    // clear chat window and reset the id
    document.getElementById("scroll").innerHTML = "";
    lastMessageID = -1;
```

```
    }
    // retrieve the arrays from the server's response
    idArray = response.getElementsByTagName("id");
    colorArray = response.getElementsByTagName("color");
    nameArray = response.getElementsByTagName("name");
    timeArray = response.getElementsByTagName("time");
    messageArray = response.getElementsByTagName("message");
    // add the new messages to the chat window
    displayMessages(idArray, colorArray, nameArray, timeArray,
                                                    messageArray);
    // the ID of the last received message is stored locally
    if(idArray.length>0)
      lastMessageID = idArray.item(idArray.length - 1).firstChild.data;
    // restart sequence
    setTimeout("requestNewMessages();", updateInterval);
}

/* function that appends the new messages to the chat list  */
function displayMessages(idArray, colorArray, nameArray,
                          timeArray, messageArray)
{
  // each loop adds a new message
  for(var i=0; i<idArray.length; i++)
  {
    // get the message details
    var color = colorArray.item(i).firstChild.data.toString();
    var time = timeArray.item(i).firstChild.data.toString();
    var name = nameArray.item(i).firstChild.data.toString();
    var message = messageArray.item(i).firstChild.data.toString();
    // compose the HTML code that displays the message
    var htmlMessage = "";
    htmlMessage += "<div class=\"item\" style=\"color:" + color + "\">";
    htmlMessage += "[" + time + "] " + name + " said: <br/>";
    htmlMessage += message.toString();
    htmlMessage += "</div>";
    // display the message
    displayMessage (htmlMessage);
  }
}

// displays a message
function displayMessage(message)
{
  // get the scroll object
  var oScroll = document.getElementById("scroll");
  // check if the scroll is down
  var scrollDown = (oScroll.scrollHeight - oScroll.scrollTop <=
                    oScroll.offsetHeight );
  // display the message
  oScroll.innerHTML += message;
  // scroll down the scrollbar
  oScroll.scrollTop = scrollDown ? oScroll.scrollHeight :
oScroll.scrollTop;
}

// function that displays an error message
function displayError(message)
{
  // display error message, with more technical details if debugMode is true
  displayMessage("Error accessing the server! "+
              (debugMode ? "<br/>" + message : ""));
}

/* handles keydown to detect when enter is pressed */
```

```
function handleKey(e)
{
  // get the event
  e = (!e) ? window.event : e;
  // get the code of the character that has been pressed
  code = (e.charCode) ? e.charCode :
         ((e.keyCode) ? e.keyCode :
         ((e.which) ? e.which : 0));
  // handle the keydown event
  if (e.type == "keydown")
  {
    // if enter (code 13) is pressed
    if(code == 13)
    {
      // send the current message
      sendMessage();
    }
  }
}

/* removes leading and trailing spaces from the string */
function trim(s)
{
    return s.replace(/(^\s+)|(\s+$)/g, "")
}

/* function that computes the mouse's coordinates in page */
function getMouseXY(e)
{
  // browser specific
  if(window.ActiveXObject)
  {
    mouseX = window.event.x + document.body.scrollLeft;
    mouseY = window.event.y + document.body.scrollTop;
  }
  else
  {
    mouseX = e.pageX;
    mouseY = e.pageY;
  }
}

/* makes a server call to get the RGB code of the chosen color */
function getColor(e)
{
  getMouseXY(e);
  // don't do anything if the XMLHttpRequest object is null
  if(xmlHttpGetColor)
  {
    // initialize the offset position with the mouse current position
    var offsetX = mouseX;
    var offsetY = mouseY;
    // get references
    var oPalette = document.getElementById("palette");
    var oTd = document.getElementById("colorpicker");
    // compute the offset position in our window
    if(window.ActiveXObject)
    {
      offsetX = window.event.offsetX;
      offsetY = window.event.offsetY;
    }
    else
    {
      offsetX -= oPalette.offsetLeft + oTd.offsetLeft;
      offsetY -= oPalette.offsetTop + oTd.offsetTop;
```

```
    }
    // call server asynchronously to find out the clicked color
    try
    {
      if (xmlHttpGetColor.readyState == 4 ||
          xmlHttpGetColor.readyState == 0)
      {
        params = "?offsetx=" + offsetX + "&offsety=" + offsetY;
        xmlHttpGetColor.open("GET", getColorURL+params, true);
        xmlHttpGetColor.onreadystatechange = handleGettingColor;
        xmlHttpGetColor.send(null);
      }
    }
    catch(e)
    {
      // display error message
      displayError(xmlHttp.statusText);
    }
  }
}

/* function that handles the http response */
function handleGettingColor()
{
  // if the process is completed, decide to do with the returned data
  if (xmlHttpGetColor.readyState == 4)
  {
    // only if HTTP status is "OK"
    if (xmlHttpGetColor.status == 200)
    {
      try
      {
        //change the color
        changeColor();
      }
      catch(e)
      {
        // display error message
        displayError(xmlHttpGetColor.statusText);
      }
    }
    else
    {
      // display error message
      displayError(xmlHttpGetColor.statusText);
    }
  }
}

/* function that changes the color used for displaying messages */
function changeColor()
{
  response=xmlHttpGetColor.responseText;
  // server error?
  if (response.indexOf("ERRNO") >= 0
      || response.indexOf("error:") >= 0
      || response.length == 0)
    throw(response.length == 0 ? "Can't change color!" : response);
  // change color
  var oColor = document.getElementById("color");
  var oSampleText = document.getElementById("sampleText");
  oColor.value = response;
  oSampleText.style.color = response;
}
```

12. After having talked about it, it is time to see it in action. Let's see how the chat window looks in the beginning. Load `http://localhost/ajax/chat/index.html` with a web browser.

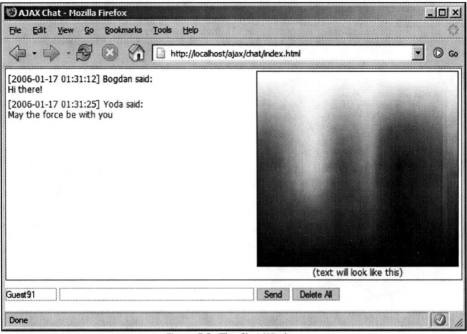

Figure 5.3: The Chat Window

You can observe the default color of your messages is black (RGB code: #000000). In Figure 5.3 we can also see a default random name Guest91. When initially loading the chat window, all previously posted messages are displayed. You can change your messages' color by simply clicking on the `palette` image on the desired color.

What just happened?

Technically, the application is split in two smaller applications that build our final solution:

- The chat application
- Choosing a color application

The chat application implements the basic functions of posting and retrieving messages. Each user can choose a nickname and post a message. The chat window containing all the posted messages is updated by retrieving the messages asynchronously from the server.

We use a `palette` containing the entire spectrum of colors to allow the user pick a color for the text he or she writes. When clicking on the palette, the mouse coordinates are sent to the server, which obtains the color code.

If you analyze the code for a bit, the details will become clear. Let's have a look at it starting with the `index.html` file. The only part that is really interesting in this script is a scroll region that can be implemented in DHTML. A little piece of information regarding scrolling can be found at `http://www.dyn-web.com/dhtml/scroll/`. Basically, the idea for having a part of the page with a scrollbar next to it is to have two layers one inside another. In our example, the `div scroll` and its inner layers do the trick.

The outer layer is `scroll`. It has a fixed `width` and `height` and the most useful property of it is `overflow`. Generally, the content of a block box is confined to the content edges of the box. In certain cases, a box may overflow, meaning its content lies partly or entirely outside of the box. In CSS, this property specifies what happens when an element overflows its area. For more details, please see `overflow`'s specification, at `http://www.w3.org/TR/REC-CSS2/visufx.html`.

OK, now that we have defined our block box and what happens when its content exceeds its area, we can easily guess that the inner content of the block box is the one that will eventually exceed the dimensions of the box. The inner content contains the messages written in the chat.

Next, we move to the `chat.js` file containing the JavaScript part for our application.

The whole file can be divided in two parts: the one that handles choosing a color and the other that handles chat messages.

We will start by choosing a color. This part, which, in the beginning, might seem pretty difficult proves to be far easier to implement. Let's have a panoramic view of the entire process. First, we have a palette image that contains the entire spectrum of visible colors. PHP has two functions that will help us in finding the RGB code of the chosen color, `imagecreatefrompng` and `imagecolorat`. When talking about the `get_color.php` page we will see more about these functions. For now all we need to know is that these two functions allow us to obtain the RGB code of a pixel given the x and y position in the image. The position of the pixel is retrieved in the `getMouseXY` function.

The `getColor` function retrieves the RGB code of the color chosen by the user when clicking the palette image. First of all it retrieves the mouse coordinates from the event. Then, it computes the coordinates where the click event has been produced as relative values within the image. This is done by subtracting from the positions obtained by the `getMouseXY` function the relative position of the image inside the `td` element and the `td` position in the window. Having computed the relative coordinates as the `offsetx` and `offsety`, the server page that will return the RGB code of the chosen color is called. The change of state of the HTTP request object is handled by the `handleGettingColor` function.

The `handleGettingColor` function checks to see when the request to the server is completed and if no errors occurred, the `changeColor` function is called. This function populates the text field with the RGB code returned by the server and colors the sample text with the given code.

OK, let's now see how the chat works.

By default when the page initializes and the `onblur` event occurs, the `checkUsername` function is called. This function ensures that the name of the user isn't empty by generating an arbitrary username.

On pressing the send button, the sendMessage function is called. This function adds the current message to the message queue to be sent to the server. Before adding it into the queue the function trims the message by calling the trim function, and we encode the message using encodeURIComponent to make sure it gets through successfully.

The handleKey function is called whenever a keydown event occurs. When the *Enter* key is pressed the sendMessage function is called so that both pressing the send button and pressing *Enter* within the messageBox control have the same effect.

The deleteMessages function adds the delete message to the messages to be sent to the server.

The requestNewMessages function is responsible for sending chat messages. It retrieves a message from the queue and sends it to the server. The change of state of the HTTP request object is handled by the handleReceivingMessages function.

The handleReceivingMessages checks to see when the request to the server is completed and if no errors occurred then the readMessages function is called.

The readMessages function checks to see if someone else erased all the chat messages and if so the client's chat window is also emptied. In order to append new messages to the chat, we call the displayMessages function. This function takes as parameters the arrays that correspond to the new messages. It composes the new messages as HTML and it appends them to those already in the chat by calling the displayMessage function. In the beginning, the displayMessage function checks to see if the scroll bar is at the bottom of the list of messages. This is necessary in order to reposition it at the end of the function so that the focus is now on the last new messages.

The last function presented is the init function. Its role is to retrieve the chat messages, to ensure that the username is not null, to set the text's color to black, and to turn off the auto complete functionality.

For the error handling part, we use the displayError function, which calls the displayMessage function in turn with the error message as parameter.

Let's move on to the server side of the application by first presenting the chat.php file. The server deals with clients' requests like this:

- Retrieves the client's parameters
- Identifies the operations that need to be performed
- Performs the necessary operations
- Sends the results back to the client

The request includes the mode parameter that specifies one of the following operations to be performed by the server:

- SendAndRetrieve: First the new messages are inserted in the database and then all new messages are retrieved and sent back to the client.
- DeleteAndRetrieve: All messages are erased and the new messages that might exist are fetched and sent back to the client.
- Retrieve: The new messages are fetched and sent back to the client.

The business logic behind chat.php lies in the chat.class.php script, which contains the Chat class.

The deleteMessages method truncates the data table erasing all the information.

The postMessages method inserts all the new messages into the database.

The isDatabaseCleared method checks to see if all messages have been erased. Basically, by providing the ID of the last message retrieved from the server and by checking if it still exists, we can detect if all messages have been erased.

The retrieveNewMessages method gets all new messages since the last message (identified by its id) retrieved from the server during the last request (if a last request exists; or all messages in other cases) and also checks to see if the database has been emptied by calling the isDatabaseCleared method. This function composes the response for the client and sends it.

The config.php file contains the database configuration parameters and the error_handler.php file contains the module for handling errors.

Now, let's see how the color-choosing functionality is implemented on the server side in the get_color.php file.

We mentioned above two PHP functions that we used to retrieve the RGB code of a pixel in an image. Let's see how they work:

- imagecreatefrompng(string filename) returns an image identifier representing the image in PNG format obtained from the given filename.

- int imagecolorat(resource image, int x, int y) returns the index of the color of the pixel at the specified location in the image specified by *image*. Returns the index of the color of the pixel at the specified location in the image specified by image. If PHP is compiled against GD library 2.0 or higher and the image is a true-color image, this function returns the RGB value of that pixel as an integer.

The first 8 bits of the result contains the blue code, the next 8 bits the green code and the next 8 bits the red code. Using bit shifting and masking we obtain the distinct red, green, and blue components as integer values. All that's left for us to do is to convert them to their hexadecimal value, to concatenate these values, and to send them to the client.

Let's wrap things up! We started with the interface that is presented to the user, *the client side of the application* composed by the HTML, CSS, and JavaScript files implemented in the index.html, chat.css, and chat.js files. After having seen how the interface looks and how the data retrieved from the web server is processed in order to be presented to the user, we went one step further and took a look at the server side of the application.

We saw the files that are called by the client side, chat.php and get_color.php. The last step consisted in presenting the parameters to connect to the database (config.php), the error handling module (error_handler.php), and the script containing the core of the functionality (chat.class.php).

Summary

At the beginning of the chapter we saw why one can face problems when communicating with other people in a dynamic way over the Internet. We saw what the solutions for these problems are and how AJAX chat solutions can bring something new, useful, and ergonomic. After seeing some other AJAX chat implementations, we started building our own solution. Step by step we have implemented our AJAX chat solution keeping it simple, easily extensible, and modular.

After reading this chapter, you can try improving the solution, by adding new features like:

- Chat rooms
- Simple command lines (joining/leaving a chat room, switching between chat room)
- Private messaging

6

AJAX Suggest and Autocomplete

Suggest and Autocomplete are popular features implemented in most modern browsers, email clients, source-code editors, word processors, and operating systems. Suggest and Autocomplete are the two sides of the same coin—they go hand in hand. Usually, there is no distinction made between the two of them, but "autocomplete" is used more frequently.

Autocomplete refers to the application's ability to predict the word or phrase the user wants to type. This feature is very useful because it speeds up the interaction making the user interface friendlier, it helps in using the right vocabulary, and it helps avoiding typing errors.

In browsers, you can see autocomplete in action when you type a new address in the address bar or when you fill in some form, and the autocomplete engine of that particular browser is triggered. In email programs, it is very useful be able to choose the recipient by typing only a few letters.

In source-code text editors, I'm sure you appreciate the *code completion* feature. Long variable names make the code easier to understand, but harder to type, unless your editor supports code completion. In some editors, after typing an object's name followed by a period, you get a scrolling list of the object's public members. It is like having the documentation at your fingertips. Microsoft has implemented it in the **Visual Studio Integrated Development Environment**, and has patented it under the name of **IntelliSense**. The **GNU Emacs** editor was supporting the autocomplete feature long before Microsoft introduced it.

In operating systems' shells such as Unix's bash, sh, or the Windows command prompt, autocomplete for command names, filenames, and paths is usually done by pressing the *Tab* key after typing the first few letters of the word. I'm sure you find this feature very useful when you have a very long path to type!

Introducing AJAX Suggest and Autocomplete

Autocomplete is yet another good example of a feature that was traditionally used only in desktop applications. Popular implementations of this feature in web applications are very recent. (Note that the typical form autocompletion in web browsers, or the remember-password feature, is implemented locally by the web browsers, it's not a feature of the site.)

It's all about enriching web applications' user interfaces with features that have already been integrated into desktop applications. See a nice autocomplete example that implements this feature at `http://demo.script.aculo.us/ajax/autocompleter`.

The most popular example of this feature is Google Suggest.

Google Suggest

Why Google Suggest? Because it is the most popular web implementation of suggest and autocomplete using AJAX. Believe it or not, Google was not the first to implement this technology. Christian Stocker used it in his Bitflux Blog `http://blog.bitflux.ch/archive/2004/07/13/livesearch_roundup.html` in April 2004, seven months prior to Google's release. One article that describes exactly how autocomplete textboxes can be implemented in a web page using JavaScript goes as back as September 2003, `http://www.sitepoint.com/article/life-autocomplete-textboxes`. `XMLHttpRequest` is known to have been in use for a couple of years now. Therefore, Google didn't invent anything; it just put together a perfect example.

The web address where Google Suggest can be accessed is `http://www.google.com/webhp?complete=1&hl=en`

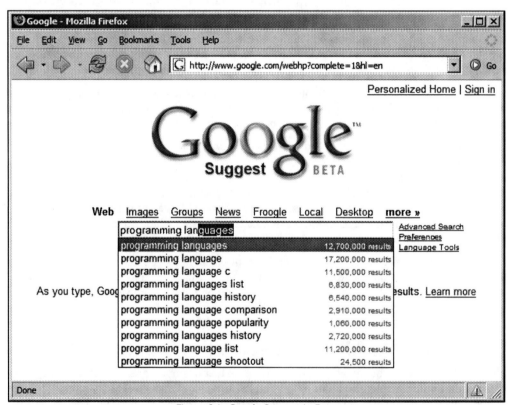

Figure 6.1: Google Suggest in Beta

The clever part of the JavaScript script in an application like Google Suggest is that it caches a table of previous suggestions received for a certain keyword. Therefore, if you type a keyword and then erase back a few characters, the old suggestions received from the request will have been cached and hence there will be no need to fetch them again.

The same technique has also been implemented in Gmail (www.gmail.com) and Google Maps (http://maps.google.com). .

Implementing AJAX Suggest and Autocomplete

In this chapter we'll develop a suggest and autocomplete feature that helps the user to find PHP functions and their official help page from http://www.php.net. The PHP functions database required for this chapter includes all the PHP functions from http://www.php.net/quickref.php.

We will implement the following features in our application:

- The matching functions are retrieved as you type and displayed in a scrollable drop-down list.

- The current keyword is autocompleted with the missing letters from the first suggestion returned as result. The added letters are highlighted.

- The initial letters matching the search keyword are bolded in the drop-down list.

- The drop-down list is scrollable, but the scroll bar appears only if the list of results exceeds a predefined number of suggestions.

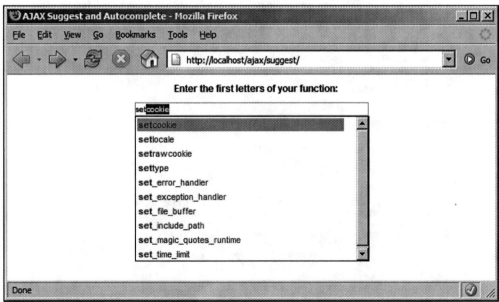

Figure 6.2: Many Interesting Functions

Time for Action—AJAX Suggest and Autocomplete

1. As always, we start by creating the necessary database structures. Create a new table named suggest in the ajax database that contains a single field (name), which is also the primary key:

```
CREATE TABLE suggest
(
  name VARCHAR(100) NOT NULL DEFAULT '',
  PRIMARY KEY (name)
);
```

2. The suggest table will be populated with the complete list of PHP functions that we took from http://www.php.net/quickref.php; because the table contains over 4,000 records, we are listing only the first ten here. Please use the script from the code download for the complete list:

```
INSERT INTO suggest (name) VALUES
  ('abs'),
  ('acos'),
  ('acosh'),
  ('addcslashes'),
  ('addslashes'),
  ('aggregate'),
  ('aggregate_info'),
  ('aggregate_methods'),
  ('aggregate_methods_by_list'),
  ('aggregate_methods_by_regexp');
```

3. Create a new folder named suggest, under the ajax folder.

4. We will start by creating the code for the server side. In the suggest folder, create a file named config.php, and add the database configuration code to it (change these values to match your configuration):

```
<?php
// defines database connection data
define('DB_HOST', 'localhost');
define('DB_USER', 'ajaxuser');
define('DB_PASSWORD', 'practical');
define('DB_DATABASE', 'ajax');
?>
```

5. Then add the standard error-handling file error_handler.php:

```
<?php
// set the user error handler method to be error_handler
set_error_handler('error_handler', E_ALL);
// error handler function
function error_handler($errNo, $errStr, $errFile, $errLine)
{
  // clear any output that has already been generated
  if(ob_get_length()) ob_clean();
  // output the error message
  $error_message = 'ERRNO: ' . $errNo . chr(10) .
                   'TEXT: ' . $errStr . chr(10) .
                   'LOCATION: ' . $errFile .
                   ', line ' . $errLine;
  echo $error_message;
  // prevent processing any more PHP scripts
  exit;
}
?>
```

6. Create another file named suggest.php, and add this code to it:

```php
<?php
// reference the file containing the Suggest class
require_once('suggest.class.php');
// create a new Suggest instance
$suggest = new Suggest();
// retrieve the keyword passed as parameter
$keyword = $_GET['keyword'];
// clear the output
if(ob_get_length()) ob_clean();
// headers are sent to prevent browsers from caching
header('Expires: Mon, 26 Jul 1997 05:00:00 GMT' );
header('Last-Modified: ' . gmdate('D, d M Y H:i:s') . 'GMT');
header('Cache-Control: no-cache, must-revalidate');
header('Pragma: no-cache');
header('Content-Type: text/xml');
// send the results to the client
echo $suggest->getSuggestions($keyword);
?>
```

7. Create another file named suggest.class.php, and add this code to it:

```php
<?php
// load error handling module
require_once('error_handler.php');
// load configuration file
require_once('config.php');

// class supports server-side suggest & autocomplete functionality
class Suggest
{
  // database handler
  private $mMysqli;

  // constructor opens database connection
  function __construct()
  {
    // connect to the database
    $this->mMysqli = new mysqli(DB_HOST, DB_USER, DB_PASSWORD,
                                                 DB_DATABASE);
  }

  // destructor, closes database connection
  function __destruct()
  {
    $this->mMysqli->close();
  }

  // returns all PHP functions that start with $keyword
  public function getSuggestions($keyword)
  {
    // escape the keyword string
    $patterns = array('/\s+/', '/"+/', '/%+/');
    $replace = array('');
    $keyword = preg_replace($patterns, $replace, $keyword);
    // build the SQL query that gets the matching functions from the database
    if($keyword != '')
      $query = 'SELECT name ' .
               'FROM suggest ' .
               'WHERE name LIKE "' . $keyword . '%"';
    // if the keyword is empty build a SQL query that will return no results
    else
      $query = 'SELECT name ' .
```

```
                          'FROM suggest ' .
                          'WHERE name=""';
      // execute the SQL query
      $result = $this->mMysqli->query($query);
      // build the XML response
      $output = '<?xml version="1.0" encoding="UTF-8" standalone="yes"?>';
      $output .= '<response>';
      // if we have results, loop through them and add them to the output
      if($result->num_rows)
        while ($row = $result->fetch_array(MYSQLI_ASSOC))
          $output .= '<name>' . $row['name'] . '</name>';
      // close the result stream
      $result->close();
      // add the final closing tag
      $output .= '</response>';
      // return the results
      return $output;
    }
  //end class Suggest
}
?>
```

8. Create a new file named index.html, and add this code to it:

```
<!DOCTYPE html PUBLIC "-//W3C//DTD XHTML 1.0 Transitional//EN"
"http://www.w3.org/TR/xhtml1/DTD/xhtml1-transitional.dtd">
<html xmlns="http://www.w3.org/1999/xhtml" xml:lang="en" lang="en">
  <head>
    <title>AJAX Suggest and Autocomplete</title>
    <meta http-equiv="Content-Type" content="text/html; charset=UTF-8" />
    <link href="suggest.css" rel="stylesheet" type="text/css" />
    <script type="text/javascript" src="suggest.js"></script>
  </head>
  <body>
    <noscript>
      Your browser does not support JavaScript!!
    </noscript>
    <div id="content" onclick="hideSuggestions();">
      <div id="message">Enter the first letters of your function:</div>
      <input type="text" name="keyword" id="keyword" maxlength="70"
             size="69" onkeyup = "handleKeyUp(event)" value="" />
      <div id="scroll">
        <div id="suggest">
        </div>
      </div>
    </div>
  </body>
</html>
```

9. Create another file named suggest.css, and add this code to it:

```
 body
{
  font-family: helvetica, sans-serif;
  margin: 0px;
  padding: 0px;
  font-size: 12px
}

#content
{
  height: 100%;
  width: 100%;
  text-align:center
}

#message
```

```
{
  font-weight: bold;
  text-align: center;
  margin-left: 10px;
  margin-bottom: 10px;
  margin-top: 10px
}

a
{
  text-decoration: none;
  margin: 0px;
  color: #173f5f
}

input
{
  border: #999 1px solid;
  font-family: helvetica, sans-serif;
  font-weight: normal;
  font-size: 10px
}

#scroll
{
  position: relative;
  margin: 0 auto;
  visibility: hidden;
  background-color: white;
  z-index: 1;
  width: 300px;
  height: 180px;
  border-top-style: solid;
  border-right-style: solid;
  border-left-style: solid;
  border-collapse: collapse;
  border-bottom-style: solid;
  border-color: #000000;
  border-width: 1px;
  overflow: auto
}

#scroll div
{
  margin: 0 auto;
  text-align:left
}

#suggest table
{
  width: 270px;
  font-size: 11px;
  font-weight: normal;
  color: #676767;
  text-decoration: none;
  border: 0px;
  padding: 0px;
  text-align:left;
  margin: 0px
}

.highlightrow
{
  background-color: #999999;
  cursor: pointer
}
```

10. Create another file named `suggest.js`, and add this code to it:

```javascript
/* URL to the PHP page called for receiving suggestions for a keyword*/
var getFunctionsUrl = "suggest.php?keyword=";
/* URL for seeing the results for the selected suggestion */
var phpHelpUrl="http://www.php.net/manual/en/function.";
/* the keyword for which an HTTP request has been initiated */
var httpRequestKeyword = "";
/* the last keyword for which suggests have been requested */
var userKeyword = "";
/* number of suggestions received as results for the keyword */
var suggestions = 0;
/* the maximum number of characters to be displayed for a suggestion */
var suggestionMaxLength = 30;
/* flag that indicates if the up or down arrow keys were pressed
   the last time a keyup event occurred   */
var isKeyUpDownPressed = false;
/* the last suggestion that has been used for autocompleting the keyword
*/
var autocompletedKeyword = "";
/* flag that indicates if there are results for the current requested
keyword*/
var hasResults = false;
/* the identifier used to cancel the evaluation with the clearTimeout
method. */
var timeoutId = -1;
/* the currently selected suggestion (by arrow keys or mouse)*/
var position = -1;
/* cache object containing the retrieved suggestions for different
keywords */
var oCache = new Object();
/* the minimum and maximum position of the visible suggestions */
var minVisiblePosition = 0;
var maxVisiblePosition = 9;
// when set to true, display detailed error messages
var debugMode = true;
/* the XMLHttp object for communicating with the server */
var xmlHttpGetSuggestions = createXmlHttpRequestObject();
/* the onload event is handled by our init function */
window.onload = init;

// creates an XMLHttpRequest instance
function createXmlHttpRequestObject()
{
  // will store the reference to the XMLHttpRequest object
  var xmlHttp;
  // this should work for all browsers except IE6 and older
  try
  {
    // try to create XMLHttpRequest object
    xmlHttp = new XMLHttpRequest();
  }
  catch(e)
  {
    // assume IE6 or older
    var XmlHttpVersions = new Array("MSXML2.XMLHTTP.6.0",
                                    "MSXML2.XMLHTTP.5.0",
                                    "MSXML2.XMLHTTP.4.0",
                                    "MSXML2.XMLHTTP.3.0",
                                    "MSXML2.XMLHTTP",
                                    "Microsoft.XMLHTTP");
    // try every prog id until one works
    for (var i=0; i<XmlHttpVersions.length && !xmlHttp; i++)
    {
      try
```

```
    {
      // try to create XMLHttpRequest object
      xmlHttp = new ActiveXObject(xmlHttpVersions[i]);
    }
    catch (e) {}
  }
}
// return the created object or display an error message
if (!xmlHttp)
  alert("Error creating the XMLHttpRequest object.");
else
  return xmlHttp;
}

/* function that initializes the page */
function init()
{
  // retrieve the input control for the keyword
  var oKeyword = document.getElementById("keyword");
  // prevent browser from starting the autofill function
  oKeyword.setAttribute("autocomplete", "off");
  // reset the content of the keyword and set the focus on it
  oKeyword.value = "";
  oKeyword.focus();
  // set the timeout for checking updates in the keyword's value
  setTimeout("checkForChanges()", 500);
}

/* function that adds to a keyword an array of values */
function addToCache(keyword, values)
{
  // create a new array entry in the cache
  oCache[keyword] = new Array();
  // add all the values to the keyword's entry in the cache
  for(i=0; i<values.length; i++)
    oCache[keyword][i] = values[i];
}

/*
    function that checks to see if the keyword specified as parameter is in
    the cache or tries to find the longest matching prefixes in the cache
    and adds them in the cache for the current keyword parameter
*/
function checkCache(keyword)
{
  // check to see if the keyword is already in the cache
  if(oCache[keyword])
    return true;
  // try to find the biggest prefixes
  for(i=keyword.length-2; i>=0; i--)
  {
    // compute the current prefix keyword
    var currentKeyword = keyword.substring(0, i+1);
    // check to see if we have the current prefix keyword in the cache
    if(oCache[currentKeyword])
    {
      // the current keyword's results already in the cache
      var cacheResults = oCache[currentKeyword];
      // the results matching the keyword in the current cache results
      var keywordResults = new Array();
      var keywordResultsSize = 0;
      // try to find all matching results starting with the current prefix
      for(j=0;j<cacheResults.length;j++)
      {
```

```
                if(cacheResults[j].indexOf(keyword) == 0)
                    keywordResults[keywordResultsSize++] = cacheResults[j];
            }
            // add all the keyword's prefix results to the cache
            addToCache(keyword, keywordResults);
            return true;
        }
    }
    // no match found
    return false;
}

/* initiate HTTP request to retrieve suggestions for the current keyword
*/
function getSuggestions(keyword)
{
    /* continue if keyword isn't null and the last pressed key wasn't up or
       down */
    if(keyword != "" && !isKeyUpDownPressed)
    {
        // check to see if the keyword is in the cache
        isInCache = checkCache(keyword);
        // if keyword is in cache...
        if(isInCache == true)
        {
            // retrieve the results from the cache
            httpRequestKeyword=keyword;
            userKeyword=keyword;
            // display the results in the cache
            displayResults(keyword, oCache[keyword]);
        }
        // if the keyword isn't in cache, make an HTTP request
        else
        {
            if(xmlHttpGetSuggestions)
            {
                try
                {
                    /* if the XMLHttpRequest object isn't busy with a previous
                       request... */
                    if (xmlHttpGetSuggestions.readyState == 4 ||
                        xmlHttpGetSuggestions.readyState == 0)
                    {
                        httpRequestKeyword = keyword;
                        userKeyword = keyword;
                        xmlHttpGetSuggestions.open("GET",
                                    getFunctionsUrl + encode(keyword), true);
                        xmlHttpGetSuggestions.onreadystatechange =
                                                handleGettingSuggestions;
                        xmlHttpGetSuggestions.send(null);
                    }
                    // if the XMLHttpRequest object is busy...
                    else
                    {
                        // retain the keyword the user wanted
                        userKeyword = keyword;
                        // clear any previous timeouts already set
                        if(timeoutId != -1)
                            clearTimeout(timeoutId);
                        // try again in 0.5 seconds
                        timeoutId = setTimeout("getSuggestions(userKeyword);", 500);
                    }
                }
                catch(e)
```

```
            {
                displayError("Can't connect to server:\n" + e.toString());
            }
          }
        }
      }
    }
}

/* transforms all the children of an xml node into an array */
function xmlToArray(resultsXml)
{
    // initiate the resultsArray
    var resultsArray= new Array();
    // loop through all the xml nodes retrieving the content
    for(i=0;i<resultsXml.length;i++)
      resultsArray[i]=resultsXml.item(i).firstChild.data;
    // return the node's content as an array
    return resultsArray;
}

/* handles the server's response containing the suggestions
   for the requested keyword   */
function handleGettingSuggestions()
{
    //if the process is completed, decide what to do with the returned data
    if (xmlHttpGetSuggestions.readyState == 4)
    {
      // only if HTTP status is "OK"
      if (xmlHttpGetSuggestions.status == 200)
      {
        try
        {
          // process the server's response
          updateSuggestions();
        }
        catch(e)
        {
          // display the error message
          displayError(e.toString());
        }
      }
      else
      {
        displayError("There was a problem retrieving the data:\n" +
                      xmlHttpGetSuggestions.statusText);
      }
    }
}

/* function that processes the server's response */
function updateSuggestions()
{
    // retrieve the server's response
    var response = xmlHttpGetSuggestions.responseText;
    // server error?
    if (response.indexOf("ERRNO") >= 0
        || response.indexOf("error:") >= 0
        || response.length == 0)
      throw(response.length == 0 ? "Void server response." : response);
    // retrieve the document element
    response = xmlHttpGetSuggestions.responseXML.documentElement;
    // initialize the new array of functions' names
    nameArray = new Array();
    // check to see if we have any results for the searched keyword
```

```
            if(response.childNodes.length)
            {
                /* we retrieve the new functions' names from the document element as
                   an array */
                nameArray= xmlToArray(response.getElementsByTagName("name"));
            }
            // check to see if other keywords are already being searched for
            if(httpRequestKeyword == userKeyword)
            {
                // display the results array
                displayResults(httpRequestKeyword, nameArray);
            }
            else
            {
                // add the results to the cache
                // we don't need to display the results since they are no longer useful
                addToCache(httpRequestKeyword, nameArray);
            }
        }

        /* populates the list with the current suggestions */
        function displayResults(keyword, results_array)
        {
            // start building the HTML table containing the results
            var div = "<table>";
            // if the searched for keyword is not in the cache then add it to the cache
            if(!oCache[keyword] && keyword)
                addToCache(keyword, results_array);
            // if the array of results is empty display a message
            if(results_array.length == 0)
            {
                div += "<tr><td>No results found for <strong>" + keyword +
                       "</strong></td></tr>";
                // set the flag indicating that no results have been found
                // and reset the counter for results
                hasResults = false;
                suggestions = 0;
            }
            // display the results
            else
            {
                // resets the index of the currently selected suggestion
                position = -1;
                // resets the flag indicating whether the up or down key has been pressed
                isKeyUpDownPressed = false;
                /* sets the flag indicating that there are results for the searched
                   for keyword */
                hasResults = true;
                // get the number of results from the cache
                suggestions = oCache[keyword].length;
                // loop through all the results and generate the HTML list of results
                for (var i=0; i<oCache[keyword].length; i++)
                {
                    // retrieve the current function
                    crtFunction = oCache[keyword][i];
                    // set the string link for the for the current function
                    // to the name of the function
                    crtFunctionLink = crtFunction;
                    // replace the _ with - in the string link
                    while(crtFunctionLink.indexOf("_") !=-1)
                        crtFunctionLink = crtFunctionLink.replace("_","-");
                    // start building the HTML row that contains the link to the
                    // PHP help page of the current function
```

```
                    div += "<tr id='tr" + i +
                            "' onclick='location.href=document.getElementById(\"a" + i +
                            "\").href;' onmouseover='handleOnMouseOver(this);' " +
                            "onmouseout='handleOnMouseOut(this);'>" +
                            "<td align='left'><a id='a" + i +
                            "' href='" + phpHelpUrl + crtFunctionLink + ".php";
                    // check to see if the current function name length exceeds the maximum
                    // number of characters that can be displayed for a function name
                    if(crtFunction.length <= suggestionMaxLength)
                    {
                        // bold the matching prefix of the function name and of the keyword
                        div += "'><b>" +
                                crtFunction.substring(0, httpRequestKeyword.length) +
                                "</b>"
                        div += crtFunction.substring(httpRequestKeyword.length,
                                                    crtFunction.length) +
                                "</a></td></tr>";
                    }
                    else
                    {
                        // check to see if the length of the current keyword exceeds
                        // the maximum number of characters that can be displayed
                        if(httpRequestKeyword.length < suggestionMaxLength)
                        {
                            /* bold the matching prefix of the function name and that of the
                               keyword */
                            div += "'><b>" +
                                    crtFunction.substring(0, httpRequestKeyword.length) +
                                    "</b>"
                            div += crtFunction.substring(httpRequestKeyword.length,
                                                        suggestionMaxLength) +
                                    "</a></td></tr>";
                        }
                        else
                        {
                            // bold the entire function name
                            div += "'><b>" +
                                    crtFunction.substring(0,suggestionMaxLength) +
                                    "</b></td></tr>"
                        }
                    }
                }
            }
            // end building the HTML table
            div += "</table>";
            // retrieve the suggest and scroll object
            var oSuggest = document.getElementById("suggest");
            var oScroll = document.getElementById("scroll");
            // scroll to the top of the list
            oScroll.scrollTop = 0;
            // update the suggestions list and make it visible
            oSuggest.innerHTML = div;
            oScroll.style.visibility = "visible";
            // if we had results we apply the type ahead for the current keyword
            if(results_array.length > 0)
                autocompleteKeyword();
        }

        /* function that periodically checks to see if the typed keyword has
        changed */
        function checkForChanges()
        {
            // retrieve the keyword object
```

```
        var keyword = document.getElementById("keyword").value;
        // check to see if the keyword is empty
        if(keyword == "")
        {
            // hide the suggestions
            hideSuggestions();
            // reset the keywords
            userKeyword="";
            httpRequestKeyword="";
        }
        // set the timer for a new check
        setTimeout("checkForChanges()", 500);
        // check to see if there are any changes
        if((userKeyword != keyword) &&
           (autocompletedKeyword != keyword) &&
           (!isKeyUpDownPressed))
           // update the suggestions
           getSuggestions(keyword);
    }

    /* function that handles the keys that are pressed */
    function handleKeyUp(e)
    {
        // get the event
        e = (!e) ? window.event : e;
        // get the event's target
        target = (!e.target) ? e.srcElement : e.target;
        if (target.nodeType == 3)
            target = target.parentNode;
        // get the character code of the pressed button
        code = (e.charCode) ? e.charCode :
               ((e.keyCode) ? e.keyCode :
               ((e.which) ? e.which : 0));
        // check to see if the event was keyup
        if (e.type == "keyup")
        {
            isKeyUpDownPressed =false;
            // check to see we if are interested in the current character
            if ((code < 13 && code != 8) ||
                (code >=14 && code < 32) ||
                (code >= 33 && code <= 46 && code != 38 && code != 40) ||
                (code >= 112 && code <= 123))
            {
                // simply ignore non-interesting characters
            }
            else
            /* if Enter is pressed we jump to the PHP help page of the current
               function */
            if(code == 13)
            {
                // check to see if any function is currently selected
                if(position>=0)
                {
                    location.href = document.getElementById("a" + position).href;
                }
            }
            else
            // if the down arrow is pressed we go to the next suggestion
              if(code == 40)
              {
                  newTR=document.getElementById("tr"+(++position));
                  oldTR=document.getElementById("tr"+(--position));
                  // deselect the old selected suggestion
                  if(position>=0 && position<suggestions-1)
                      oldTR.className = "";
```

```
                  // select the new suggestion and update the keyword
                  if(position < suggestions - 1)
                  {
                    newTR.className = "highlightrow";
                    updateKeywordValue(newTR);
                    position++;
                  }
                  e.cancelBubble = true;
                  e.returnValue = false;
                  isKeyUpDownPressed = true;
                  // scroll down if the current window is no longer valid
                  if(position > maxVisiblePosition)
                  {
                    oScroll = document.getElementById("scroll");
                    oScroll.scrollTop += 18;
                    maxVisiblePosition += 1;
                    minVisiblePosition += 1;
                  }
                }
                else
                // if the up arrow is pressed we go to the previous suggestion
                if(code == 38)
                {
                  newTR=document.getElementById("tr"+(--position));
                  oldTR=document.getElementById("tr"+(++position));
                  // deselect the old selected position
                  if(position>=0 && position <= suggestions - 1)
                  {
                    oldTR.className = "";
                  }
                  // select the new suggestion and update the keyword
                  if(position > 0)
                  {
                    newTR.className = "highlightrow";
                    updateKeywordValue(newTR);
                    position--;
                    // scroll up if the current window is no longer valid
                    if(position<minVisiblePosition)
                    {
                      oScroll = document.getElementById("scroll");
                      oScroll.scrollTop -= 18;
                      maxVisiblePosition -= 1;
                      minVisiblePosition -= 1;
                    }
                  }
                  else
                    if(position == 0)
                      position--;
                  e.cancelBubble = true;
                  e.returnValue = false;
                  isKeyUpDownPressed = true;
                }
              }
            }

/* function that updates the keyword value with the value
   of the currently selected suggestion */
function updateKeywordValue(oTr)
{
  // retrieve the keyword object
  var oKeyword = document.getElementById("keyword");
  // retrieve the link for the current function
  var crtLink = document.getElementById("a" +
                        oTr.id.substring(2,oTr.id.length)).toString();
  // replace - with _ and leave out the .php extension
```

```
        crtLink = crtLink.replace("-", "_");
        crtLink = crtLink.substring(0, crtLink.length - 4);
        // update the keyword's value
        oKeyword.value = unescape(crtLink.substring(phpHelpUrl.length,
    crtLink.length));
    }

    /* function that removes the style from all suggestions*/
    function deselectAll()
    {
        for(i=0; i<suggestions; i++)
        {
            var oCrtTr = document.getElementById("tr" + i);
            oCrtTr.className = "";
        }
    }

    /* function that handles the mouse entering over a suggestion's area
        event */
    function handleOnMouseOver(oTr)
    {
        deselectAll();
        oTr.className = "highlightrow";
        position = oTr.id.substring(2, oTr.id.length);
    }

    /* function that handles the mouse exiting a suggestion's area event */
    function handleOnMouseOut(oTr)
    {
        oTr.className = "";
        position = -1;
    }

    /* function that escapes a string */
    function encode(uri)
    {
        if (encodeURIComponent)
        {
            return encodeURIComponent(uri);
        }

        if (escape)
        {
            return escape(uri);
        }
    }

    /* function that hides the layer containing the suggestions */
    function hideSuggestions()
    {
        var oScroll = document.getElementById("scroll");
        oScroll.style.visibility = "hidden";
    }

    /* function that selects a range in the text object passed as parameter */
    function selectRange(oText, start, length)
    {
        // check to see if in IE or FF
        if (oText.createTextRange)
        {
            //IE
            var oRange = oText.createTextRange();
            oRange.moveStart("character", start);
            oRange.moveEnd("character", length - oText.value.length);
            oRange.select();
```

```
        }
      else
        // FF
        if (oText.setSelectionRange)
        {
          oText.setSelectionRange(start, length);
        }
      oText.focus();
    }

    /* function that autocompletes the typed keyword*/
    function autocompleteKeyword()
    {
      //retrieve the keyword object
      var oKeyword = document.getElementById("keyword");
      // reset the position of the selected suggestion
      position=0;
      // deselect all suggestions
      deselectAll();
      // highlight the selected suggestion
      document.getElementById("tr0").className="highlightrow";
      // update the keyword's value with the suggestion
      updateKeywordValue(document.getElementById("tr0"));
      // apply the type-ahead style
      selectRange(oKeyword,httpRequestKeyword.length,oKeyword.value.length);
      // set the autocompleted word to the keyword's value
      autocompletedKeyword=oKeyword.value;
    }

    /* function that displays an error message */
    function displayError(message)
    {
      // display error message, with more technical details if debugMode is true
      alert("Error accessing the server! "+
          (debugMode ? "\n" + message : ""));
    }
```

11. The code is ready for testing now. Load the address `http://localhost/ajax/`
    `suggest/` with a web browser. Let's say, you're looking for the help page of `strstr`.
    After typing **s**, you're shown a list of functions that start with this letter:

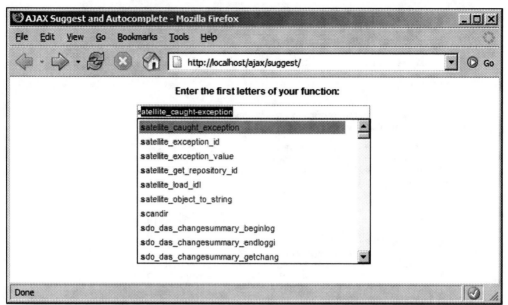

Figure 6.3: PHP Knows Many Functions That Start with "s"

12. OK, PHP has many functions that start with letter **s**. Observe that the first matching function is autocompleted in the search box and that you have a long list of functions to scroll through. Let's type the second letter of the word strstr: t.

13. The list of functions has diminished as expected. Find the function you are interested in by continuing to type its name, or by using the keyboard's up and down arrows, or using the mouse. When you have found it, press *Enter* or click it using the mouse.

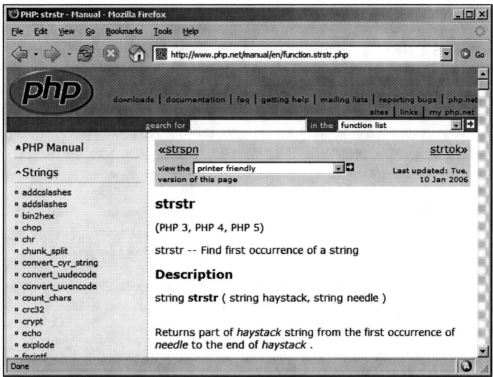

Figure 6.4: PHP Documentation for strstr

What Just Happened?

Let us start with the index.html file.

The interesting part in this script is that a scroll region can be implemented in DHTML. A little piece of heaven regarding scrolling can be found at http://www.dyn-web.com/dhtml/scroll/. The idea for having a part of the page with a scrollbar next to it is to have two layers one inside another. In our example the div scroll and the div suggest do the trick.

The outer layer is scroll. It has a fixed width and height and its most useful property is overflow. Generally, the content of a block box is confined to just the content edges of the box. In certain cases, a box may overflow, meaning that part of its content lies outside the box. In CSS, the overflow property specifies what happens when an element overflows its area. You can find the possible values of overflow at http://www.w3.org/TR/REC-CSS2/visufx.html.

Another thing that can be interesting is how we can center an object horizontally. The classic align = center attribute is not valid in XHTML 1.0 and therefore a workaround needs to be found. The solution is to use the margin attribute set to auto for the element you want centered. If you have a valid doctype, Internet Explorer 6 will render an element having auto margins centered; otherwise, as is the case with the earlier versions, the attribute will be ignored. For earlier versions of Internet Explorer, you need to have the text-align attribute set to center for the parent of the element you want centered. This is because Internet Explorer incorrectly applies the `text-align` attribute to all block elements instead of only inline elements making things work.

The input control handles the `keyup` event, which in fact triggers the process of fetching and displaying the suggestions for the current keyword. The content `div` handles the `click` event so that when the user clicks outside the suggestions area, the suggestions won't be displayed until the user modifies the current keyword.

For this application, almost everything is about JavaScript, DOM, and CSS. The server side is very simple and it does not imply any significant effort, but the client-side code in `suggest.js` is a bit more complex. Let's enumerate the client features we implemented:

1. When a user starts typing, a drop-down list with suggestions appears; the list is updated as the user types new characters or erases some of them.

2. The first matching characters are in "Bold" in the list of suggestions.

3. The first matching suggestion is autocompleted in the keyword box.

4. By moving through the suggestions with the up and down arrow keys the keyword box is completed with the current selected suggestion.

5. By moving with the mouse over the suggestions nothing happens.

6. By pressing *Enter* or by clicking the mouse on a suggestion the page is redirected to the PHP help page on the php.net site.

7. The page is also redirected to php.net when the user presses *Enter* in the keyword box.

8. When the mouse is clicked outside the suggestions' list or the keyword box the list of suggestions is hidden.

9. The suggestions are cached on the client side.

We have a function that periodically checks to see if the keyword has changed. If so, an HTTP request to the server page containing the current keyword is initiated. In response, the server page returns the matching PHP functions as suggestions for that keyword. The client browser displays the suggestions in a drop-down list. The user can navigate through the suggestions using the up and down arrow keys or the mouse. On typing a new letter or on erasing one, the list of suggestions is updated. After seeing the images in the previous section and after a short overview of the process, it is time for us to see exactly how all these can be implemented.

The `createXmlHttpRequestObject` is the function that we use for creating our `XMLHttpRequest` object.

The `init` function does nothing more than setting off the `autocomplete` attribute for the keyword box. This is done in order to prevent browsers initiating their own autocomplete engine. Because setting `"autocomplete"="off"` is not a valid attribute according to XHTML specifications, the HTML is invalidated. This attribute was introduced by Microsoft and has been adopted by the majority of browsers.

The function that checks to see if the keyword has changed is `checkForUpdates`. If so, it starts the process of updating the suggestions list. For navigating through the list of suggestions, the function `handleKeyUp` is used. We will see more about this function later in this chapter.

We have talked about caching the results. Yes, this is a very good optimization technique for this kind of application. Therefore, we have two functions that deal with the cache object—`checkCache` and `addToCache`.

The `checkCache` function checks to see if a given keyword is in the cache. If it's not in the cache, it tries to find the longest matching prefixes for our keyword in the list of cached values. Those matching prefixes are added to the cache by calling the `addToCache` function.

The `addToCache` function inserts in the cache for a given keyword a list of values that represent the suggestions for the keyword.

The `getSuggestions` function is called for fetching new suggestions. If the current keyword is already in the cache (`checkCache` function), we populate the suggestions list directly with those suggestions that have been cached. If a request is already in progress, the keyword that we would have wanted to use for a new call is saved and a timeout for this function is set. This way, we make sure that we save the last keyword for which we could not make a server call and as soon as the current request completes a new server call is initiated with the last keyword.

The `handleGettingSuggestions` function checks to see when the request to the server is completed and if there are no errors, the `updateSuggestions` function is called.

The `updateSuggestions` function checks to see if it is necessary to update the suggestion list. We check to see if during the server call there was another attempt to initiate a server call. By this we know if the user modified the current keyword and if so we don't need to display the retrieved suggestions since they are no longer interesting for the user. Nevertheless, the client caches all the suggestions from the server.

The `xmlToArray` function is the one that converts a collection of XML nodes into an array.

The function that actually builds the list of suggestions is `displayResults`. It receives as parameters the keyword and the list of available functions as an array. The first thing to do is to cache the current results, so that if we want to search again the same keyword, we don't have to make another call to the web server. We go through all the suggestions in the array and we dynamically build a table containing the suggestions. If no suggestions are available, a message is displayed.

The `updateKeywordValue` function is responsible for updating the current keyword with the value contained in the suggestion currently selected given as a `tr` object.

The `hideSuggestions` function hides the `div` element containing all suggestions for the current keyword.

The `deselectAll` function deselects the currently selected suggestions.

The `handleOnMouseOver` and `handleOnMouseOut` functions handle the events that occur when the mouse cursor enters or exits the `tr` area of a suggestion. These functions update the style of the suggestion where the event takes place accordingly.

The `encode` function escapes the string passed as a parameter and it is used by the `getSuggestions` function when calling the server page.

Next, we will talk about the handlekeyup function. This is the function used for navigation through the results and submission. Since we are interested only in few keys, the others are ignored. Before getting there we need to make sure the code works on every browser. In order for this to happen, we need to write a few lines as we can see for ourselves.

In order to know which characters to consider, we need to know the codes of the keys. The event object received as parameter has a property keyCode that has the code of the pressed key. In the following table, you can find a list of most of the special keys:

Table 1: Key codes

Key	Code	Key	Code
Backspace	8	Print Screen	44
Tab	9	Delete	46
Enter	13	F1	112
Shift	16	F2	113
Ctrl	17	F3	114
Alt	18	F4	115
Pause/Break	19	F5	116
Caps Lock	20	F6	117
Esc	27	F7	118
Page Up	33	F8	119
Page Down	34	F9	120
End	35	F10	121
Home	36	F11	122
Left Arrow	37	F12	123
Up Arrow	38		
Right Arrow	39		
Down Arrow	40		

On pressing *Enter* (code 13), the page submits to the php.net help with the specification for the currently selected suggestion if any is selected. On pressing the up or down arrow keys the currently selected suggestion moves one position up or down if possible. The current keyword is also updated with the value of the current selected suggestion. We do not handle any other pressed keys since they modify the keyword and we have already presented the checkForChanges function that handles this part.

Another problem that arises when having more than ten suggestions available is that we have a scrollable div region. As we stated before, we want the user to be able to navigate through the results by using the up and down arrow keys. If the user reaches a result that is not currently visible, we need to scroll in the region in order to make that result visible. In order to implement this, we keep minimum and maximum positions of the results that are currently visible. It's as if we had a window that moves through the results according to the arrows' movements and the current selected result.

The `selectRange` and `autocompleteKeyword` functions do the trick for the type-ahead look by autocompleting the current keyword with the rest of the missing letters up to the first suggestion. The part that is missing is added as highlighted text to the current keyword. The `select()` method selects all the text, and hence selecting only a part of a text is not possible. In order to do this, Internet Explorer offers one solution while Mozilla / Firefox offers another one. It is not for the first time that issues are not the same in all browsers, so we have to take each case and solve it separately. In Firefox, issues are simple because there is just one function that does all the work for us—`setSelectionRange`. This function takes two parameters—the start position of the selection and the length of the selection. In Internet Explorer, we have to use the `TextRange` object in order to achieve the same goal. Let us take a closer look at it because it might be useful for us in the future and for this, we need to know what it can do.

The `TextRange` object can carry out tasks such as searching or selecting text. Text ranges let you pick out characters, words, and sentences from the text. Each of these three is a logical unit of the object. In order to use such an object you have to follow these steps:

- Create the text range
- Apply a method to the selected text

You can copy the text, search in the text, and select a part of the text, as in our case.

To create such an object you can call the `createTextRange` method on a `body`, `textarea`, or `button` element.

Each object has a start and an end position defining the scope of the text. When you create a new text range, the start and end positions contain the entire content by default. To modify the scope of the text range we can use the `move`, `moveStart`, and `moveEnd` functions. Each of them takes two parameters—the first parameter specifies the logical unit and the second one the number of units to move. The result contains the numbers of units moved. The `select` method makes the selection equal to the current object. In order to have a complete view of its capabilities check the following link on MSDN: `http://msdn.microsoft.com/library/default.asp?url=/workshop/author/dyncontent/textrange.asp`.

After receiving the suggestions and inserting them into the page, we need to autocomplete the keyword with the value of the first suggestion. This is accomplished by using the `selectRange` function described above.

For the error-handling part, we use the `displayError` function that displays an alert with the error message as parameter.

OK, now we have seen how it goes for the client side of the application. Let's check the server side.

For the server side, things are very simple. The `suggest.php` file retrieves the parameter passed by the client and that represents the searched for keyword. Then it calls a method of the `Suggest` class in `suggest.class.php` to find the matching suggestions for our keyword. The web server returns an XML response containing the PHP functions that match the current keyword. As we can see for ourselves, the effort resides on the client side and almost nothing on the server side.

The PHP help implemented as an AJAX suggest and autocomplete solution has proven to be far more challenging than we would have thought at the beginning. As mentioned above, we had many things to deal with. Hopefully, these problems also brought useful solutions for our application and can be used as a learning base for other applications.

Summary

In the beginning of the chapter, we gave a definition of autocomplete and suggest. We have seen how popular these notions are in domains from code editors to operating systems' consoles.

The application developed throughout this chapter offers an online PHP help with links to the official help on www.php.net.

The functionality offered here resembles to that offered by Google Suggest from many points of view, but it also has some additional features.

7

AJAX Real-Time Charting with SVG

Scalable Vector Graphics (SVG) is one of the emerging technologies with a good chance of becoming the next "big thing" for web graphics, as was the case with Flash. SVG is a language for defining two-dimensional graphics. SVG isn't necessarily related to web development, but it fits very well into the picture because it complements the features offered naturally by web browsers. Today, there are more SVG implementations and standardization isn't great, but things are expected to improve in the future.

SVG is a **World Wide Web Consortium (W3C)** recommendation since January 2003. Among the big names that have contributed to its creation we can mention Sun Microsystems, Adobe, Apple, IBM, and Kodak to name just a few. The current specification is SVG 1.2. SVG Mobile, SVG Print, and sXBL are other recommendations under work at W3C that are likely to get support on most browsers and platforms.

The main features of SVG are:

- SVG graphics are defined in XML format, so the files can be easily manipulated with existing editors, parsers, etc.
- SVG images are scalable; they can zoomed, resized, and reoriented without losing quality.
- SVG includes font elements so that both text and graphical appearance are preserved.
- SVG includes declarative animation elements.
- SVG allows a multi-namespace XML application.
- SVG allows the script-based manipulation of the document tree using a subset of the XML DOM and the SVG uDOM.

For a primer on the world of SVG, check out these resources:

- The SVG W3C page at `http://www.w3.org/Graphics/SVG/`.
- An SVG introduction at `http://www.w3schools.com/svg/svg_intro.asp`.
- A very useful list of SVG links at `http://www.svgi.org/`.
- A handy SVG reference at `http://www.w3schools.com/svg/svg_reference.asp`.
- The SVG document structure is explained at `http://www.w3.org/TR/SVG/struct.html`.
- SVG examples at `http://www.carto.net/papers/svg/samples/` and `http://svg-whiz.com/samples.html`.

Implementing a Real-Time Chart with AJAX and SVG

Before continuing, please make sure your web browser supports SVG. The code in this case study has been tested with Firefox 1.5, Internet Explorer with the Adobe SVG Viewer, and Apache Batik. You can test the online demo accessing the link you can find at `http://ajaxphp.packtpub.com`.

Firefox ships with integrated SVG support. Being at its first version, this SVG implementation does have some problems that you need to take into consideration when writing the code, and the performance isn't excellent.

To load SVG in Internet Explorer, you need to install an external SVG plug-in. The SVG plug-in we used in our tests is the one from Adobe, which you can download at `http://www.adobe.com/svg/viewer/install/main.html`. The installation process is very simple; you just need to download a small file named `svgview.exe`, and execute it. The first time you load an SVG page, you will be asked to confirm the terms of agreement.

Finally, we also tested the application with Apache's Batik SVG viewer, in which case you need to load the `svg` file directly, because it doesn't support loading the HTML file that loads the SVG script. (You may want to check Batik for its good DOM viewer, which nicely displays the SVG nodes in a hierarchical structure.)

In this chapter's case study, we'll create a simple chart application whose input data is retrieved asynchronously from a PHP script. The generated data can be anything, and in our case we'll have a simple algorithm that generates random data. Figure 7.1 shows sample output from the application:

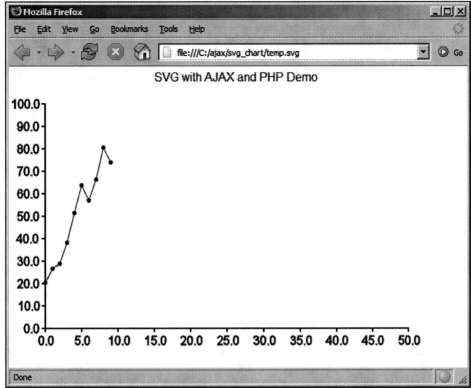

Figure 7.1: SVG Chart

The chart in Figure 7.1 is actually a static SVG file called temp.svg, which represents a snapshot of the output generated by the running application; it is not a screenshot of the actual running application. The script is saved as `temp.svg` in this chapter's folder in the code download, and you can load it directly into your web browser (not necessarily through a web server), after you've made sure your browser supports SVG.

We will first have a look at the contents of `temp.svg`, to get a feeling about what we want to generate dynamically from our JavaScript code. Note that the SVG script can be generated either at the client side or at the server side. For our application, the server only generates random coordinates, and the JavaScript client uses these coordinates to compose the SVG output.

Have a look at a stripped version of the `temp.svg` file:

```
<svg width="100%" height="100%" xmlns="http://www.w3.org/2000/svg"
xmlns:xlink="http://www.w3.org/1999/xlink" onload="init(evt)">
   <a xlink:href="http://ajaxphp.packtpub.com">
     <text x="200" y="20">
       SVG with AJAX and PHP Demo
     </text>
   </a>
   <!-- All chart elements are grouped and translated by 50, 50 -->
   <g transform="translate(50, 50)">
```

```
<!-- Group all axis elements (lines and text nodes) -->
<g>
  <!-- Path draws the grid axes and unit delimiters -->
  <path stroke="black" stroke-width="2" d=" ... path definition here ..."/>

  <!-- Text nodes that display horizontal unit numbers -->
  <text x="-10" y="322" stroke="black">0.0</text>
  ...
  ... more text nodes here that draw horizontal and vertical unit numbers
  ...
</g>

<!-- Draw the lines between chart nodes as a single -->
<path stroke="black" stroke-width="1" fill="none" d="... definition ..."/>

<!-- Draw the chart nodes as filled blue circles -->
<circle cx="00" cy="239.143" r="3" fill="blue" />
...
... more circle nodes here that draw filled blue circles for chart nodes
...
</g>
</svg>
```

Have a closer look at this code snippet to identify all the chart elements. The SVG format supports the notion of element groups, which are elements grouped under a <g> element. In temp.svg we have two groups: the first group contains all the charts' elements, translating them by (50, 50) pixels, while the second <g> element group is a child of the first group, and it contains the chart's axis lines and numbers.

SVG knows how to handle many element types, which can also be animated (yes, SVG is very powerful). In our example, we make use of some of the very basic ones: path (to draw the axis lines and chart lines), text (to draw the axis numbers, and to dynamically display chart node coordinates when the mouse cursor hovers over them—this latter feature isn't included in the code snippet), and circle (to draw the blue dots on the chart that represent the chart nodes).

You can find documentation for these elements at:

- http://www.w3schools.com/svg/svg_path.asp
- http://www.w3schools.com/svg/svg_circle.asp
- http://www.w3schools.com/svg/svg_text.asp

The paths are described by a path definition. The complete code for the path element that draws the chart lines you can see in Figure 7.1 looks like this:

```
<!-- Draw the lines between chart nodes -->
<path stroke="black" stroke-width="1" fill="none"
  d="M0,239.143 L10,220.286 L20,213.429 L30,185.571 L40,145.714
     L50,108.857 L60,129 L70,101.143 L80,58.2857 L90,78.4286"/>
```

A detail that was stripped from the code snippet was the mouseover and mouseout events of the chart node circles. In our code, the mouseover event (which fires when you move the mouse pointer over a node) will call a JavaScript function that displays a text above the node specifying its coordinates. The mouseout event makes that text disappear. You can see this feature in action in Figure 7.2, which displays the SVG chart application in action.

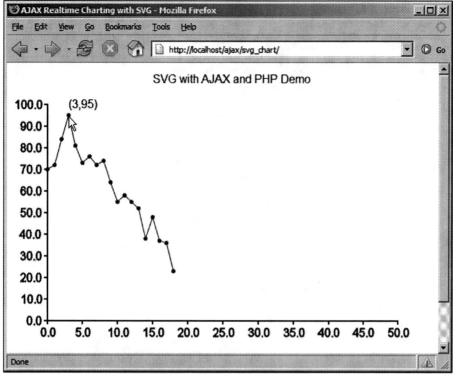

Figure 7.2: SVG Charting in Action

To get the dynamically generated contents of the SVG chart at any given time with Firefox, right click the chart, click Select All, then right-click the chart again, and choose View Selection Source.

Now that you have a good idea about what you are going to implement, let's get to work. It's time for action!

Time for Action—Building the Real-Time SVG Chart

1. Start by creating a new subfolder of the ajax folder, called svg_chart.

2. In the svg_chart folder, create a new file named index.html with the following contents:

```
<!DOCTYPE html PUBLIC "-//W3C//DTD XHTML 1.1//EN"
"http://www.w3.org/TR/xhtml11/DTD/xhtml11.dtd">
<html>
  <head>
    <title>AJAX Realtime Charting with SVG</title>
  </head>
  <body>
    <embed src="chart.svg" width="600" height="450" type="image/svg+xml" />
  </body>
</html>
```

3. Then create a file named chart.svg, and add the following code to it:

```
<svg width="100%" height="100%" xmlns="http://www.w3.org/2000/svg"
xmlns:xlink="http://www.w3.org/1999/xlink" onload="init(evt)">
  <script type="text/ecmascript" xlink:href="ajaxRequest.js"/>
  <script type="text/ecmascript" xlink:href="realTimeChart.js"/>
  <a xlink:href="http://ajaxphp.packtpub.com">
    <text x="200" y="20">
      SVG with AJAX and PHP Demo
    </text>
  </a>
</svg>
```

4. Create a file named ajaxrequest.js with the following contents:

```
// will store reference to the XMLHttpRequest object
var xmlHttp = null;

// creates an XMLHttpRequest instance
function createXmlHttpRequestObject()
{
  // will store the reference to the XMLHttpRequest object
  var xmlHttp;
  // this should work for all browsers except IE6 and older
  try
  {
    // try to create XMLHttpRequest object
    xmlHttp = new XMLHttpRequest();
  }
  catch(e)
  {
    // assume IE6 or older
    var XmlHttpVersions = new Array("MSXML2.XMLHTTP.6.0",
                                    "MSXML2.XMLHTTP.5.0",
                                    "MSXML2.XMLHTTP.4.0",
                                    "MSXML2.XMLHTTP.3.0",
                                    "MSXML2.XMLHTTP",
                                    "Microsoft.XMLHTTP");
    // try every prog id until one works
    for (var i=0; i<XmlHttpVersions.length && !xmlHttp; i++)
    {
      try
      {
        // try to create XMLHttpRequest object
        xmlHttp = new ActiveXObject(XmlHttpVersions[i]);
      }
      catch (e) {}
    }
  }
  // return the created object or display an error message
  if (!xmlHttp)
    alert("Error creating the XMLHttpRequest object.");
  else
    return xmlHttp;
}

// initiates an AJAX request
function ajaxRequest(url, callback)
{
  // stores a reference to the function to be called when the response
  // from the server is received
  var innerCallback = callback;
  // create XMLHttpRequest object when this method is first called
  if (!xmlHttp) xmlHttp = createXmlHttpRequestObject();
  // if the connection is clear, initiate new server request
  if (xmlHttp && (xmlHttp.readyState == 4 || xmlHttp.readyState == 0))
```

```
    {
        xmlHttp.onreadystatechange = handleGettingResults;
        xmlHttp.open("GET", url, true);
        xmlHttp.send(null);
    }
    else
        // if the connection is busy, retry after 1 second
        setTimeout("ajaxRequest(url,callback)", 1000);

    // called when the state of the request changes
    function handleGettingResults()
    {
        // move forward only if the transaction has completed
        if (xmlHttp.readyState == 4)
        {
            // a HTTP status of 200 indicates the transaction completed
            // successfully
            if (xmlHttp.status == 200)
            {
                // execute the callback function, passing the server response
                innerCallback(xmlHttp.responseText)
            }
            else
            {
                // display error message
                alert("Couldn't connect to server");
            }
        }
    }
}
```

5. The bulk of the client-side work is done by RealTimeChart.js:

```
// SVG namespace
var svgNS = "http://www.w3.org/2000/svg";
// the SVG document handler
var documentSVG = null;
// will store the root <g> element that groups all chart elements
var chartGroup = null;
// how often to request new data from server?
var updateInterval = 1000;
// coordinates (in pixels) used to translate the chart
var x = 50, y = 50;
// chart's dimension (in pixels)
var height = 300, width = 500;
// chart's axis origin
var xt1 = 0, yt1 = 0;
// chart's axis maximum values
var xt2 = 50, yt2 = 100;
// number of horizontal and vertical axis divisions
var xDivisions = 10, yDivisions = 10;
// default text width and height for initial display (recalculated
// afterwards)
var defaultTextWidth = 30, defaultTextHeight = 20;
// will retain references to the chart units for recalculating positions
var xIndexes = new Array(xDivisions + 1);
var yIndexes = new Array(yDivisions + 1);
// will store the text node that displays the selected chart node
var currentNodeInfo;
// retains the latest values generated by server
var lastX = -1, lastY = -1;
// shared svg elements
var chartGroup, dataGroup, dataPath;
```

```
// initializes chart
function init(evt)
{
  /**** Prepare the group that will contain all chart data  ****/
  // obtain SVG document handler
  documentSVG = evt.target.ownerDocument;
  // create the <g> element that groups all chart elements
  chartGroup = documentSVG.createElementNS(svgNS, "g");
  chartGroup.setAttribute("transform", "translate(" + x + " " + y + ")");

  /**** Prepare the group that will store the Y and Y axis and numbers ****/
  axisGroup = documentSVG.createElementNS(svgNS, "g");
  // create the X axis line as a <path> element
  axisPath = documentSVG.createElementNS(svgNS, "path");
  // the axis lines will be black, 2 pixels wide
  axisPath.setAttribute("stroke", "black");
  axisPath.setAttribute("stroke-width", "2");

  /**** Create the division lines for the X and Y axis  ****/
  // create the path definition text for the X axis division lines
  pathText = "M 0 " + height;
  // adds divisions to the X axis (differently for last division)
  for (var i = 0; i <= xDivisions; i++)
    pathText += "l 0 5 l 0 -5 " +
      ((i == xDivisions) ? "" : ("l " + width/xDivisions + " 0"));
  // create the path definition text for the Y axis division lines
  pathText += "M 0 " + height;
  // adds one division to the Y axis (differently for last division)
  for (var i = 0; i <= yDivisions; i++)
    pathText += "l -5 0 l 5 0 " +
      ((i == yDivisions) ? "" : ("l 0 -" + height / yDivisions));
  // add the path definition (the <d> attribute) to the path
  axisPath.setAttribute("d", pathText);
  // add the path to the axis group
  axisGroup.appendChild(axisPath);

  /**** Create the text nodes for the X and Y axis  ****/
  // adds text nodes for the X axis
  for (var i = 0; i <= xDivisions; i++)
  {
    // creates the <text> node for the division
    t = documentSVG.createElementNS(svgNS, "text");
    // stores the node for future reference
    xIndexes[i] = t;
    // creates the text for the <text> node
    t.appendChild(documentSVG.createTextNode(
                  (xt1 + i * ((xt2 - xt1) / xDivisions)).toFixed(1)));
    // sets the X and Y attributes for the <text> node
    t.setAttribute("x", i * width / xDivisions - defaultTextWidth / 2);
    t.setAttribute("y", height + 30 + defaultTextHeight);
    // when the graph first loads, we want the text nodes invisible
    t.setAttribute("stroke", "white");
    // add the <text> node to the axis group
    axisGroup.appendChild(t);
  }
  // adds text nodes for the Y axis
  for (var i = 0; i <= yDivisions; i++)
  {
    // creates the <text> node for the division
    t = documentSVG.createElementNS(svgNS, "text");
    // stores the node for future reference
    yIndexes[i] = t;
    // creates the text for the <text> node
    t.appendChild(documentSVG.createTextNode(
                  (yt1 + i * ((yt2 - yt1) / yDivisions)).toFixed(1)));
```

```
      // sets the X and Y attributes for the <text> node
      t.setAttribute("x", -30 -defaultTextWidth);
      t.setAttribute("y", height - i * height / yDivisions
                          + defaultTextHeight / 2);
      // when the graph first loads, we want the text nodes invisible
      t.setAttribute("stroke", "white");
      // add the <text> node to the axis group
      axisGroup.appendChild(t);
    }

    // add the axis group to the chart
    chartGroup.appendChild(axisGroup);

    /**** Prepare the <path> element that will draw chart's data ****/
    dataPath = documentSVG.createElementNS(svgNS, "path");
    dataPath.setAttribute("stroke", "black");
    dataPath.setAttribute("stroke-width", "1");
    dataPath.setAttribute("fill", "none");
    // add the data path to the chart group
    chartGroup.appendChild(dataPath);

    /**** Final initialization steps ****/
    // add the chart group to the SVG document
    documentSVG.documentElement.appendChild(chartGroup);
    // this is needed to correctly display text nodes in Firefox
    setTimeout("refreshXYIndexes()", 500);
    // initiate repetitive server requests
    setTimeout("updateChart()", updateInterval);
}

// this function redraws the text for the axis units and makes it visible
// (this is required to correctly position the text in Firefox)
function refreshXYIndexes()
{
  // redraw text nodes on the X axis
  for (var i = 0; i <= xDivisions; i++)
    if (typeof xIndexes[i].getBBox != "undefined")
      try
      {
        textWidth = xIndexes[i].getBBox().width;
        textHeight = xIndexes[i].getBBox().height;
        xIndexes[i].setAttribute("x", i*width/xDivisions - textWidth/2);
        xIndexes[i].setAttribute("y", height + 10 + textHeight);
        xIndexes[i].setAttribute("stroke", "black");
      }
      catch(e) {}
  // redraw text nodes on the Y axis
  for (var i = 0; i <= yDivisions; i++)
    if (typeof yIndexes[i].getBBox != "undefined")
      try
      {
        twidth = yIndexes[i].getBBox().width;
        theight = yIndexes[i].getBBox().height;
        yIndexes[i].setAttribute("y", height-i*height/yDivisions
                                            +theight/2);
        yIndexes[i].setAttribute("x", -10 -twidth);
        yIndexes[i].setAttribute("stroke", "black");
      }
      catch(e) {}
}
```

```
// called when mouse hovers over chart node to display its coordinates
function createPointInfo(x, y, whereX, whereY)
{
  // make sure you don't display more coordinates at the same time
  if (currentNodeInfo) removePointInfo();
  // create text node
  currentNodeInfo = documentSVG.createElementNS(svgNS, "text");

  currentNodeInfo.appendChild(documentSVG.createTextNode("("+x+","+y+")"));
  // set coordinates
  currentNodeInfo.setAttribute("x", whereX.toFixed(1));
  currentNodeInfo.setAttribute("y", whereY - 10);
  // add the node to the group
  chartGroup.appendChild(currentNodeInfo);
}

// removes the text node that displays chart node coordinates
function removePointInfo()
{
  chartGroup.removeChild(currentNodeInfo);
  currentNodeInfo = null;
}

// draws a new point on the graph
function addPoint(X, Y)
{
  // save these values for future reference
  lastX = X;
  lastY = Y;
  // start over (reload page) after the last value was generated
  if (X == xt2)
    window.location.reload(false);
  // calculate the coordinates of the new node
  coordX = (X - xt1) * (width / (xt2 - xt1));
  coordY = height - (Y - yt1) * (height / (yt2 - yt1));
  // draw the node on the chart as a blue filled circle
  var circle = documentSVG.createElementNS(svgNS, "circle");
  circle.setAttribute("cx", coordX); // X position
  circle.setAttribute("cy", coordY); // Y position
  circle.setAttribute("r", 3); // radius
  circle.setAttribute("fill", "blue"); // color
  circle.setAttribute("onmouseover",
                      "createPointInfo(" + X + "," +
                      Y + "," + coordX + "," + coordY + ")");
  circle.setAttribute("onmouseout", "removePointInfo()");
  chartGroup.appendChild(circle);
  // add a new line to the new node on the graph
  current = dataPath.getAttribute("d"); // current path definition
  // update path definition
  if (!current || current == "")
    dataPath.setAttribute("d", " M " + coordX + " " + coordY);
  else
    dataPath.setAttribute("d", current + " L " + coordX + " " + coordY);
}

// initiates asynchronous request to retrieve new chart data
function updateChart()
{
  // builds the query string
  param = "?lastX=" + lastX + ((lastY != -1) ? "&lastY=" + lastY : "");
  // make the request through either AJAX
  if (window.getURL)
    // Supported by Adobe's SVG Viewer and Apache Batik
    getURL("svg_chart.php" + param, handleResults);
  else
```

```
        // Supported by Mozilla, implemented in ajaxRequest.js
        ajaxRequest("svg_chart.php" + param, handleResults);
}

// callback function that reads data received from server
function handleResults(data)
{
    // get the response data
    if (window.getURL)
        responseText = data.content;
    else
        responseText = data;
    // split the pair to obtain the X and Y coordinates
    var newCoords = responseText.split(",");
    // draw a new node at these coordinates
    addPoint(newCoords[0], newCoords[1]);
    // restart sequence
    setTimeout("updateChart()", updateInterval)
}
```

6. Finally, create the server-side script, named svg_chart.php:

```php
<?php
// variable initialization
$maxX = 50; // our max X
$maxY = 100; //our max Y
$maxVariation = $maxY / 7; // maximum Y variation for one step
// client tells last X value generated (defaults to -1)
if (isset($_GET['lastX']))
    $lastX = $_GET['lastX'];
else
    $lastX = -1;
// client tells last Y value generated (defaults to random)
if (isset($_GET['lastY']))
    $lastY = $_GET['lastY'];
else
    $lastY = rand(0, $maxY);
// calculate a new random number
$randomY = (int) ($lastY + $maxVariation - rand(0, $maxVariation*2));
// make sure the new Y is between 0 and $maxY
while ($randomY < 0) $randomY += $maxVariation;
while ($randomY > $maxY) $randomY -= $maxVariation;
// generate a new pair of numbers
$output = $lastX + 1 . ',' . $randomY;
// clear the output
if(ob_get_length()) ob_clean();
// headers are sent to prevent browsers from caching
header('Expires: Fri, 25 Dec 1980 00:00:00 GMT'); // time in the past
header('Last-Modified: ' . gmdate('D, d M Y H:i:s') . 'GMT');
header('Cache-Control: no-cache, must-revalidate');
header('Pragma: no-cache');
// send the results to the client
echo $output;
?>
```

7. Load http://localhost/ajax/svg_chart, and admire your brand new chart!

What Just Happened?

Let's briefly look at the important elements of the code, starting with the server. The svg_chart.php script is called asynchronously to generate a new set of (X, Y) coordinates to be displayed by the client in the chart. The client is supposed to tell the server the previously generated coordinates, and based on that data, the server generates a new set. This simulates pretty well a real-world scenario. The previously generated coordinates are sent via GET as two parameters named lastX and lastY. To test the server-side functionality independently of the rest of the solution, try loading http://localhost/ajax/svg_chart/svg_chart.php?lastX=5&lastY=44:

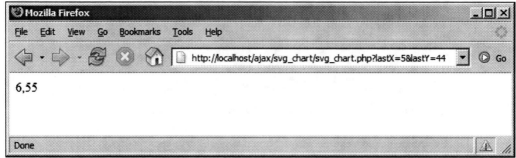

Figure 7.3: The Server generating a New Set of Coordinates for the Client

On the client, everything starts with index.html, which is really simple; all it does is to load the SVG file. The best way to do this at the moment is by using an <embed> element, which isn't supported by W3C (you can also use <object> and <iframe>, but they are more problematic—see http://www.w3schools.com/svg/svg_inhtml.asp):

```
<body>
  <embed src="chart.svg" width="600" height="450" type="image/svg+xml" />
</body>
```

And here it comes—chart.svg. This file isn't very impressive by itself, because it uses functionality provided by the JavaScript files (notice the onload event), but it includes the chart title:

```
<svg width="100%" height="100%" xmlns="http://www.w3.org/2000/svg"
xmlns:xlink="http://www.w3.org/1999/xlink" onload="init(evt)">
  <script type="text/ecmascript" xlink:href="ajaxRequest.js"/>
  <script type="text/ecmascript" xlink:href="realTimeChart.js"/>
  <a xlink:href="http://ajaxphp.packtpub.com">
    <text x="200" y="20">
      SVG with AJAX and PHP Demo
    </text>
  </a>
</svg>
```

chart.svg references two JavaScript files:

ajaxRequest.js contains the engine that implements asynchronous HTTP request functionality using the XMLHttpRequest object. This engine is used by realTimeChart.js to get new chart data from the server when the Firefox web browser is used. For the Adobe SVG and Apache Batik implementations, we use specific functionality provided by these engines through their getURL methods instead. See the updateChart method in realTimeChart.js for details.

The code in ajaxRequest.js contains a different coding pattern than what you've met so far in the book. What is important to understand is:

- All HTTP requests go through a single XMLHttpRequest instance, rather than automatically creating new XMLHttpRequest objects for each call, as implemented in other patterns. This way we are guaranteed to receive responses in the same order as they were requested, which is important for our charting application (and for any other application where the responses must come in order). If the connection is busy processing a previous request, our code waits for one second, and then retries. This technique is also friendly in its use of the web server resources.

- The ajaxRequest() method receives as parameter the URL to connect to, and a reference to the callback function to be called when the server response is received. This is a good technique to implement when you need the flexibility to access the same functionality from several sources.

- The handleGettingResults() method is defined inside the ajaxRequest method. This is one of JavaScript's features that enable emulating OOP functionality. So far we haven't used these features because we think they bring real benefits only when writing large applications and they require a longer learning curve for programmers inexperienced in OOP techniques. If you like this technique, you'll find it easy to implement it in your applications.

realTimeChart.js contains all the functionality that generates the SVG chart. The code contains detailed comments about the specific techniques. Here is a short description of each of the methods:

- init() is called when the page loads to perform the chart initialization. This method generates the SVG code for the chart axis and builds the initial structure for the whole chart. Initially, the numbers for the axis units are drawn with white font to make them invisible. We need this because of a problem in the Firefox SVG implementation that doesn't allow calculating the text size and positioning it correctly before it is rendered on the screen. Using pre-calculated values isn't an option because the grid is configurable and its axis can be populated with different values. To overcome this problem, init() uses setTimeout() to execute refreshXYIndexes() after half a second.

- refreshXYIndexes() is able to calculate the correct positions for the text on the axis units, even with Firefox 1.5. After it sets the new coordinates, it changes the color of the text from white to black, making it visible.

- createPointInfo() is called from the onmouseover function of the chart nodes to display the node coordinates.

- removePointInfo() is called from the onmouseout event to remove the displayed node coordinates.

- updateChart() is the function that initiates the asynchronous request. The getURL method is used if available (this method is supported by Adobe SVG and Apache Batik). Otherwise, the ajaxRequest method (from ajaxRequest.js) is used to make the request. When calling the server, the pair of previously generated coordinates is sent via GET, which the server uses to calculate the new values.

- `handleResults()` is the callback method that is called by `ajaxRequest` when the response from the server is received. This response is read (again, with SVG implementation-specific code), and the coordinates generated by the server are sent to `addPoint()`.

- `addPoint()` receives a set of coordinates used to generate a new node on the chart. These coordinates are saved for later, because on the next request they will be sent to the server. The server will use these coordinates to calculate the new ones for the client, enabling the simple mechanism of managing state: with each new request the X coordinate is increased by one and the Y is calculated randomly, but with a function that takes into account the previously generated Y coordinate.

Summary

Whether you like SVG or not (especially in the light of the recent SVG versus Flash wars), you must admit it allows implementing powerful functionality in web pages. Having tasted its functionality, you'll now know in which projects you might consider using it. If you are serious about SVG, be sure to check out the visual editors around, which make SVG creation a lot easier. You may also consider purchasing one of the numerous SVG books.

8
AJAX Grid

Data grids have always been one of the areas where web applications have had a serious disadvantage compared to desktop programs. The fact that the page needed a full reload when switching between grid pages, or when updating grid details, harmed the application from a usability point of view. Technically, fully reloading the page has bad effects as well, unnecessarily wasting network resources.

But now you know there is a smarter solution to this problem. You can use AJAX to update the grid content without refreshing the page. You can keep your beautiful design in the client browser without even one page blink. Only the table data is refreshed, not the whole page.

The novelty in this chapter is that we'll use **Extensible Stylesheet Language Transformation (XSLT)** and **XML Path Language (XPath)** to generate the client output. XSLT and XPath are part of the **Extensible Stylesheet Language (XSL)** family. XSLT allows defining rules to transform an XML document to another format and XPath is a very powerful query language that allows performing searches and retrieving data from XML documents. When used to create web front ends, XSLT permits implementing a very flexible architecture, in which the server outputs the data in XML format, and that data is transformed to HTML using an XSL transformation. You can find an introduction to XSL in Appendix C at `http://ajaxphp.packtpub.com`, and a good description at `http://en.wikipedia.org/wiki/Extensible_Stylesheet_Language`.

> Note the XSL transformation can be applied at both client side and server side. The implementation in this chapter relies on client functionality to perform the transformation. This doesn't require any special features of the server, but it poses some constraints for the client. In Chapter 9, you will see how to apply the transformation at the server side using PHP functionality, in which case you require this feature to be enabled in PHP, but the solution works with any client, as the client receives directly the HTML code it is supposed to display.

In this chapter, you'll use:

- XSL to generate an HTML data grid based on XML data received from the server.
- AJAX to implement the editable data grid. The user should be able to switch between product pages and edit product details without experiencing any page reloads.

Implementing the AJAX Grid Using Client-Side XSLT

In this case study, you will build an AJAX-enabled editable data grid. The products used to populate the grid were kindly provided to us by http://www.the-joke-shop.com/.

Figure 8.1 shows the second page of products and Figure 8.2 shows how the grid looks after the Edit link is clicked, and one of the products enters edit mode.

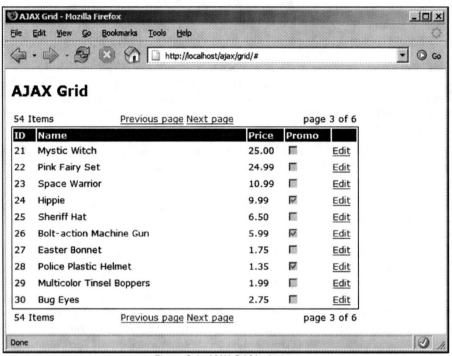

Figure 8.1: AJAX Grid in Action

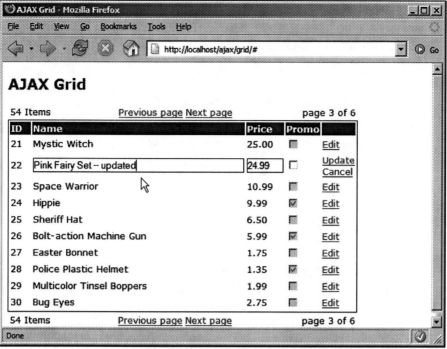

Figure 8.2: AJAX Grid in Edit Mode

Because there's a lot of dynamically output data to generate, this is a good opportunity to learn about XSLT.

Let's first write the code so you'll have a working solution, and then we will comment upon it. The program will be composed of the following files:

- `grid.php`
- `grid.class.php`
- `error_handler.php`
- `config.php`
- `grid.css`
- `index.html`
- `grid.xsl`
- `grid.js`

Time for Action—AJAX Grid

1. Let's start by preparing the database for this exercise. We basically need a table with products. You can either execute the SQL script `product.sql` from the code download, or you can type it (the code snippet below creates only the first 10 products; please use the code download for the complete list of products):

```
CREATE TABLE product
(
  product_id INT UNSIGNED NOT NULL AUTO_INCREMENT,
  name VARCHAR(50) NOT NULL DEFAULT '',
  price DECIMAL(10,2) NOT NULL DEFAULT '0.00',
  on_promotion TINYINT NOT NULL DEFAULT '0',
  PRIMARY KEY (product_id)
);
INSERT INTO product(name, price, on_promotion)
          VALUES('Santa Costume', 14.99, 0);
INSERT INTO product(name, price, on_promotion)
          VALUES('Medieval Lady', 49.99, 1);
INSERT INTO product(name, price, on_promotion)
          VALUES('Caveman', 12.99, 0);
INSERT INTO product(name, price, on_promotion)
          VALUES('Costume Ghoul', 18.99, 0);
INSERT INTO product(name, price, on_promotion)
          VALUES('Ninja', 15.99, 0);
INSERT INTO product(name, price, on_promotion)
          VALUES('Monk', 13.99, 0);
INSERT INTO product(name, price, on_promotion)
          VALUES('Elvis Black Costume', 35.99, 0);
INSERT INTO product(name, price, on_promotion)
          VALUES('Robin Hood', 18.99, 0);
INSERT INTO product(name, price, on_promotion)
          VALUES('Pierot Clown', 22.99, 1);
INSERT INTO product(name, price, on_promotion)
          VALUES('Austin Powers', 49.99, 0);
```

2. Create a new subfolder called grid under your ajax folder.

3. We'll start writing the code with the server side. In the grid folder, create a new file called grid.php, which will respond to client's asynchronous requests:

```php
<?php
// load error handling script and the Grid class
require_once('error_handler.php');
require_once('grid.class.php');
// the 'action' parameter should be FEED_GRID_PAGE or UPDATE_ROW
if (!isset($_GET['action']))
{
  echo 'Server error: client command missing.';
  exit;
}
else
{
  // store the action to be performed in the $action variable
  $action = $_GET['action'];
}
// create Grid instance
$grid = new Grid($action);
// valid action values are FEED_GRID_PAGE and UPDATE_ROW
if ($action == 'FEED_GRID_PAGE')
{
  // retrieve the page number
  $page = $_GET['page'];
  // read the products on the page
  $grid->readPage($page);
}
else if ($action == 'UPDATE_ROW')
{
  // retrieve parameters
  $id = $_GET['id'];
  $on_promotion = $_GET['on_promotion'];
  $price = $_GET['price'];
```

```php
$name = $_GET['name'];
// update the record
$grid->updateRecord($id, $on_promotion, $price, $name);
}
else
  echo 'Server error: client command unrecognized.';
// clear the output
if(ob_get_length()) ob_clean();
// headers are sent to prevent browsers from caching
header('Expires: Fri, 25 Dec 1980 00:00:00 GMT'); // time in the past
header('Last-Modified: ' . gmdate('D, d M Y H:i:s') . 'GMT');
header('Cache-Control: no-cache, must-revalidate');
header('Pragma: no-cache');
header('Content-Type: text/xml');
// generate the output in XML format
header('Content-type: text/xml');
echo '<?xml version="1.0" encoding="ISO-8859-1"?>';
echo '<data>';
echo '<action>' . $action . '</action>';
echo $grid->getParamsXML();
echo $grid->getGridXML();
echo '</data>';
?>
```

4. Create a new file called grid.class.php, and add the following code to it:

```php
<?php
// load configuration file
require_once('config.php');
// start session
session_start();

// includes functionality to manipulate the products list
class Grid
{
  // grid pages count
  public $mTotalPages;
  // grid items count
  public $mItemsCount;
  // index of page to be returned
  public $mReturnedPage;
  // database handler
  private $mMysqli;
  // database handler
  private $grid;

  // class constructor
  function __construct()
  {
    // create the MySQL connection
    $this->mMysqli = new mysqli(DB_HOST, DB_USER, DB_PASSWORD,
                                DB_DATABASE);
    // call countAllRecords to get the number of grid records
    $this->mItemsCount = $this->countAllRecords();
  }

  // class destructor, closes database connection
  function __destruct()
  {
    $this->mMysqli->close();
  }
  // read a page of products and save it to $this->grid
  public function readPage($page)
  {
    // create the SQL query that returns a page of products
    $queryString = $this->createSubpageQuery('SELECT * FROM product',
                                             $page);
```

```
      // execute the query
      if ($result = $this->mMysqli->query($queryString))
      {
        // fetch associative array
        while ($row = $result->fetch_assoc())
        {
          // build the XML structure containing products
          $this->grid .= '<row>';
          foreach($row as $name=>$val)
            $this->grid .= '<' . $name . '>' .
                           htmlentities($val) .
                           '</' . $name . '>';
          $this->grid .= '</row>';
        }
        // close the results stream
        $result->close();
      }
    }

    // update a product
    public function updateRecord($id, $on_promotion, $price, $name)
    {
      // escape input data for safely using it in SQL statements
      $id = $this->mMysqli->real_escape_string($id);
      $on_promotion = $this->mMysqli->real_escape_string($on_promotion);
      $price = $this->mMysqli->real_escape_string($price);
      $name = $this->mMysqli->real_escape_string($name);
      // build the SQL query that updates a product record
      $queryString =  'UPDATE product SET name="' . $name . '", ' .
                      'price=' . $price . ',' .
                      'on_promotion=' . $on_promotion .
                      ' WHERE product_id=' . $id;
      // execute the SQL command
      $this->mMysqli->query($queryString);
    }

    // returns data about the current request (number of grid pages, etc)
    public function getParamsXML()
    {
      // calculate the previous page number
      $previous_page =
        ($this->mReturnedPage == 1) ? '' : $this->mReturnedPage-1;
      // calculate the next page number
      $next_page = ($this->mTotalPages == $this->mReturnedPage) ?
                   '' : $this->mReturnedPage + 1;
      // return the parameters
      return '<params>' .
             '<returned_page>' . $this->mReturnedPage . '</returned_page>'.
             '<total_pages>' . $this->mTotalPages . '</total_pages>'.
             '<items_count>' . $this->mItemsCount . '</items_count>'.
             '<previous_page>' . $previous_page . '</previous_page>'.
             '<next_page>' . $next_page . '</next_page>' .
             '</params>';
    }

    // returns the current grid page in XML format
    public function getGridXML()
    {
      return '<grid>' . $this->grid . '</grid>';
    }

    // returns the total number of records for the grid
    private function countAllRecords()
    {
      /* if the record count isn't already cached in the session,
         read the value from the database */
```

```php
        if (!isset($_SESSION['record_count']))
        {
          // the query that returns the record count
          $count_query = 'SELECT COUNT(*) FROM product';
          // execute the query and fetch the result
          if ($result = $this->mMysqli->query($count_query))
          {
            // retrieve the first returned row
            $row = $result->fetch_row();
            /* retrieve the first column of the first row (it represents the
               records count that we were looking for), and save its value in
               the session */
            $_SESSION['record_count'] = $row[0];
            // close the database handle
            $result->close();
          }
        }
        // read the record count from the session and return it
        return $_SESSION['record_count'];
    }

    // receives a SELECT query that returns all products and modifies it
    // to return only a page of products
    private function createSubpageQuery($queryString, $pageNo)
    {
      // if we have few products then we don't implement pagination
      if ($this->mItemsCount <= ROWS_PER_VIEW)
      {
        $pageNo = 1;
        $this->mTotalPages = 1;
      }
      // else we calculate number of pages and build new SELECT query
      else
      {
        $this->mTotalPages = ceil($this->mItemsCount / ROWS_PER_VIEW);
        $start_page = ($pageNo - 1) * ROWS_PER_VIEW;
        $queryString .= ' LIMIT ' . $start_page . ',' . ROWS_PER_VIEW;
      }
      // save the number of the returned page
      $this->mReturnedPage = $pageNo;
      // returns the new query string
      return $queryString;
    }
// end class Grid
}
?>
```

5. Add the configuration file, config.php:

```php
<?php
// defines database connection data
define('DB_HOST', 'localhost');
define('DB_USER', 'ajaxuser');
define('DB_PASSWORD', 'practical');
define('DB_DATABASE', 'ajax');
// defines the number of visible rows in grid
define('ROWS_PER_VIEW', 10);
?>
```

6. Create the error-handling script, error_handler.php with the following contents:

```php
<?php
// set the user error handler method to be error_handler
set_error_handler('error_handler', E_ALL);
// error handler function
function error_handler($errNo, $errStr, $errFile, $errLine)
{
```

```
       // clear any output that has already been generated
       ob_clean();
       // output the error message
       $error_message = 'ERRNO: ' . $errNo . chr(10) .
                        'TEXT: ' . $errStr . chr(10) .
                        'LOCATION: ' . $errFile .
                        ', line ' . $errLine;
       echo $error_message;
       // prevent processing any more PHP scripts
       exit;
    }
    ?>
```

7. It's time for the client now. Start by creating index.html:

```html
<!DOCTYPE html PUBLIC "-//W3C//DTD XHTML 1.0 Transitional//EN"
"http://www.w3.org/TR/xhtml1/DTD/xhtml1-transitional.dtd">
<html>
  <head>
    <title>AJAX Grid</title>
    <script type="text/javascript" src="grid.js"></script>
    <link href="grid.css" type="text/css" rel="stylesheet"/>
  </head>
    <body onload="init();">
    <div id="gridDiv" />
  </body>
</html>
```

8. Now let's create the XSLT file named grid.xsl that will be used in the JavaScript code to generate the output:

```xml
<?xml version="1.0" encoding="ISO-8859-1"?>
<xsl:stylesheet version="1.0"
xmlns:xsl="http://www.w3.org/1999/XSL/Transform">
  <xsl:template match="/">
    <h2>AJAX Grid</h2>
    <xsl:call-template name="menu"/>
    <form id="grid_form_id">
      <table class="list">
        <tr>
          <th class="th1">ID</th>
          <th class="th2">Name</th>
          <th class="th3">Price</th>
          <th class="th4">Promo</th>
          <th class="th5"></th>
        </tr>
        <xsl:for-each select="data/grid/row">
          <xsl:element name="tr">
            <xsl:attribute name="id">
              <xsl:value-of select="product_id" />
            </xsl:attribute>
            <td><xsl:value-of select="product_id" /></td>
            <td><xsl:value-of select="name" /> </td>
            <td><xsl:value-of select="price" /></td>
            <td>
              <xsl:choose>
                <xsl:when test="on_promotion &gt; 0">
                  <input type="checkbox" name="on_promotion"
                         disabled="disabled" checked="checked"/>
                </xsl:when>
                <xsl:otherwise>
                  <input type="checkbox" name="on_promotion"
                  disabled="disabled"/>
                </xsl:otherwise>
              </xsl:choose>
            </td>
```

```
                    <td>
                      <xsl:element name="a">
                        <xsl:attribute name = "href">#</xsl:attribute>
                        <xsl:attribute name = "onclick">
                          editId(<xsl:value-of select="product_id" />, true)
                        </xsl:attribute>
                        Edit
                      </xsl:element>
                    </td>
                  </xsl:element>
                </xsl:for-each>
              </table>
            </form>
            <xsl:call-template name="menu" />
          </xsl:template>
          <xsl:template name="menu">
            <xsl:for-each select="data/params">
              <table>
                <tr>
                  <td class="left">
                    <xsl:value-of select="items_count" /> Items
                  </td>
                  <td class="right">
                    <xsl:choose>
                      <xsl:when test="previous_page>0">
                        <xsl:element name="a" >
                          <xsl:attribute name="href" >#</xsl:attribute>
                          <xsl:attribute name="onclick">
                            loadGridPage(<xsl:value-of select="previous_page"/>)
                          </xsl:attribute>
                          Previous page
                        </xsl:element>
                      </xsl:when>
                    </xsl:choose>
                  </td>
                  <td class="left">
                    <xsl:choose>
                      <xsl:when test="next_page>0">
                        <xsl:element name="a">
                          <xsl:attribute name = "href" >#</xsl:attribute>
                          <xsl:attribute name = "onclick">
                            loadGridPage(<xsl:value-of select="next_page"/>)
                          </xsl:attribute>
                          Next page
                        </xsl:element>
                      </xsl:when>
                    </xsl:choose>
                  </td>
                  <td class="right">
                    page <xsl:value-of select="returned_page" />
                    of <xsl:value-of select="total_pages" />
                  </td>
                </tr>
              </table>
            </xsl:for-each>
          </xsl:template>
        </xsl:stylesheet>
```

9. Create `grid.js`:

```
// stores the reference to the XMLHttpRequest object
var xmlHttp = createXmlHttpRequestObject();
// the name of the XSLT file
var xsltFileUrl = "grid.xsl";
// the file that returns the requested data in XML format
var feedGridUrl = "grid.php";
```

```
        // the id of the grid div
        var gridDivId = "gridDiv";
        // the grid of the status div
        var statusDivId = "statusDiv";
        // stores temporary row data
        var tempRow;
        // the ID of the product being edited
        var editableId = null;
        // the XSLT document
        var stylesheetDoc;

        // eveything starts here
        function init()
        {
          // test if user has browser that supports native XSLT functionality
          if(window.XMLHttpRequest && window.XSLTProcessor && window.DOMParser)
          {
            // load the grid
            loadStylesheet();
            loadGridPage(1);
            return;
          }
          // test if user has Internet Explorer with proper XSLT support
          if (window.ActiveXObject && createMsxml2DOMDocumentObject())
          {
            // load the grid
            loadStylesheet();
            loadGridPage(1);
            // exit the function
            return;
          }
          // if browser functionality testing failed, alert the user
          alert("Your browser doesn't support the necessary functionality.");
        }

        function createMsxml2DOMDocumentObject()
        {
          // will store the reference to the MSXML object
          var msxml2DOM;
          // MSXML versions that can be used for our grid
          var msxml2DOMDocumentVersions = new Array("Msxml2.DOMDocument.6.0",
                                                    "Msxml2.DOMDocument.5.0",
                                                    "Msxml2.DOMDocument.4.0");
          // try to find a good MSXML object
          for (var i=0; i<msxml2DOMDocumentVersions.length && !msxml2DOM; i++)
          {
            try
            {
              // try to create an object
              msxml2DOM = new ActiveXObject(msxml2DOMDocumentVersions[i]);
            }
            catch (e) {}
          }
          // return the created object or display an error message
          if (!msxml2DOM)
            alert("Please upgrade your MSXML version from \n" +
                  "http://msdn.microsoft.com/XML/XMLDownloads/default.aspx");
          else
            return msxml2DOM;
        }

        // creates an XMLHttpRequest instance
        function createXmlHttpRequestObject()
        {
          // will store the reference to the XMLHttpRequest object
          var xmlHttp;
```

```
    // this should work for all browsers except IE6 and older
    try
    {
      // try to create XMLHttpRequest object
      xmlHttp = new XMLHttpRequest();
    }
    catch(e)
    {
      // assume IE6 or older
      var XmlHttpVersions = new Array("MSXML2.XMLHTTP.6.0",
                                      "MSXML2.XMLHTTP.5.0",
                                      "MSXML2.XMLHTTP.4.0",
                                      "MSXML2.XMLHTTP.3.0",
                                      "MSXML2.XMLHTTP",
                                      "Microsoft.XMLHTTP");
      // try every prog id until one works
      for (var i=0; i<XmlHttpVersions.length && !xmlHttp; i++)
      {
        try
        {
          // try to create XMLHttpRequest object
          xmlHttp = new ActiveXObject(XmlHttpVersions[i]);
        }
        catch (e) {}
      }
    }
    // return the created object or display an error message
    if (!xmlHttp)
      alert("Error creating the XMLHttpRequest object.");
    else
      return xmlHttp;
}

// loads the stylesheet from the server using a synchronous request
function loadStylesheet()
{
  // load the file from the server
  xmlHttp.open("GET", xsltFileUrl, false);
  xmlHttp.send(null);
  // try to load the XSLT document
  if (this.DOMParser) // browsers with native functionality
  {
    var dp = new DOMParser();
    stylesheetDoc = dp.parseFromString(xmlHttp.responseText, "text/xml");
  }
  else if (window.ActiveXObject) // Internet Explorer?
  {
    stylesheetDoc = createMsxml2DOMDocumentObject();
    stylesheetDoc.async = false;
    stylesheetDoc.load(xmlHttp.responseXML);
  }
}

// makes asynchronous request to load a new page of the grid
function loadGridPage(pageNo)
{
  // disable edit mode when loading new page
  editableId = false;
  // continue only if the XMLHttpRequest object isn't busy
  if (xmlHttp && (xmlHttp.readyState == 4 || xmlHttp.readyState == 0))
  {
    var query = feedGridUrl + "?action=FEED_GRID_PAGE&page=" + pageNo;
    xmlHttp.open("GET", query, true);
    xmlHttp.onreadystatechange = handleGridPageLoad;
    xmlHttp.send(null);
  }
}
```

```
// handle receiving the server response with a new page of products
function handleGridPageLoad()
{
  // when readyState is 4, we read the server response
  if (xmlHttp.readyState == 4)
  {
    // continue only if HTTP status is "OK"
    if (xmlHttp.status == 200)
    {
      // read the response
      response = xmlHttp.responseText;
      // server error?
      if (response.indexOf("ERRNO") >= 0
          || response.indexOf("error") >= 0
          || response.length == 0)
      {
        // display error message
        alert(response.length == 0 ? "Server serror." : response);
        // exit function
        return;
      }
      // the server response in XML format
      xmlResponse = xmlHttp.responseXML;
      // browser with native functionality?
      if (window.XMLHttpRequest && window.XSLTProcessor &&
          window.DOMParser)
      {
        // load the XSLT document
        var xsltProcessor = new XSLTProcessor();
        xsltProcessor.importStylesheet(stylesheetDoc);
        // generate the HTML code for the new page of products
        page = xsltProcessor.transformToFragment(xmlResponse, document);
        // display the page of products
        var gridDiv = document.getElementById(gridDivId);
        gridDiv.innerHTML = "";
        gridDiv.appendChild(page);
      }
      // Internet Explorer code
      else if (window.ActiveXObject)
      {
        // load the XSLT document
        var theDocument = createMsxml2DOMDocumentObject();
        theDocument.async = false;
        theDocument.load(xmlResponse);
        // display the page of products
        var gridDiv = document.getElementById(gridDivId);
        gridDiv.innerHTML = theDocument.transformNode(stylesheetDoc);
      }
    }
    else
    {
      alert("Error reading server response.")
    }
  }
}

// enters the product specified by id into edit mode if editMode is true,
// and cancels edit mode if editMode is false
function editId(id, editMode)
{
  // gets the <tr> element of the table that contains the table
  var productRow = document.getElementById(id).cells;
  // are we enabling edit mode?
  if(editMode)
  {
    // we can have only one row in edit mode at one time
```

```
    if(editableId) editId(editableId, false);
    // store current data, in case the user decides to cancel the changes
    save(id);
    // create editable text boxes
    productRow[1].innerHTML =
        '<input class="editName" type="text" name="name" ' +
        'value="' + productRow[1].innerHTML+'">';
    productRow[2].innerHTML =
        '<input class="editPrice" type="text" name="price" ' +
        'value="' + productRow[2].innerHTML+'">';
    productRow[3].getElementsByTagName("input")[0].disabled = false;
    productRow[4].innerHTML = '<a href="#" ' +
        'onclick="updateRow(document.forms.grid_form_id,' + id +
        ')">Update</a><br/><a href="#" onclick="editId(' + id +
        ',false)">Cancel</a>';
    // save the id of the product being edited
    editableId = id;
  }
  // if disabling edit mode...
  else
  {
    productRow[1].innerHTML = document.forms.grid_form_id.name.value;
    productRow[2].innerHTML = document.forms.grid_form_id.price.value;
    productRow[3].getElementsByTagName("input")[0].disabled = true;
    productRow[4].innerHTML = '<a href="#" onclick="editId(' + id +
                              ',true)">Edit</a>';
    // no product is being edited
    editableId = null;
  }
}

// saves the original product data before editing row
function save(id)
{
  // retrieve the product row
  var tr = document.getElementById(id).cells;
  // save the data
  tempRow = new Array(tr.length);
  for(var i=0; i<tr.length; i++)
    tempRow[i] = tr[i].innerHTML;
}

// cancels editing a row, restoring original values
function undo(id)
{
  // retrieve the product row
  var tr = document.getElementById(id).cells;
  // copy old values
  for(var i=0; i<tempRow.length; i++)
    tr[i].innerHTML = tempRow[i];
  // no editable row
  editableId = null;
}

// update one row in the grid if the connection is clear
function updateRow(grid, productId)
{
  // continue only if the XMLHttpRequest object isn't busy
  if (xmlHttp && (xmlHttp.readyState == 4 || xmlHttp.readyState == 0))
  {
    var query = feedGridUrl + "?action=UPDATE_ROW&id=" + productId +
                "&" + createUpdateUrl(grid);
    xmlHttp.open("GET", query, true);
    xmlHttp.onreadystatechange = handleUpdatingRow;
    xmlHttp.send(null);
  }
}
```

```
          // handle receiving a response from the server when updating a product
          function handleUpdatingRow()
          {
            // when readyState is 4, we read the server response
            if(xmlHttp.readyState == 4)
            {
              // continue only if HTTP status is "OK"
              if(xmlHttp.status == 200)
              {
                // read the response
                response = xmlHttp.responseText;
                // server error?
                if (response.indexOf("ERRNO") >= 0
                    || response.indexOf("error") >= 0
                    || response.length == 0)
                  alert(response.length == 0 ? "Server serror." : response);
                // if everything went well, cancel edit mode
                else
                  editId(editableId, false);
              }
              else
              {
                // undo any changes in case of error
                undo(editableId);
                alert("Error on server side.");
              }
            }
          }

          // creates query string parameters for updating a row
          function createUpdateUrl(grid)
          {
            // initialize query string
            var str = "";
            // build a query string with the values of the editable grid elements
            for(var i=0; i<grid.elements.length; i++)
              switch(grid.elements[i].type)
              {
                case "text":
                case "textarea":
                  str += grid.elements[i].name + "=" +
                         escape(grid.elements[i].value) + "&";
                  break;
                case "checkbox":
                  if (!grid.elements[i].disabled)
                    str += grid.elements[i].name + "=" +
                           (grid.elements[i].checked ? 1 : 0) + "&";
                  break;
              }
            // return the query string
            return str;
          }
```

10. Finally, create grid.css:

```
body
{
  font-family: Verdana, Arial;
  font-size: 10pt
}

table
{
  width: 500px;
}

td.right
{
```

```
      color: darkblue;
      text-align: right;
      width: 125px
}

td.left
{
      color: darkblue;
      text-align: left;
      width: 125px
}

table.list
{
      border: black 1px solid;
}

th
{
      text-align: left;
      background-color: navy;
      color: white
}

th.th1
{
      width: 30px
}

th.th2
{
      width: 300px
}

input.editName
{
      border: black 1px solid;
      width: 300px
}

input.editPrice
{
      border: black 1px solid;
      width: 50px
}
```

11. Load `http://localhost/ajax/grid` in your web browser, and test its functionality to make sure it works as expected (see Figures 8.1 and 8.2 for reference).

What Just Happened?

Let's dissect the code starting with the server-side functionality. At the heart of the server lies the database. In our case, we have a table called `product` with the following fields:

- `product_id` is the table's primary key, containing the numeric ID of the product.
- `name` is the product's name.
- `price` is the product's price.
- `on_promotion` is a bit field (should only take values of 0 or 1, although MySQL may permit more, depending on the version), which specifies if the product is on promotion. We used this field for our grid because it allows us to show how to use a checkbox to display the bit value.

217

As usual on the server, we have a PHP script, which in this case is named grid.php, that is the main access point for all asynchronous client requests.

grid.php expects to receive a query string parameter called action that tells it what action it is expected to perform. The possible values are:

- FEED_GRID_PAGE: This value is used to retrieve a page of products. Together with this parameter, the server also expects a parameter named page, which specifies what page of products to return.

- UPDATE_ROW: This value is used to update the details of a row that was edited by the user. For this action, the server also expects to receive the new values for the product, in four parameters named id, name, price, and on_promotion.

To see the data generated by the server, make a simple call to http://localhost/ajax/grid/grid.php?action=FEED_GRID_PAGE&page=1. Using the default database information, the output will look like Figure 8.3:

Figure 8.3: Server Returning the First Page of Products

On the client, this data will be parsed and transformed to the HTML grid using an XSL transformation. This code was tested with Mozilla and Internet Explorer, which at the time of writing supported the required functionality. Opera is expected to support XSL Transformations starting with version 9.

The XSL transformation code is defined in `grid.xsl`. Please see Appendix C at `http://ajaxphp.packtpub.com` for a primer into the world of XSL, and refer one of the many available books and online resources for digging into the details. XSL is a really big subject, so be prepared for a lot of learning if you intend to master it.

The first function in the client script, `grid.js`, is `init()`. This function checks if the user's browser has the necessary features to perform the XSL transformation:

```
// eveything starts here
function init()
{
  // test if user has browser that supports native XSLT functionality
  if(window.XMLHttpRequest && window.XSLTProcessor && window.DOMParser)
  {
    // load the grid
    loadStylesheet();
    loadGridPage(1);
    return;
  }
  // test if user has Internet Explorer with proper XSLT support
  if (window.ActiveXObject && createMsxml2DOMDocumentObject())
  {
    // load the grid
    loadStylesheet();
    loadGridPage(1);
    // exit the function
    return;
  }
  // if browser functionality testing failed, alert the user
  alert("Your browser doesn't support the necessary functionality.");
}
```

This function allows continuing if the browser is either Internet Explorer (in which case the user also needs a recent MSXML version), or a browser that natively supports the XMLHttpRequest, XSLTProcessor, and DOMParser classes.

The second function that is important to understand is `loadStylesheet()`. This function is called once when the page loads, to request the `grid.xsl` file from the server, which is loaded locally. The `grid.xls` file is loaded using a synchronous call, and then is stored using techniques specific to the user's browser, depending on whether the browser has native functionality, or it is Internet Explorer, in which case an `ActiveXObject` is used:

```
// loads the stylesheet from the server using a synchronous request
function loadStylesheet()
{
  // load the file from the server
  xmlHttp.open("GET", xsltFileUrl, false);
  xmlHttp.send(null);
  // try to load the XSLT document
  if (this.DOMParser) // browsers with native functionality
  {
    var dp = new DOMParser();
    stylesheetDoc = dp.parseFromString(xmlHttp.responseText, "text/xml");
  }
  else if (window.ActiveXObject) // Internet Explorer?
```

```
    {
      stylesheetDoc = createMsxml2DOMDocumentObject();
      stylesheetDoc.async = false;
      stylesheetDoc.load(xmlHttp.responseXML);
    }
  }
```

The loadGridPage function is called once when the page loads, and then each time the user clicks Previous Page or Next Page, to load a new page of data. This function calls the server asynchronously, specifying the page of products that needs to be retrieved:

```
// makes asynchronous request to load a new page of the grid
function loadGridPage(pageNo)
{
  // disable edit mode when loading new page
  editableId = false;
  // continue only if the XMLHttpRequest object isn't busy
  if (xmlHttp && (xmlHttp.readyState == 4 || xmlHttp.readyState == 0))
  {
    var query = feedGridUrl + "?action=FEED_GRID_PAGE&page=" + pageNo;
    xmlHttp.open("GET", query, true);
    xmlHttp.onreadystatechange = handleGridPageLoad;
    xmlHttp.send(null);
  }
}
```

The handleGridPageLoad callback function is called to handle the server response. After the typical error handling mechanism, it reveals the code that effectively transforms the XML structure received from the server to HTML code that is displayed to the client. The transformation code is, again, browser-specific, performing functionality differently for Internet Explorer and for the browsers with native XLS support:

```
// the server response in XML format
xmlResponse = xmlHttp.responseXML;
// browser with native functionality?
if (window.XMLHttpRequest && window.XSLTProcessor && window.DOMParser)
{
  // load the XSLT document
  var xsltProcessor = new XSLTProcessor();
  xsltProcessor.importStylesheet(stylesheetDoc);
  // generate the HTML code for the new page of products
  page = xsltProcessor.transformToFragment(xmlResponse, document);
  // display the page of products
  var gridDiv = document.getElementById(gridDivId);
  gridDiv.innerHTML = "";
  gridDiv.appendChild(page);
}
// Internet Explorer code
else if (window.ActiveXObject)
{
  // load the XSLT document
  var theDocument = createMsxml2DOMDocumentObject();
  theDocument.async = false;
  theDocument.load(xmlResponse);
  // display the page of products
  var gridDiv = document.getElementById(gridDivId);
  gridDiv.innerHTML = theDocument.transformNode(stylesheetDoc);
}
```

Then we have the editId function, which is called when the Edit or Cancel links are clicked in the grid, to enable or disable edit mode. When edit mode is enabled, the product name, its price, and its promotion checkbox are transformed to editable controls. When disabling edit mode, the same elements are changed back to their non-editable state.

save() and undo() are helper functions used for editing rows. The save function saves the original product values, which are loaded back to the grid by undo if the user changes her or his mind about the change and clicks the Cancel link.

Row updating functionality is supported by the updateRow function, which is called when the Update link is clicked. updateRow() makes an asynchronous call to the server, specifying the new product values, which are composed into the query string using the createUpdateUrl helper function:

```
// update one row in the grid if the connection is clear
function updateRow(grid, productId)
{
  // continue only if the XMLHttpRequest object isn't busy
  if (xmlHttp && (xmlHttp.readyState == 4 || xmlHttp.readyState == 0))
  {
    var query = feedGridUrl + "?action=UPDATE_ROW&id=" + productId +
                "&" + createUpdateUrl(grid);
    xmlHttp.open("GET", query, true);
    xmlHttp.onreadystatechange = handleUpdatingRow;
    xmlHttp.send(null);
  }
}
```

The handleUpdatingRow callback function has the responsibility to ensure that the product change is performed successfully, in which case it disables edit mode for the row, or displays an error message if an error happened on the server side:

```
// continue only if HTTP status is "OK"
if(xmlHttp.status == 200)
{
  // read the response
  response = xmlHttp.responseText;
  // server error?
  if (response.indexOf("ERRNO") >= 0
      || response.indexOf("error") >= 0
      || response.length == 0)
    alert(response.length == 0 ? "Server serror." : response);
  // if everything went well, cancel edit mode
  else
    editId(editableId, false);
}
```

The technique for displaying the error was implemented in other exercises as well. If the server returned a specific error message, that message is displayed to the user. If PHP is configured not to output errors, the response from the server will be void, in which case we simply display a generic error message.

Summary

In this chapter you have implemented already familiar AJAX techniques to build a data grid. You have met XSL, which allows implementing very powerful architectures where the server side of your application doesn't need to deal with presentation.

Having XSL deal with formatting the data to be displayed to your visitors is the professional way to deal with these kinds of tasks, and if you are serious about web development, it is recommended to learn XSL well. Beware; this will be time and energy consuming, but in the end the effort will be well worth it.

AJAX RSS Reader

In the last few years, the Web has become much more active than it used to be. Today, we see an explosion of new sources of information, such as news sites appearing every day (such as http://www.digg.com and http://www.newsvine.com), and the growing trend of web life—weblogs (every person seems to have a weblog these days).

As a natural reaction to this invasion of information, many systems that allow grouping, filtering, and aggregating this information have appeared. This is implemented in practice through **web syndication**, which is that form of syndication where parts of a website (such as news, weblog posts, articles, and so on) are made available for other sites or applications to use.

In order to be usable by other parties, the data to be shared must be in a generic format that can be laid out in different formats than in the original source, and when it comes to such formats, **RSS 2.0** and **Atom** are the most popular choices.

Learn more about the history of RSS and Atom in the Wikipedia—the link to the RSS page is http://en.wikipedia.org/wiki/RSS_(protocol).

In this chapter, we'll analyze the RSS file format, then take a look at Google Reader (Google's RSS aggregator), and then build our own RSS aggregator web page with AJAX and PHP.

Working with RSS

RSS is a widely used XML-based standard, used to exchange information between applications on the Internet. One of the great advantages of XML is that it is plain text, thus easily read by any application. RSS feeds can be viewed as plain text files, but it doesn't make much sense to use them like that, as they are meant to be read by specialized software that generates web content based on their data.

While RSS is not the only standard for expressing feeds as XML, we've chosen to use this format in the case study because it's very widely used. In order to better understand RSS, we need to see what lies underneath the name; the RSS document structure, that is.

The RSS Document Structure

The first version of RSS was created in 1999. This is known as version 0.9. Since then it has evolved to the current 2.0.1 version, which has been *frozen* by the development community, as future development is expected to be done under a different name.

A typical RSS feed might look like this:

```
<rss version="2.0">
  <channel>
    <title>CNN.com</title>
    <link>http://www.example.org</link>
    <description>A short description of this feed</description>
    <language>en</language>
    <pubDate>Mon, 17 Oct 2005 07:56:23 EDT</pubDate>
    <item>
      <title>Catchy Title</title>
      <link>http://www.example.org/2005/11/catchy-title.html</link>
      <description>
        The description can hold any content you wish, including XHTML.
      </description>
      <pubDate>Mon, 17 Oct 2005 07:55:28 EDT</pubDate>
    </item>
    <item>
      <title>Another Catchy Title</title>
      <link>http://www.example.org/2005/11/another-catchy-title.html</link>
      <description>
        The description can hold any content you wish, including XHTML.
      </description>
      <pubDate>Mon, 17 Oct 2005 07:55:28 EDT</pubDate>
    </item>
  </chanel>
</rss>
```

The feed may contain any number of `<item>` items, each item holding different news or blog entries or whatever content you wish to store.

This is all plain text, but as we stated above, we need special software that will parse the XML and return the information we want. An RSS parser is called an **aggregator** because it can usually extract and aggregate information from more than one RSS source.

Such an application is Google Reader, an online service from Google, launched in fall 2005. A veteran web-based RSS reader service is the one at `http://www.bloglines.com`.

Google Reader

Google Reader (`http://reader.google.com`) provides a simple and intuitive AJAX-enabled interface that helps users keep track of their RSS subscriptions and reading. It hasn't been long since this service was launched (it's still in beta at the moment of writing), but it has already got a great deal of attention from users. Figure 9.1 shows the Google Reader in action, reading a news item from Packt Publishing's RSS feed.

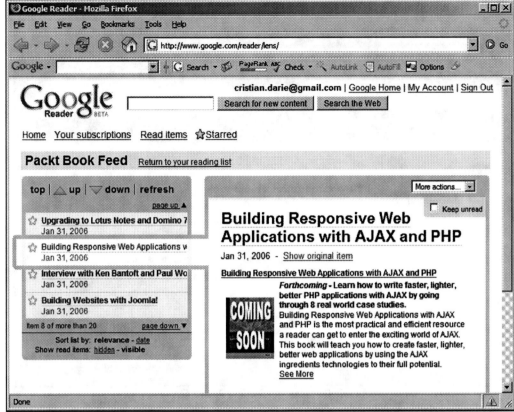

Figure 9.1: Managing RSS Subscriptions (Feeds) on Google Reader

Implementing the AJAX RSS Reader

In order for this exercise to function correctly, you need to enable XSL support in your PHP installation. Appendix A contains installation instructions that include XSL support.

In the exercise that will follow we will build our own AJAX-enabled RSS reader application. The main characteristics for the application are:

1. We'll keep the application simple. The list of feeds will be hard-coded in a PHP file on the server.

2. We'll use XSLT to transform the RSS feed data into something that we can display to the visitor. In this chapter, the XSL transformation will be performed on the server side, using PHP code.

3. We'll use the SimpleXML library to read the XML response from the news server. SimpleXML was introduced in PHP 5, and you can find its official documentation at http://php.net/simplexml. SimpleXML is an excellent library that can make reading XML sources much easier than using the DOM.

4. The application will look like Figure 9.2:

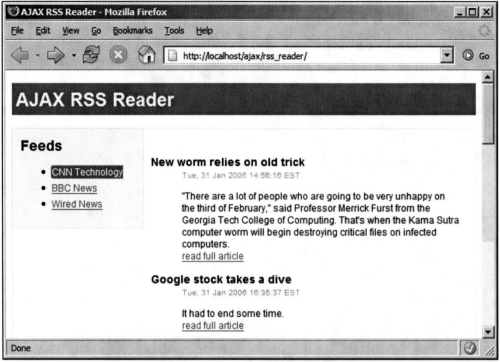

Figure 9.2: Our AJAX-enabled RSS Reader Start Page

Feeds are loaded dynamically and are displayed as links in the left column. Clicking on a feed will trigger an HTTP request and the server script will acquire the desired RSS feed.

The server then formats the feed with XSL and returns an XML string. Results are then displayed in a human-readable form.

Time for Action—Building the RSS Reader Application

1. In your ajax folder, create a new folder named rss_reader.

2. Let's start with the server. Create a new file named rss_reader.php, and add this code to it:

```php
<?php
// load helper scripts
require_once ('error_handler.php');
require_once ('rss_reader.class.php');
// create a new RSS Reader instance
$reader = new CRssReader(urldecode($_POST['feed']));
// clear the output
if(ob_get_length()) ob_clean();
// headers are sent to prevent browsers from caching
header('Expires: Fri, 25 Dec 1980 00:00:00 GMT'); // time in the past
header('Last-Modified: ' . gmdate( 'D, d M Y H:i:s') . 'GMT');
header('Cache-Control: no-cache, must-revalidate');
```

```
header('Pragma: no-cache');
header('Content-Type: text/xml');
// return the news to the client
echo $reader->getFormattedXML();
?>
```

3. Create a new file named rss_reader.class.php, and add this code to it:

```php
<?php
// this class retrieves an RSS feed and performs a XSLT transformation
class CRssReader
{
  private $mXml;
  private $mXsl;

  // Constructor - creates an XML object based on the specified feed
  function __construct($szFeed)
  {
    // retrieve the RSS feed in a SimpleXML object
    $this->mXml = simplexml_load_file(urldecode($szFeed));
    // retrieve the XSL file contents in a SimpleXML object
    $this->mXsl = simplexml_load_file('rss_reader.xsl');
  }

  // Creates a formatted XML document based on retrieved feed
  public function getFormattedXML()
  {
    // create the XSLTProcessor object
    $proc = new XSLTProcessor;
    // attach the XSL
    $proc->importStyleSheet($this->mXsl);
    // apply the transformation and return formatted data as XML string
    return $proc->transformToXML($this->mXml);
  }
}
?>
```

4. Create a new file named rss_reader.xsl, and add this code to it:

```xml
<?xml version="1.0" encoding="UTF-8"?>
<xsl:stylesheet version="1.0"
xmlns:xsl="http://www.w3.org/1999/XSL/Transform">
  <xsl:template match="/">
    <dl>
      <xsl:for-each select="rss/channel/item">
        <dt><h3><xsl:value-of select="title" /></h3></dt>
        <dd>
          <span class="date"><xsl:value-of select="pubDate" /></span>
          <p>
            <xsl:value-of select="description" />
            <br />
            <xsl:element name="a">
              <xsl:attribute name = "href">
                <xsl:value-of select="link" />
              </xsl:attribute>
              read full article
            </xsl:element>
          </p>
        </dd>
      </xsl:for-each>
    </dl>
  </xsl:template>
</xsl:stylesheet>
```

5. Now add the standard error-handling file, error_handler.php. Feel free to copy this file from the previous chapter. Anyway, here's the code for it:

```php
<?php
// set the user error handler method to be error_handler
set_error_handler('error_handler', E_ALL);

// error handler function
function error_handler($errNo, $errStr, $errFile, $errLine)
{
    // clear any output that has already been generated
    if(ob_get_length()) ob_clean();
    // output the error message
    $error_message = 'ERRNO: ' . $errNo . chr(10) .
                     'TEXT: ' . $errStr . chr(10) .
                     'LOCATION: ' . $errFile .
                     ', line ' . $errLine;
    echo $error_message;
    // prevent processing any more PHP scripts
    exit;
}
?>
```

6. In the `rss_reader` folder, create a file named `config.php`, where we'll add the feeds our application will aggregate.

```php
<?php
// Set up some feeds
$feeds = array ('0' => array('title' => 'CNN Technology',
                             'feed' =>
'http://rss.cnn.com/rss/cnn_tech.rss'),
                '1' => array('title' => 'BBC News',
                             'feed' =>
'http://news.bbc.co.uk/rss/newsonline_uk_edition/front_page/rss.xml'),
                '2' => array('title' => 'Wired News',
                             'feed' =>
'http://wirednews.com/news/feeds/rss2/0,2610,3,00.xml'));
?>
```

7. Create a new file named `index.php`, and add this code to it:

```php
<?php
// load the list of feeds
require_once ('config.php');
?>
<!DOCTYPE html PUBLIC "-//W3C//DTD XHTML 1.0 Transitional//EN"
"http://www.w3.org/TR/xhtml1/DTD/xhtml1-transitional.dtd">
<html xmlns="http://www.w3.org/1999/xhtml">
  <head>
    <meta http-equiv="Content-Type" content="text/html; charset=utf-8" />
    <title>AJAX RSS Reader</title>
    <link rel="stylesheet" type="text/css" href="rss_reader.css"/>
    <script src="rss_reader.js" type="text/javascript"></script>
  </head>
  <body>
    <h1>AJAX RSS Reader</h1>
    <div id="feeds">
      <h2>Feeds</h2>
      <ul id="feedList">
      <?php
        // Display feeds
        for ($i = 0; $i < count($feeds); $i++)
        {
          echo '<li id="feed-' . $i . '"><a href="javascript:void(0);" ';
          echo 'onclick="getFeed(document.getElementById(\'feed-' . $i .
               '\'), \'' . urlencode($feeds[$i]['feed']) . '\');">';
          echo $feeds[$i]['title'] . '</a></li>';
        }
      ?>
```

```
            </ul>
          </div>
          <div id="content">
            <div id="loading" style="display:none">Loading feed...</div>
            <div id="feedContainer" style="display:none"></div>
            <div id="home">
              <h2>About the AJAX RSS Reader</h2>
              <p>
                The AJAX RSS reader is only a simple application that provides
                basic functionality for retrieving RSS feeds.
              </p>
              <p>
                This application is presented as a case study in
                <a href="https://www.packtpub.com/ajax_php/book"> Building
                Responsive Web Applications with AJAX and PHP</a>
                (Packt Publishing, 2006).
              </p>
            </div>
          </div>
        </body>
      </html>
```

8. Create a new file named rss_reader.js, and add this code to it:

```javascript
// holds an instance of XMLHttpRequest
var xmlHttp = createXmlHttpRequestObject();
// when set to true, display detailed error messages
var showErrors = true;

// creates an XMLHttpRequest instance
function createXmlHttpRequestObject()
{
  // will store the reference to the XMLHttpRequest object
  var xmlHttp;
  // this should work for all browsers except IE6 and older
  try
  {
    // try to create XMLHttpRequest object
    xmlHttp = new XMLHttpRequest();
  }
  catch(e)
  {
    // assume IE6 or older
    var XmlHttpVersions = new Array("MSXML2.XMLHTTP.6.0",
                                    "MSXML2.XMLHTTP.5.0",
                                    "MSXML2.XMLHTTP.4.0",
                                    "MSXML2.XMLHTTP.3.0",
                                    "MSXML2.XMLHTTP",
                                    "Microsoft.XMLHTTP");
    // try every prog id until one works
    for (var i=0; i<XmlHttpVersions.length && !xmlHttp; i++)
    {
      try
      {
        // try to create XMLHttpRequest object
        xmlHttp = new ActiveXObject(XmlHttpVersions[i]);
      }
      catch (e) {} // ignore potential error
    }
  }
  // return the created object or display an error message
  if (!xmlHttp)
    alert("Error creating the XMLHttpRequest object.");
  else
```

```
        return xmlHttp;
}

// function that displays an error message
function displayError($message)
{
  // ignore errors if showErrors is false
  if (showErrors)
  {
    // turn error displaying Off
    showErrors = false;
    // display error message
    alert("Error encountered: \n" + $message);
  }
}

// Retrieve titles from a feed and display them
function getFeed(feedLink, feed)
{
  // only continue if xmlHttp isn't void
  if (xmlHttp)
  {
    // try to connect to the server
    try
    {
      if (xmlHttp.readyState == 4 || xmlHttp.readyState == 0)
      {
        /* Get number of feeds and loop through each one of them to
           change the class name of their container (<li>). */
        var numberOfFeeds =
                document.getElementById("feedList").childNodes.length;
        for (i = 0; i < numberOfFeeds; i++)
          document.getElementById("feedList").childNodes[i].className = "";
        // Change the class name for the clicked feed so it becomes
        // highlighted
        feedLink.className = "active";
        // Display "Loading..." message while loading feed
        document.getElementById("loading").style.display = "block";
        // Call the server page to execute the server-side operation
        params = "feed=" + feed;
        xmlHttp.open("POST", "rss_reader.php", true);
        xmlHttp.setRequestHeader("Content-Type",
                                 "application/x-www-form-urlencoded");
        xmlHttp.onreadystatechange = handleHttpGetFeeds;
        xmlHttp.send(params);
      }
      else
      {
        // if connection was busy, try again after 1 second
        setTimeout("getFeed('" + feedLink + "', '" + feed + "');", 1000);
      }
    }
    // display the error in case of failure
    catch (e)
    {
      displayError(e.toString());
    }
  }
}

// function that retrieves the HTTP response
function handleHttpGetFeeds()
{
```

```
     // continue if the process is completed
     if (xmlHttp.readyState == 4)
     {
      // continue only if HTTP status is "OK"
       if (xmlHttp.status == 200)
       {
         try
         {
           displayFeed();
         }
         catch(e)
         {
           // display error message
           displayError(e.toString());
         }
       }
       else
       {
         displayError(xmlHttp.statusText);
       }
     }
   }

   // Processes server's response
   function displayFeed()
   {
     // read server response as text, to check for errors
     var response = xmlHttp.responseText;
     // server error?
     if (response.indexOf("ERRNO") >= 0
           || response.indexOf("error:") >= 0
           || response.length == 0)
       throw(response.length == 0 ? "Void server response." : response);
     // hide the "Loading..." message upon feed retrieval
     document.getElementById("loading").style.display = "none";
     // append XSLed XML content to existing DOM structure
     var titlesContainer = document.getElementById("feedContainer");
     titlesContainer.innerHTML = response;
     // make the feed container visible
     document.getElementById("feedContainer").style.display = "block";
     // clear home page text
     document.getElementById("home").innerHTML = "";
   }
```

9. Create a new file named rss_reader.css, and add this code to it:

```css
body
{
   font-family: Arial, Helvetica, sans-serif;
   font-size: 12px;
}

h1
{
   color: #ffffff;
   background-color: #3366CC;
   padding: 5px;
}

h2
{
   margin-top: 0px;
}

h3
{
```

```
   margin-bottom: 0px;
}

li
{
   margin-bottom: 5px;
}

div
{
   padding: 10px;
}

a, a:visited
{
   color: #3366CC;
   text-decoration: underline;
}

a:hover
{
   color: #ffffff;
   background-color: #3366CC;
   text-decoration: none;
}

.active a
{
   color: #ffffff;
   background-color: #3366CC;
   text-decoration: none;
}

.active a:visited
{
   color: #ffffff;
   background-color:#3366CC;
   text-decoration:none;
}

.active a:hover
{
   color:#ffffff;
   background-color: #3366CC;
   text-decoration: none;
}

#feeds
{
   display: inline;
   float: left;
   width: 150px;
   background-color: #f4f4f4;
   border:1px solid #e6e6e6;
}

#content
{
   padding-left:170px;
   border:1px solid #f1f1f1;
}

#loading
{
   float: left;
   display: inline;
```

```
        width: 410px;
        background-color: #fffbb8;
        color: #FF9900;
        border: 1px solid #ffcc00;
        font-weight: bold;
    }

    .date
    {
        font-size: 10px;
        color: #999999;
    }
```

10. Load `http://localhost/ajax/rss_reader` in your web browser. The initial page should look like Figure 9.3. If you click one of the links, you should get something like Figure 9.2.

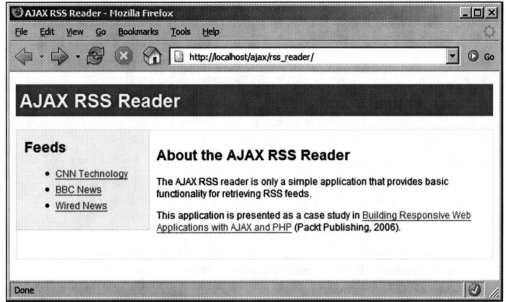

Figure 9.3: The First Page of the AJAX RSS Reader

What Just Happened?

It's not a really professional application at this state, but the point is proven. It doesn't take much code to accomplish such a result and any features you might think of can be added easily.

The user interface of this application is pretty basic, all set up in `index.php`. We first need to include `config.php`—where our `feeds` are defined, in order to display the list of feeds on the left panel. Feeds are defined as an associative array of arrays. The main array's keys are numbers starting from 0 and its values are arrays, with keys being the feeds' titles and values being the feeds' URLs. The `$feeds` array looks like this:

```
$feeds = array ("0" => array("title" => "CNN Technology",
                             "feed" => "http://rss.cnn.com/rss/cnn_tech.rss"),
```

```
            "1" => array("title" => "BBC News",
                         "feed" =>
   "http://news.bbc.co.uk/rss/newsonline_uk_edition/front_page/rss.xml"),
            "2" => array("title" => "Wired News",
                         "feed" =>
   "http://wirednews.com/news/feeds/rss2/0,2610,3,00.xml"));
```

Translated into a more meaningful form, this is how the $feeds array looks like:

ID	Feed Title (title)	Feed URL (feed)
0	CNN Technology	http://rss.cnn.com/rss/cnn_tech.rss
1	BBC News	http://news.bbc.co.uk/rss/newsonline_uk_edition/front_page/rss.xml
2	Wired News	http://wirednews.com/news/feeds/rss2/0,2610,3,00.xml

We have decided to store the feeds like this for simplicity, but it's easy to extend the code and store them in a database, if you need to.

In index.php we loop through these feeds and display them all as an un-ordered list, each feed being a link inside an <li> element. We assign each link an onclick event function where getFeed function will be called. This function takes two parameters: the <li>'s ID and the feed's URL. We need the ID in order to highlight that link in the list and we need the feed's URL to send it as a parameter in our HTTP request to the server. The urlencode function ensures that the URL is safely sent to the server, which will use urldecode to decode it.

Two more things about index.php:

- Initially hidden, the <div> with id="loading" will be displayed while retrieving the feed, to inform the user that the feed is loading. This is useful when working with a slow connection or with slow servers, when the retrieval time will be long.

  ```
  <div id="loading" style="display:none">Loading feed...</div>
  ```

- The <div> with id="feedContainer" is the actual container where the feed will be loaded. The feed will be dynamically inserted inside this div element.

  ```
  <div id="feedContainer"></div>
  ```

rss_reader.js contains the standard XMLHttpRequest initialization, request sending, and response retrieval code. The getFeed function handles the sending of the HTTP request. First it loops through all feed links and un-highlights the links by setting their CSS class to none. It then highlights the active feed link:

```
/* Get number of feeds and loop through each one of them to
   change the class name of their container (<li>). */
var numberOfFeeds =
            document.getElementById("feedList").childNodes.length;
for (i = 0; i < numberOfFeeds; i++)
   document.getElementById("feedList").childNodes[i].className = "";
// Change the class name for the clicked feed to highlight it
feedLink.className = "active";
```

OK, the next step is to display the Loading feed... message:

```
// Display "Loading..." message while loading feed
document.getElementById("loading").style.display = "block";
```

And finally, we send the HTTP request with the feed's title as parameter:

```
// Call the server page to execute the server-side operation
params = "feed=" + feed;
xmlHttp.open("POST", "rss_reader.php", true);
xmlHttp.setRequestHeader("Content-Type",
                         "application/x-www-form-urlencoded");
xmlHttp.onreadystatechange = handleHttpGetFeeds;
xmlHttp.send(params);
```

The `rss_reader.php` script creates an instance of the `CRssReader` class and displays an XSL-formatted XML document, which is returned back to the client. The following lines do the hard work (the code that clears the output and prevents browser caching was stripped):

```
$reader = new CRssReader(urldecode($_POST['feed']));
echo $reader->getFormattedXML();
```

`CRssReader` is defined in `rss_reader.class.php`. This PHP class handles XML retrieval and formatting. Getting a remote XML file is a piece of cake with PHP 5's new extension: SimpleXML. We'll also load the XSL template and apply it to the retrieved XML.

The constructor of this class retrieves the XML and saves it in a class member named `$mXml` and the XSL file in a class member named `$mXsl`:

```
// Constructor - creates an XML object based on the specified feed
function __construct($szFeed)
{
    // retrieve the RSS feed in a SimpleXML object
    $this->mXml = simplexml_load_file(urldecode($szFeed));
    // retrieve the XSL file contents in a SimpleXML object
    $this->mXsl = simplexml_load_file('rss_reader.xsl');
}
```

The `getFormattedXML()` function creates a new `XSLTProcessor` object in order to apply the XSL transformation. The `transformToXML` method simply returns a formatted XML document, after the XSL has been applied.

```
// Creates a formatted XML document based on retrieved feed
public function getFormattedXML()
{
    // create the XSLTProcessor object
    $proc = new XSLTProcessor;
    // attach the XSL
    $proc->importStyleSheet($this->mXsl);
    // apply the transformation and return formatted data as XML string
    return $proc->transformToXML($this->mXml);
}
```

What we need to accomplish with XSL is to loop through each "record" of the XML and display the data inside. A record is delimited by `<item>` and `</item>` tags.

In `rss_reader.xsl` we define a loop like this:

```
<xsl:for-each select="rss/channel/item">
```

For example, to display the current title, we write:

```
<h3><xsl:value-of select="title" /></h3>
```

Notice how we create a new <a> element with XSLT:

```
<xsl:element name="a">
  <xsl:attribute name = "href">
    <xsl:value-of select="link" />
  </xsl:attribute>
  read full article
</xsl:element>
```

We use this technique to build links to full articles on their actual websites.

There's also a bit of CSS code that will format the output according to our wish. Everything should be pretty clear if you take a quick look at rss_reader.css.

Summary

Today's Web is different than yesterday's Web and tomorrow's Web will certainly be different than today's. Yesterday's Web was a collection of pages linked together. All static, and everybody kept things for themselves. The main characteristic of today's Web is information exchange between websites and/or applications.

Based on what you've learned in this chapter, you'll be able to build an even better RSS Reader, but why stop here? You hold some great tools that allow you to build great applications that could impact on tomorrow's Web!

10
AJAX Drag and Drop

When **drag-and-drop** capability was first introduced to websites, people looked at it with astonishment. This was really a great feature to provide via your website! Since then, JavaScript has evolved in people's eyes from a "check-out-that-snow-on-my-website" scripting language to a standardized and powerful "do-powerful-stuff-with-it" language.

Many frameworks and JavaScript toolkits have been developed, with new ones appearing frequently. **script.aculo.us** is one of the most popular JavaScript toolkits, and it allows implementing amazing effects in web pages—check out the examples on its official web page at http://script.aculo.us/. Script.aculo.us is an open-source JavaScript framework, distributed under an MIT-style license, so you can use it for anything you like, as long as you include the copyright notice. You can download script.aculo.us from http://script.aculo.us/downloads. Check out the documentation on http://wiki.script.aculo.us

In this chapter, you will learn how to integrate **script.aculo.us** features into your website, by building an AJAX database-enabled sortable list.

Using Drag and Drop on the Web

While exploring some existing web applications with drag-and-drop capability, we found out that there are at least two situations where drag and drop smoothes up the user interface and the interactivity between human and machine. Drag and drop can be successfully used in:

- Shopping carts
- Sortable lists

Shopping Carts

You're probably familiar with traditional e-commerce websites. In the light of the new AJAX boom, a new generation of shopping carts has appeared, where visitors have to use drag and drop to add products to their carts, instead of clicking an "Add to Cart" button. While one could argue the real usefulness of this "feature" (my grandmother still prefers the button, she doesn't know how to drag and drop), the visual effect is pretty impressive.

A few websites have already put this into practice. One such example is Panic Goods—selling t-shirts! The URL for this is: http://www.panic.com/goods.

Notice the light blue bar on the bottom of the screen? That's the actual shopping cart. Just *drag* some t-shirts from the catalog, and *drop* them into the shopping cart, to see how the cart performs. Products are lined up in the cart and it's easy to see what you have chosen and for what amount. Drag items outside the light blue bar to remove them from the cart. Pretty impressive, isn't it?

Sortable Lists

There's a type of list we probably use daily, namely, a **to-do list**. We usually use yellow Post-its and some of us even use specialized software.

But with so many new web applications available out there, surely there must be a dozen to-do list applications! I'll just mention **Ta-da Lists** (http://www.tadalist.com), created by **37signals**. This company has actually reinvented the entire concept of web applications and has taken it to the next level. Ta-da Lists, one of its first products, is a tool that allows you to create several to-do lists, each with its own items (things to do, that is). It's a really helpful tool and a lot of people use it, although most of them have upgraded to other 37signals products like Basecamp (http://www.basecamphq.com) and Backpack (http://www.backpackit.com).

Despite its intuitive user interface and easy-to-use actions, Ta-da Lists lacks a very basic feature that would greatly increase its usability: dragging and dropping list items, thus reordering the list. To reorder a list in Ta-da Lists, you have to click on a link that will refresh the page and display four arrow buttons (bring to front, move up, move down, and send to back).

Although this implementation works well, a drag-and-drop system would make it faster and easier to use. 37signals have improved this functionality in Basecamp, though, and the to-do lists in there have draggable items—an upgrade that proves the usability of the drag-and-drop concept.

Building the AJAX Drag-and-Drop Sortable List Application

One thing that sets this application apart from other applications we've built in this book is that in this case, we are going to use two external JavaScript frameworks: **Prototype** and **script.aculo.us**.

"Prototype is a JavaScript framework that aims to ease development of dynamic web applications." It was created by Sam Stephenson and is quickly becoming *the* JavaScript framework, because of its great functionality.

> Prototype is distributed under an MIT-style license and it can be downloaded from http://prototype.conio.net.
>
> If you want to learn more about Prototype, check out the tutorial on http://www.particletree.com/features/quick-guide-to-prototype.

The Prototype features are:

- Complete object-orientation
- Utility functions
- Form helper functions
- AJAX support
- Periodical executer

Another pioneer of JavaScript development is Thomas Fuchs, the man who built the great JavaScript library—script.aculo.us—a library that provides spectacular visual effects. We'll be using some of these features in our drag-and-drop application (more specifically, the dragging and dropping features). Script.aculo.us is built on top of Prototype, thus inheriting all Prototypes' features.

Features of Script.aculo.us are:

- Complete object-orientation
- Visual effects (fade in, fade out, grow, shrink, blind down, blind up, shake, etc.)
- Drag-and-drop support
- Autocompletion
- In-place editing
- Slider controls

The application we're about to build will be a small task management application and will allow us to create new tasks, reorder existing tasks, and delete tasks. Summarizing the features:

- Database back end
- Drag-and-drop items
- Add new tasks with AJAX
- Instant database update when drag and dropping
- Delete a task by dragging and dropping it into a special designated area

Let's take a look at how this is going to look:

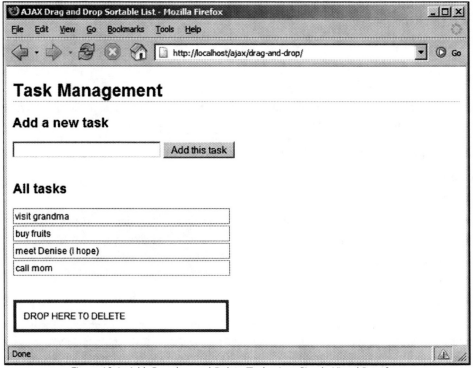

Figure 10.1: Add, Reorder, and Delete Tasks, in a Simple Visual Interface

Dragging items around the screen makes the other items switch positions.

When dropping a task on the DROP HERE TO DELETE area, a confirmation is required before the application proceeds with the actual deletion; as shown in the following figure:

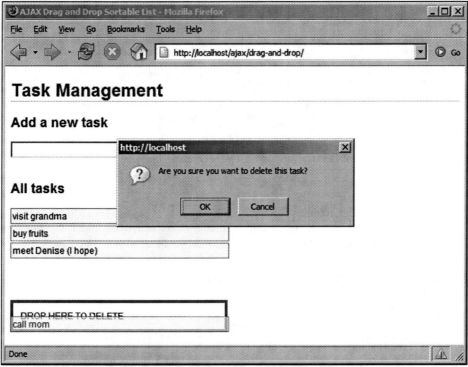

Figure 10.2: Confirmation Required Before Deleting a Task

Time for Action—Task Management Application with AJAX

1. Connect to the ajax database, and create a table named tasks with the following code:

```
CREATE TABLE tasks (
  id INT UNSIGNED NOT NULL AUTO_INCREMENT,
  order_no INT UNSIGNED NOT NULL default '0',
  description VARCHAR(100) NOT NULL default '',
  PRIMARY KEY (id)
);
```

2. In your ajax folder, create a new folder named drag-and-drop.

3. In the drag-and-drop folder, create a file named config.php, and add the database configuration code to it:

```
<?php
// defines database connection data
define('DB_HOST', 'localhost');
define('DB_USER', 'ajaxuser');
define('DB_PASSWORD', 'practical');
define('DB_DATABASE', 'ajax');
?>
```

4. Now add the standard error-handling file, `error_handler.php`. Feel free to copy this file from previous chapters. Anyway, here's the code for it:

```php
<?php
// set the user error handler method to be error_handler
set_error_handler('error_handler', E_ALL);

// error handler function
function error_handler($errNo, $errStr, $errFile, $errLine)
{
  // clear any output that has already been generated
  if(ob_get_length()) ob_clean();
  // output the error message
  $error_message = 'ERRNO: ' . $errNo . chr(10) .
                   'TEXT: ' . $errStr . chr(10) .
                   'LOCATION: ' . $errFile .
                   ', line ' . $errLine;
  echo $error_message;
  // prevent processing any more PHP scripts
  exit;
}
?>
```

5. Download the script.aculo.us library from `http://script.aculo.us/downloads` and unzip/untar the downloaded archive to your `drag-and-drop` folder. Change the script.aculo.us folder name from something like `scriptaculous-js-x.y.z` to simply `scriptaculous`.

6. Create a new file named `index.php`, and add this code to it:

```php
<?php
  require_once ('taskslist.class.php');
?>
<!DOCTYPE html PUBLIC "-//W3C//DTD XHTML 1.0 Transitional//EN"
"http://www.w3.org/TR/xhtml1/DTD/xhtml1-transitional.dtd">
<html xmlns="http://www.w3.org/1999/xhtml">
  <head>
    <meta http-equiv="Content-Type" content="text/html; charset=utf-8" />
    <title>AJAX Drag and Drop Sortable List</title>
    <link href="drag-and-drop.css" rel="stylesheet" type="text/css" />
    <script src="drag-and-drop.js" type="text/javascript"></script>
    <script src="scriptaculous/lib/prototype.js" type="text/javascript">
    </script>
    <script src="scriptaculous/src/scriptaculous.js" type="text/javascript">
    </script>
  </head>
  <body onload="startup()">
    <h1>Task Management</h1>
    <h2>Add a new task</h2>
    <div>
      <input type="text" id="txtNewTask" name="txtNewTask"
          size="30" maxlength="100" onkeydown="handleKey(event)"/>
      <input type="button" name="submit" value="Add this task"
          onclick="process('txtNewTask', 'addNewTask')" />
    </div>
    <br />
    <h2>All tasks</h2>
    <ul id="tasksList" class="sortableList"
        onmouseup="process('tasksList', 'updateList')">
      <?php
        $myTasksList = new TasksList();
        echo $myTasksList->BuildTasksList();
      ?>
```

```
        </ul>
        <br /><br />
        <div id="trash">
          DROP HERE TO DELETE
          <br /><br />
        </div>
      </body>
</html>
```

7. Create a new file named `tasks1ist.class.php`, and add this code to it:

```php
<?php
// load error handler and database configuration
require_once ('error_handler.php');
require_once ('config.php');

// This class builds a tasks list and
// performs add/delete/reorder actions on it
class TasksList
{
  // stored database connection
  private $mMysqli;

  // constructor opens database connection
  function __construct()
  {
    // connect to the database
    $this->mMysqli = new mysqli(DB_HOST, DB_USER, DB_PASSWORD,
                                DB_DATABASE);
  }

  // destructor closes database connection
  public function __destruct()
  {
    $this->mMysqli->close();
  }

  // Builds the tasks list
  public function BuildTasksList()
  {
    // initialize output
    $myList = '';
    // build query
    $result = $this->mMysqli->query('SELECT * FROM tasks ' .
                                    'ORDER BY order_no ASC');
    // build task list as <li> elements
    while ($row = $result->fetch_assoc())
    {
      $myList .= '<li id="' . htmlentities($row['id']) . '">' .
                 htmlentities($row['description']) . '</li>';
    }
    // return the list
    return $myList;
  }

  // Handles the server-side data processing
  public function Process($content, $action)
  {
    // perform action requested by client
    switch($action)
    {
      // Reorder task list
      case 'updateList':
        // retrieve update details
        $new_order = explode('_', $content);
        // update list
```

243

```php
        for ($i=0; $i < count($new_order); $i++)
        {
            // escape data received from client
            $new_order[$i] =
                        $this->mMysqli->real_escape_string($new_order[$i]);
            // update task
            $result = $this->mMysqli->query('UPDATE tasks SET order_no="' .
                            $i . '" WHERE id="' . $new_order[$i] . '"');
        }
        $updatedList = $this->BuildTasksList();
        return $updatedList;
        break;

    // Add a new task
    case 'addNewTask':
        // escape input data
        $task = trim($this->mMysqli->real_escape_string($content));
        // continue only if task name is not null
        if ($task)
        {
            // obtain the highest order_no
            $result = $this->mMysqli->query('SELECT (MAX(order_no) + 1) ' .
                                        'AS order_no FROM tasks');
            $row = $result->fetch_assoc();
            // if the table is empty, order_no will be null
            $order = $row['order_no'];
            if (!$order) $order = 1;
            // insert the new task as the bottom of the list
            $result = $this->mMysqli->query
                            ('INSERT INTO tasks (order_no, description) ' .
                            'VALUES ("' . $order . '", "' . $task . '")');
            // return the updated tasks list
            $updatedList = $this->BuildTasksList();
            return $updatedList;
        }
        break;

    // Delete task
    case 'delTask':
        // escape input data
        $content = trim($this->mMysqli->real_escape_string($content));
        // delete the task
        $result = $this->mMysqli->query('DELETE FROM tasks WHERE id="' .
                                    $content . '"');
        $updatedList = $this->BuildTasksList();
        return $updatedList;
        break;
        }
    }
}
?>
```

8. Create a new file named `drag-and-drop.php`, and add this code to it:

```php
<?php
// load helper class
require_once ('taskslist.class.php');
// create TasksList object
$myTasksList = new TasksList();
// read parameters
$action = $_GET['action'];
$content = $_GET['content'];
// clear the output
if(ob_get_length()) ob_clean();
// headers are sent to prevent browsers from caching
```

```
header('Expires: Fri, 25 Dec 1980 00:00:00 GMT'); // time in the past
header('Last-Modified: ' . gmdate( 'D, d M Y H:i:s') . 'GMT');
header('Cache-Control: no-cache, must-revalidate');
header('Pragma: no-cache');
header('Content-Type: text/html');
// execute the client request and return the updated tasks list
echo $myTasksList->Process($content, $action);
?>
```

9. Create a new file named drag-and-drop.js, and add this code to it:

```
// holds an instance of XMLHttpRequest
var xmlHttp = createXmlHttpRequestObject();
// when set to true, display detailed error messages
var showErrors = true;
// initialize the requests cache
var cache = new Array();

// creates an XMLHttpRequest instance
function createXmlHttpRequestObject()
{
  // will store the reference to the XMLHttpRequest object
  var xmlHttp;
  // this should work for all browsers except IE6 and older
  try
  {
    // try to create XMLHttpRequest object
    xmlHttp = new XMLHttpRequest();
  }
  catch(e)
  {
    // assume IE6 or older
    var XmlHttpVersions = new Array("MSXML2.XMLHTTP.6.0",
                                   "MSXML2.XMLHTTP.5.0",
                                   "MSXML2.XMLHTTP.4.0",
                                   "MSXML2.XMLHTTP.3.0",
                                   "MSXML2.XMLHTTP",
                                   "Microsoft.XMLHTTP");
    // try every prog id until one works
    for (var i=0; i<XmlHttpVersions.length && !xmlHttp; i++)
    {
      try
      {
        // try to create XMLHttpRequest object
        xmlHttp = new ActiveXObject(XmlHttpVersions[i]);
      }
      catch (e) {} // ignore potential error
    }
  }
  // return the created object or display an error message
  if (!xmlHttp)
    alert("Error creating the XMLHttpRequest object.");
  else
    return xmlHttp;
}

// function that displays an error message
function displayError($message)
{
  // ignore errors if showErrors is false
  if (showErrors)
  {
    // turn error displaying off
    showErrors = false;
    // display error message
    alert("Error encountered: \n" + $message);
```

```
    }
  }

  // Scriptaculous-specific code to define a sortable list and a drop zone
  function startup()
  {
    // Transform an unordered list into a sortable list with draggable items
    Sortable.create("tasksList", {tag:"li"});

    // Define a drop zone used for deleting tasks
    Droppables.add("trash",
    {
      onDrop: function(element)
      {
        var deleteTask =
                    confirm("Are you sure you want to delete this task?")
        if (deleteTask)
        {
          Element.hide(element);
          process(element.id, "delTask");
        }
      }
    });
  }

  // Serialize the id values of list items (<li>s)
  function serialize(listID)
  {
    // count the list's items
    var length = document.getElementById(listID).childNodes.length;
    var serialized = "";
    // loop through each element
    for (i = 0; i < length; i++)
    {
      // get current element
      var li = document.getElementById(listID).childNodes[i];
      // get current element's id without the text part
      var id = li.getAttribute("id");
      // append only the number to the ids array
      serialized += encodeURIComponent(id) + "_";
    }
    // return the array with the trailing '_' cut off
    return serialized.substring(0, serialized.length - 1);
  }

  // Send request to server
  function process(content, action)
  {
    // only continue if xmlHttp isn't void
    if (xmlHttp)
    {
      // initialize the request query string to empty string
      params = "";
      // escape the values to be safely sent to the server
      content = encodeURIComponent(content);
      // send different parameters depending on action
      if (action == "updateList")
        params = "?content=" + serialize(content) + "&action=updateList";
      else if (action == "addNewTask")
      {
        // prepare the task for sending to the server
        var newTask =
          trim(encodeURIComponent(document.getElementById(content).value));
        // don't add void tasks
        if (newTask)
          params = "?content=" + newTask + "&action=addNewTask";
```

```
  }
  else if (action =="delTask")
    params = "?content=" + content + "&action=delTask";
  // don't add null params to cache
  if (params) cache.push(params);

  // try to connect to the server
  try
  {
    // only continue if the connection is clear and cache is not empty
    if ((xmlHttp.readyState == 4 || xmlHttp.readyState == 0)
        && cache.length>0)
    {
      // get next set of values from cache
      var cacheEntry = cache.shift();
      // initiate the request
      xmlHttp.open("GET", "drag-and-drop.php" + cacheEntry, true);
      xmlHttp.setRequestHeader("Content-Type",
                               "application/x-www-form-urlencoded");
      xmlHttp.onreadystatechange = handleRequestStateChange;
      xmlHttp.send(null);
    }
    else
    {
      setTimeout("process();", 1000);
    }
  }
  // display the error in case of failure
  catch (e)
  {
    displayError(e.toString());
  }
  }
}

// function that retrieves the HTTP response
function handleRequestStateChange()
{
  // when readyState is 4, we also read the server response
  if (xmlHttp.readyState == 4)
  {
    // continue only if HTTP status is "OK"
    if (xmlHttp.status == 200)
    {
      try
      {
        postUpdateProcess();
      }
      catch(e)
      {
        // display error message
        displayError(e.toString());
      }
    }
    else
    {
      displayError(xmlHttp.statusText);
    }
  }
}
// Processes server's response
function postUpdateProcess()
{
  // read the response
  var response = xmlHttp.responseText;
  // server error?
```

```
          if (response.indexOf("ERRNO") >= 0 || response.indexOf("error") >= 0)
            alert(response);
          // update the tasks list
          document.getElementById("tasksList").innerHTML = response;
          Sortable.create("tasksList");
          document.getElementById("txtNewTask").value = "";
          document.getElementById("txtNewTask").focus();
        }
        /* handles keydown to detect when enter is pressed */
        function handleKey(e)
        {
          // get the event
          e = (!e) ? window.event : e;
          // get the code of the character that has been pressed
          code = (e.charCode) ? e.charCode :
                  ((e.keyCode) ? e.keyCode :
                  ((e.which) ? e.which : 0));
          // handle the keydown event
          if (e.type == "keydown")
          {
            // if enter (code 13) is pressed
            if(code == 13)
            {
              // send the current message
              process("txtNewTask", "addNewTask");
            }
          }
        }

        /* removes leading and trailing spaces from the string */
        function trim(s)
        {
          return s.replace(/(^\s+)|(\s+$)/g, "")
        }
```

10. Create a new file named drag-and-drop.css, and add this code to it:

```
body
{
  font-family: Arial, Helvetica, sans-serif;
  font-size: 12px;
}
ul.sortableList
{
  list-style-type: none;
  padding: 0px;
  margin: 0px;
  width: 300px;
}
ul.sortableList li
{
  cursor: move;
  padding: 2px 2px;
  margin: 2px 0px;
  border: 1px solid #00CC00;
  background-color: #F4FFF5;
}
h1
{
  border-bottom: 1px solid #cccccc;
}
#trash
{
  border: 4px solid #ff0000;
  width: 270px;
  padding: 10px;
}
```

11. Load `http://localhost/ajax/drag-and-drop` in your web browser and test its functionality to make sure it works as expected (see Figures 10.1 and 10.2 for reference).

What Just Happened?

Adding a task is performed as mentioned in the following steps:

1. The user enters task.
2. When the user clicks on Add this task button or presses *Enter*, the data is sent to the server with an asynchronous HTTP request. The server script inserts the new task into the database, and returns the updated list, which is then injected into the code with JavaScript.

When reordering the list, this is what happens:

1. Every task is an XHTML list element: an `<li>`. The user begins dragging an item; on dropping it, an HTTP request is sent to the server. This request consists of a serialized string of IDs, every list element's ID.
2. On the client you'll see the list reordered, while the server updates the order of each element in the database.

This is how deleting a task works:

1. The user drags an item and drops it on the DROP HERE TO DELETE area.
2. An HTTP request is sent to the server, which performs the task deletion from the database and the XHTML element is instantly destroyed.

We include in `index.php` the JavaScript libraries we'll be using:

```
<script src="drag-and-drop.js" type="text/javascript"></script>
<script src="scriptaculous/lib/prototype.js" type="text/javascript">
</script>
<script src="scriptaculous/src/scriptaculous.js" type="text/javascript">
</script>
```

The first line includes our custom functions and AJAX-related tasks. The second line includes the Prototype library, while the third line includes the script.aculo.us library.

The onload event inside the `<body>` tag calls the `startup()` function, which defines the unordered list with `id="tasksList"` as a sortable element (`Sortable.create`). This ensures drag-and-drop functionality for `<li>` elements inside the list. The `startup()` function also defines a droppable element `Droppables.add`; we use this as an area where we delete tasks.

Also, inside the `startup()` function, we define a behavior for dropping a list item on the drop zone:

```
onDrop: function(element)
{
  var deleteTask = confirm("Are you sure you want to delete this task?")
  if (deleteTask == true)
  {
    Element.hide(element);
    process(element, "delTask");
  }
}
```

This code asks the user for confirmation, and if this is received hides that element from the screen and calls process, which sends the HTTP request.

In index.php, there's a small block of code that dynamically creates the tasks list:

```
<ul id="tasksList" class="sortableList"
      onmouseup="process('tasksList', 'updateList')">
  <?php
    $myTasksList = new TasksList();
    echo $myTasksList->BuildTasksList();
  ?>
</ul>
```

A new task is added by clicking on the Add this task button or by pressing the *Enter* key.

The actual AJAX request is sent by the process function. This function handles the sending of requests for all three actions (reorder list / add task / delete task), by specifying the action to be performed as a parameter.

When adding a new task, the first parameter of the process function is the ID of the text field in which we've just typed a new task.

```
<input type="button" name="submit" value="Add this task"
onclick="process('txtNewTask', 'addNewTask')" />
```

The database update after list reordering is triggered by an onmouseup event inside the unordered list with id="tasksList"—our sortable list. The event calls the process function, which takes as its first parameter the list's ID.

```
<ul id="tasksList" class="sortableList" onmouseup="process('tasksList',
'updateList')">
```

Because we'll be sending an array of values to the server, we need to serialize that data and we do this through serialize, our home-made function. This function counts how many <li> elements we've got, then loops through each one of them and add its ID to the string. We also need to cut off the trailing '_' on the returned value.

```
function serialize(listID)
{
  // count the list's items
  var length = document.getElementById(listID).childNodes.length;
  var serialized = "";
  // loop through each element
  for (i = 0; i < length; i++)
  {
    // get current element
    var li = document.getElementById(listID).childNodes[i];
    // get current element's id without the text part
    var id = li.getAttribute("id");
    // append only the number to the ids array
    serialized += encodeURIComponent(id) + "_";
  }
  // return the array with the trailing '_' cut off
  return serialized.substring(0, serialized.length - 1);
}
```

Remember that XMLHttpRequest cannot make two HTTP requests at the same time, so if the object is busy processing a previous request, we save the details of the current request for later. This is particularly useful when the connection to the network or the Internet is slow. The request details are saved using a cache system with the properties of a FIFO structure. Luckily, the JavaScript's Array class offers the exact functionality we need (through its push and shift methods), and hence we use it for caching purposes:

```
var cache = new Array();
```

So, in process(), before sending a new request to the server, we save the current request to the cache.

```
// only continue if xmlHttp isn't void
if (xmlHttp)
{
  if (action)
    cache.push(content + "&" + action);
```

This adds a new element at the end of our cache array, an element that is created of two parts, a content (the ID of an HTML element) and an action to be performed by the server, separated by '&'. Note that the new element is added only if action is not null, which happens when the function is called not upon user's request, but to check if there are any pending actions to be made.

Afterwards, if the XMLHttpRequest object is free to start making other calls, we use shift() to get the last action from the cache and perform it. Note that, however, this value may not be the one just added using push—in FIFO scenarios, the oldest record is processed first.

```
// try to connect to the server
try
{
  // continue only if the XMLHttpRequest object isn't busy
  // and the cache is not empty
  if ((xmlHttp.readyState == 4 || xmlHttp.readyState == 0)
    && cache.length>0)
    {
    // get next set of values from cache
    var cacheEntry = cache.shift();
```

If the HTTP status is 0 or 4 it means that there are no active requests and we can send a new request. To send a new request we first read the data back from the cache, and split the current entry into two variables:

```
// split the array element
    var values = cacheEntry.split("&");
content = values[0];
action = values[1];
```

Depending on these variables, we'll be sending different values as parameters:

```
// send different parameters depending on action
if (action == "updateList")
  params = "content=" + serialize(content) + "&action=updateList";
else if (action == "addNewTask")

  params = "content=" + document.getElementById(content).value +
             "&action=addNewTask";
else if (action =="delTask")
  params = "content=" + content + "&action=delTask";
```

These pieces of data are then used to make the server request:

```
xmlHttp.open("POST", "drag-and-drop.php", true);
xmlHttp.setRequestHeader("Content-Type", "application/x-www-form-urlencoded");
xmlHttp.onreadystatechange = handleRequestStateChange;
xmlHttp.send(params);
```

The server's response is handled by the handleRequestStateChange function, which in turn calls postUpdateProcess(). Here we retrieve the server's response, which will either be an error message or a string containing HTML code for the updated list:

```
// read the response
var response = xmlHttp.responseText;
// server error?
if (response.indexOf("ERRNO") >= 0 || response.indexOf("error") >= 0)
  alert(response);
// update the tasks list
document.getElementById("tasksList").innerHTML = response;
Sortable.create("tasksList");
document.getElementById("txtNewTask").value = "";
document.getElementById("txtNewTask").focus();
```

The last two lines of code clear the "new task" text field and set the cursor focus on that field.

The drag-and-drop.php script is really light. We include taskslist.class.php, initiate a new TasksList object and return the updated list after we call the class method Process, which will perform one of the three possible actions: add task, reorder list, or delete task.

The taskslist.class.php file is the class we're using to perform server-side actions on our tasks list. Its constructor creates a database connection. Then, we have other two public methods:

- BuildTasksList creates list items with each task;
- Process takes two parameters, $content and $action. The first parameter holds user data and depends on the other parameter, which tells the script what actions should be performed.

When updating the list (case 'updateList'), we extract the values from the $content array, which holds a serialized string of the new order of <li> elements—the tasks, that is. Next we loop through extracted values and update the database.

To add a new task, we first escape user input with the mysqli method real_escape_string. Next, we need to get from the database the greatest order number that exists and increment it. This will be our new task's order number. We then insert the task in the database and return a string containing the order number and the task's description. This is sent back to the client, which will build a new list element, based on the received data.

When deleting a task (case 'delTask') is required, the only thing we do is delete the task from the database.

Every method returns a string with the new task list, namely a string of <li> elements.

Always filter user data

If you want to save yourself from a lot of trouble you should *always* filter user input. We used JavaScript's encodeURIComponent function when sending data to the server. On the server, we used the real_escape_string method of the mysqli object, to prevent SQL injection. Also on the server, we used the htmlentities PHP function to prepare the text that we send back to the client.

Summary

This is it! You've now got a working task management application with drag-and-drop support—all this with writing only a small amount of code. The next step in developing this application would be to make each task editable by double-clicking on it. script.aculo.us provides a great way of doing this with `Ajax.InPlaceEditor`. Check out the documentation on `http://wiki.script.aculo.us/ scriptaculous/show/Ajax.InPlaceEditor` for more information on how to accomplish this.

Another practical application for sortable lists would be in a **Content Management System (CMS)**—to manage the order of pages, projects, products, news, etc. In the end, it all depends on your imagination and how far you are willing to go to create great user interfaces.

A

Preparing Your Working Environment

In order to avoid any headaches while going through the case studies in this book, it's best to install the necessary software and configure your environment the right way from the start. Although we assume you already have some experience developing PHP applications, we'll quickly go through the steps to install your machine with the necessary software.

The good news is that all the required software is free, powerful, and (finally!) comes with installers that make the programs easy for anyone to set up and configure. The bad news is that there are many possible configurations, so the instructions written might not apply 100% to you (for example, if you are using Windows, you may prefer to use IIS instead of Apache, and so on).

We'll cover the installation instructions separately for Windows and *nix based machines. We'll also cover preparing the database that is used in many examples throughout the book; these instructions apply to both Windows and *nix users, so be sure not to miss this section at the end of the appendix.

To build websites with AJAX and PHP you will need (quite unsurprisingly) to install **PHP**. The preferred version is PHP 5, because we use some of its features in Chapter 11. You also need a web server. We will cover installing **Apache**, which is the web server preferred by most PHP developers and web hosting companies. Because we've tried to make the examples in this book as relevant as possible for real-world scenarios, many of them need a database. We cover installing **MySQL**, which is the most popular database server in the PHP world. Because we used simple SQL code, you can easily use another database server without major code changes, or older versions of MySQL.

At the end of this chapter, we'll cover installing **phpMyAdmin**, which is a very useful web tool for administering your databases. You'll then learn how to use this tool to create a new database, and then a database user with full privileges to this database.

In the following pages, you'll learn how to:

- Install Apache 2, PHP 5, and MySQL 5 on your Windows machine
- Install Apache 2, PHP 5, and MySQL 5 on your *nix machine
- Install phpMyAdmin
- Create a new database and then a database user using phpMyAdmin

TIP

Programmers who don't want to install the required software manually have the option of using a software package such as XAMPP, which bundles all of them (and many more) in a single installer file. XAMPP is packaged for Linux, Windows, Mac OS X, and Solaris, and is free of charge. You can get XAMPP from `http://www.apachefriends.org/en/xampp.html`.

If you decide to use XAMPP, you can skip directly to setting up the `ajax` database, as shown at the end of this appendix.

Preparing Your Windows Playground

Here we cover installing these software products in your Windows machine:

- Apache 2
- PHP 5
- MySQL 5

Installing Apache

You can download the latest MSI Installer version of the Apache HTTP Server from `http://httpd.apache.org/download.cgi`. Download the latest Win32 Binary (MSI Installer), which should have a name like `apache_2.x.y-win32-x86-no_ssl.msi`, then execute it.

The default installation location of Apache 2 is `c:\Program Files\Apache Group\Apache2\`, but the installer allows you to specify a different path. You can choose a more convenient location (such as `c:\Apache`), which can make your life working with Apache easier.

During installation you'll be asked to enter your server's information:

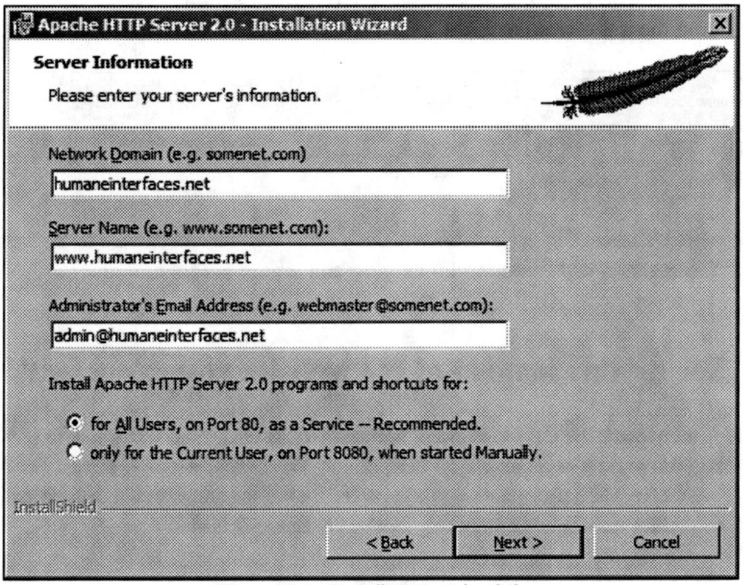

Figure A.1: Installing Apache 2.0

If you're not sure about how to complete the form, just type **localhost** for the first two fields, and write your email address for the last. You can change this information later by editing the Apache configuration file. The default location of this file is `c:\Program Files\Apache Group\Apache2\conf\httpd.conf`.

You can also choose to install Apache on Port 80, or on Port 8080. The default port is 80, but if you already have a web server (such as IIS) on your machine, you'll need to install Apache on a different port. If you choose to run Apache on Port 8080, you will need to start the Apache service manually by going to the Apache bin folder (by default `c:\Program Files\Apache Group\Apache2\bin`), and typing

```
apache -k install
```

When the web server runs on a port different than 80, you need to specify the port manually when making HTTP requests, such as in `http://localhost:8080/ajax/suggest`.

In the next setup screens, you can safely use the default options.

Along with the Apache server the installer will also start the **Apache Service Monitor** program, which is available from the taskbar. The taskbar icon reflects the current state of the web server (stopped, running, etc.), and also allows you to start, stop, or restart the Apache service.

> Keep in mind that you'll need to restart (or stop and then start) the Apache service after making any changes to the `httpd.conf` configuration file, in order for the changes to become effective.

After installing Apache 2, make sure it works OK. If you installed it on port 80, browse to http://localhost/. If you installed it on 8080, go to http://localhost:8080/. You should see an Apache welcome message similar to this:

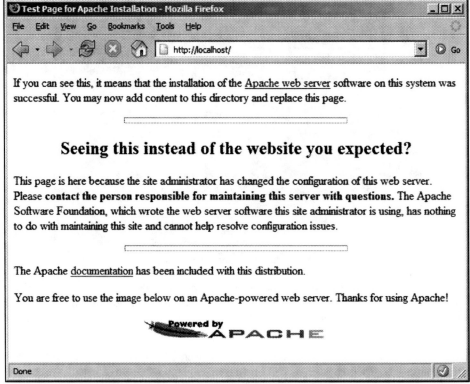

Figure A.2: Apache Installed Successfully

Installing MySQL

The official website of MySQL is http://www.mysql.com. At the time of this writing the latest stable version is MySQL 5.0, and you can download it from http://dev.mysql.com/downloads/mysql/5.0.html. However, it's good to know that we made our SQL queries compliant with the SQL 92 standard, so you should be able to reuse them with other database systems with minimum of translation effort.

In the Downloads page, scroll down to the Windows downloads section, and download the Windows Essentials file. You'll be asked to choose a mirror site, and the file will be named something like mysql-essential-5.0.xx-win32.msi. After downloading the file, simply execute it to install your MySQL Server.

After installation you'll be given the chance to configure your server. Do so. It's safe to use the default options all the way through. At some point you'll need to set the root password, which will correspond to the root@localhost user. Choose a password that's complicated enough for others not to guess and simple enough for you to remember.

Before going through any case studies in this book, remember to see the *Preparing the AJAX Database* section at the end of this appendix.

Installing PHP

The official website of PHP is `http://www.php.net`. Start by downloading from the Windows Binaries section the latest PHP 5 zip package (*not the installer!*) from `http://www.php.net/downloads.php`. We prefer not to use the installer because it doesn't include extensions that you may need for your projects, and it doesn't do much configuration work for you anyway.

After you download the Windows binaries, follow these steps to install PHP:

1. Unzip the zip package (it should be a file with a name like `php-5.x.y-win32.zip`) into a folder named `c:\PHP\`. You can choose another name or location for this folder if you want.

2. Copy `php.ini-recommended` from `c:\PHP\` to your Windows folder (`c:\windows`), renaming it as `php.ini`.

3. Open `php.ini` for editing with the text editor of your choice (such as Notepad) and uncomment the `php_gd2.dll`, `php_mysql.dll`, and `php_xsl.dll` extension lines (by removing the leading semicolons), and add a similar line for `php_mysqli`:
    ```
    extension=php_gd2.dll
    extension=php_mysql.dll
    extension=php_mysqli.dll
    extension=php_xsl.dll
    ```

4. We recommend enabling full error reporting for PHP on the development machine, but this is optional (this option is the default). Be warned that this change can alter the functionality of other scripts on your server. Find the `error_reporting` line in `php.ini` and change it to:
    ```
    error_reporting = E_ALL
    ```

5. Copy `php5ts.dll` and `libmysql.dll` located in `c:\PHP\`, to the Windows `System32` folder (by default `\windows\System32`).

6. Copy `php_mysql.dll`, `php_mysqli.dll`, `php_xsl.dll`, and `php_gd2.dll` from `c:\PHP\ext`, to the Windows `System32` folder.

7. Open the Apache configuration file for editing. By default, the location of this file is `c:\Program Files\Apache Group\Apache2\conf\httpd.conf`.

8. In `httpd.conf`, find the portion with many `LoadModule` entries, and add the following lines:
    ```
    LoadModule php5_module c:/php/php5apache2.dll
    AddType application/x-httpd-php .php
    ```

9. Also in `httpd.conf`, find the `DirectoryIndex` entry, and add `index.php` at the end of the line, like this:
    ```
    DirectoryIndex index.html index.html.var index.php
    ```

10. Save the `httpd.conf` file, and then restart the Apache 2 service, using the Apache Service Monitor by clicking its icon in the Notification Area of the taskbar. (If you get any error at this point, make sure that you followed correctly all the previous steps of the exercise.) If Apache restarts without generating any errors, that is a good sign.

11. Create a folder called `ajax` under the `htdocs` folder (by default `c:\Program Files\Apache Group\Apache2\htdocs`).

12. To make sure that your Apache instance can also correctly parse PHP code, create a file named `test.php` in the `ajax` folder, and then add the following code to it:

```
<?php
phpinfo();
?>
```

13. Point your web browser to `http://localhost/ajax/test.php` (or `http://localhost:8080/ajax/test.php` if you installed Apache to work on port 8080) to test if everything went OK with the installation. You should get a page like this:

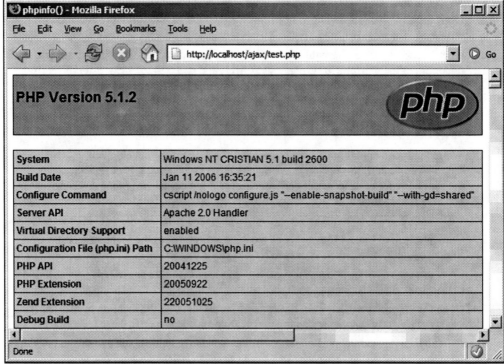

Figure A.3: PHP Installation Working

Congratulations, you just finished installing Apache, MySQL, and PHP!

The configuration set up isn't yet finished. If you're running Windows (and you probably are, since you're reading this), please skip the Preparing Your *nix Playground section, and go through the *Installing phpMyAdmin* and *Preparing the AJAX Database* sections at the end of this appendix.

Preparing Your *nix Playground

Almost all the UNIX and Linux distributions include Apache, PHP, and MySQL; however, you should check the versions of these programs. It would be good to have MySQL 4.1 or newer, and it's very important to have at least PHP 5. The code in this book will not work with older versions of PHP.

Installing Apache

To install Apache on your Unix-based server, follow these simple steps:

1. First, download the latest Apache Unix Source code for your system from `http://httpd.apache.org/download.cgi` and decompress it with a command such as:

   ```
   tar -zxvf httpd-2.0.55.tar.gz
   ```

2. To compile and install the Apache Web Server on your system, go to the folder containing the sources and execute the following commands, while logged in as root:

   ```
   ./configure --prefix=/usr/local/apache2 --enable-so --enable-ssl --with-ssl --enable-auth-digest
   ```

   ```
   make
   ```

   ```
   make install
   ```

Installing MySQL

The official website of MySQL is `http://www.mysql.com`. At the time of this writing the latest stable version is MySQL 5.0, and you can download it from `http://dev.mysql.com/downloads/mysql/5.0.html`. However, it's good to know that we made our SQL queries compliant with the SQL 92 standard, so you should be able to reuse them with other database systems with minimum of translation effort. Chapter 2 of the MySQL 5 manual covers installation procedures for all supported platforms, and you can read it here: `http://dev.mysql.com/doc/refman/5.0/en/installing.html`.

If your Linux distribution supports RPMs, you'll need to download the RPMs for Server, Client programs, and Libraries and header files. Install MySQL as explained in the manual at `http://dev.mysql.com/doc/refman/5.0/en/linux-rpm.html`. If your platform doesn't support RPMs, install MySQL as explained at `http://dev.mysql.com/doc/refman/5.0/en/installing-binary.html`.

After installing MySQL, you should change the MySQL administrator's password (the `root@localhost` user), which is blank by default. Read more about MySQL passwords at `http://dev.mysql.com/doc/mysql/en/Passwords.html`. One way to change root's password is to execute:

```
mysqladmin -u root password 'your_new_password.'
```

Alternatively, you can access MySQL through a console program or by using a database administration tool such as phpMyAdmin, and execute this command:

```
SET PASSWORD FOR root@localhost=PASSWORD('your_new_password');
```

You can now test your MySQL server by executing the following command in your console:

```
#mysql -u root -p
```

Installing PHP

Every time you want to get a new PHP library working on Linux, you need to recompile the PHP module. That's why it's recommended to make a *good* compilation, with all the needed libraries, from the start.

1. Go to http://www.php.net/downloads.php and get the complete source code archive of PHP 5.x and extract the contents into a directory. At the time of writing, the latest PHP version was 5.1.2.

2. Go to the folder where you extracted the PHP source and execute the following commands:

    ```
    ./configure --with-config-file-path=/etc --with-mysql=/usr/include/mysql
    --with-apxs2=/usr/local/apache2/bin/apxs --with-zlib --with-gd --with-xsl

    make

    make install
    ```

> If you are compiling PHP for XAMPP, you need to use the following configure command instead:
>
> ```
> ./configure --with-config-file-path=/opt/lampp/etc --with-mysql=/opt/lampp
> --with-apxs2=/opt/lampp/bin/apxs --with-zlib --with-gd
> ```
>
> After executing make and make install, you need to copy the newly created php_src/libs/libphp5.so file to /opt/lampp/modules/libphp5.so.

3. Copy php.ini-recommended to /etc/php.ini by executing the following command:
    ```
    cp php.ini-recommended /etc/php.ini.
    ```

4. Open the Apache configuration file (httpd.conf), find the DirectoryIndex entry, and make sure you have index.php at the end of the line:
    ```
    DirectoryIndex index.html index.html.var index.php
    ```

5. Restart your Apache Web Server using the following command:
    ```
    /usr/local/apache2/bin/apachectl restart
    ```

6. Create a folder called ajax under the htdocs folder (by default /usr/local/apache2/htdocs/).

7. To make sure your PHP installation works, create a file named test.php in the ajax folder you've just created, with the following contents in it:
    ```
    <?php
    phpinfo();
    ?>
    ```

8. Finally, point your web browser to `http://localhost/test.php`, to ensure PHP was correctly installed under Apache (you should get a page similar to Figure A.3).

Installing phpMyAdmin

phpMyAdmin is a very popular MySQL administration tool written in PHP. It allows you to manage your MySQL databases using a simple-to-use web interface. The official web page is `http://www.phpmyadmin.net`. Follow these steps to install and configure this program:

1. Start by downloading the latest version of phpMyAdmin from `http://www.phpmyadmin.net/home_page/downloads.php`. If you aren't sure what file to download, the safest bet is to go with the zip archive.

2. Unzip the archive somewhere on your disk. The archive contains a folder named with the complete phpMyAdmin version (for example, at the time of this writing, the folder for the beta version of phpMyAdmin is called `phpMyAdmin-2.8.0-beta1`).

3. To make your life easier, rename this folder to simply `phpMyAdmin`.

4. Move the phpMyAdmin folder to the `htdocs` folder of Apache 2 (by default `C:\Program Files\Apache Group\Apache2\htdocs`).

5. To make sure your phpMyAdmin installation is accessible by Apache, load `http://localhost/phpMyAdmin` in your favorite web browser. If everything worked OK, you should get a message such as this:

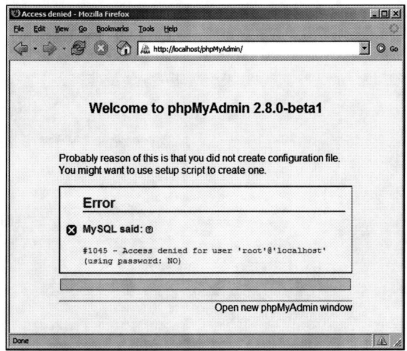

Figure A.4: phpMyAdmin Doesn't Have Access to MySQL

6. The error message is suggestive enough—you need to instruct phpMyAdmin how to access your MySQL server. Under the phpMyAdmin folder search for a file named config.inc.php. If you find this file, change its options as shown in the following code snippet. If you don't find this file, create it with the following contents:

```php
<?php
$cfg['PmaAbsoluteUri'] = "http://localhost/phpMyAdmin/";
$cfg['Servers'][1]['host'] = "localhost";
$cfg['Servers'][1]['auth_type'] = 'config';
$cfg['Servers'][1]['user'] = "root";
$cfg['Servers'][1]['password'] = "password";
?>
```

For more details on installing and using phpMyAdmin, see its documentation at http://www.phpmyadmin.net/home_page/docs.php. Packt Publishing has a separate book for those of you who want to learn more about phpMyAdmin—*Mastering phpMyAdmin for Effective MySQL Management* (ISBN: 1-904811-03-5). In case you're not a native English speaker, it's good to know that the book is also available in Czech, German, French, and Italian.

Preparing the AJAX Database

As an exercise for both using phpMyAdmin and working with MySQL, let's create a database called ajax, and create a MySQL user with full privileges to this database. You'll use this database and this user for all the exercises in this book. Follow these steps:

1. Load http://localhost/phpMyAdmin in your web browser. If the configuration data you wrote in config.inc.php was correct, you should see something like this:

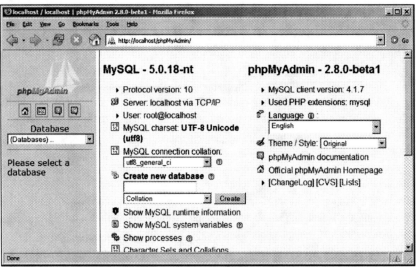

Figure A.5: phpMyAdmin in Action

2. Write ajax in the Create a new database box, and then click the Create button.

3. phpMyAdmin doesn't have the visual tools to create new users, so you'll need to write some SQL code now. You need to create a user with full access to the ajax database, which will be used in all the case studies throughout the book. This user will be called (surprise!) ajaxuser, and its password will be practical. To add this user, click the SQL tab at the top of the page, and write this code in it:

```
GRANT ALL PRIVILEGES ON ajax.*
TO ajaxuser@localhost IDENTIFIED BY "practical"
```

> SQL does sound a bit like plain English, but a few things need to be mentioned. The * in ajax.* means *all objects in the ajax database*. So this command tells MySQL "give all possible privileges to the ajax database to a user of this local machine called ajaxuser, whose password is practical".

4. Click the Go button.

Congratulations, you're all set for your journey through this book. Have fun learning AJAX!

Index

Printed in the United States
93361LV00004B/381-418/A